Give Me Winter, Give Me Dogs

Knud Rasmussen and the Fifth Thule Expedition

The title of this book, "Give me winter, give me dogs,"
is a quote from Rasmussen, "Dagboger," 102.

Published by Inhabit Media Inc.
www.inhabitmedia.com

Inhabit Media Inc. (Iqaluit) 2434 Paurngaq Cres., Iqaluit, Nunavut, X0A 2H0
(Toronto) 612 Mount Pleasant Road, Toronto, Ontario, M4S 2M8

Cover image: Photograph of Knud Rasmussen by Therkel Mathiassen, Danish Arctic Institute. Resource ID 146016.
Back cover image: Photograph of Arnarulunnguaq, Rasmussen, and Qaavigarsuaq, by Leo Hansen. Smithsonian Libraries and Archives 2005-8635.
Author photo by Andrew Balfour
Map texture at section headings: 103cia/Shutterstock.com
Wood texture on cover: stockphoto mania/Shutterstock.com
Page break element: Vector Tradition/Shutterstock.com

Editors: Neil Christopher and Anne Fullerton
Art Director: Danny Christopher

This project was made possible in part by the Government of Canada.
We acknowledge the support of the Canada Council for the Arts for our publishing program.

ISBN: 978-1-77227-550-6

Library and Archives Canada Cataloguing in Publication

Title: Give me winter, give me dogs : Knud Rasmussen and the Fifth Thule Expedition / Kenn Harper.
Names: Harper, Kenn, author.
Description: Includes bibliographical references.
Identifiers: Canadiana 20240394046 | ISBN 9781772275506 (hardcover)
Subjects: LCSH: Rasmussen, Knud, 1879-1933. | LCSH: Thule Expedition (5th : 1921-1924) | LCSH: Inuit—Canada, Northern—Social life and customs—20th century. | LCSH: Inuit—Canada, Northern—History—20th century.
Classification: LCC E99.E7 H326 2024 | DDC 971.9004/9712009042—dc23

Printed and bound in China by WKT Company Limited, July 2024, 24CB0768

Canada
Canada Council for the Arts
Conseil des Arts du Canada

Give Me Winter, Give Me Dogs

Knud Rasmussen and the Fifth Thule Expedition

KENN HARPER

INHABIT MEDIA

PART 1: BEGINNINGS

PART 2: DANISH ISLAND

Part 1:
BEGINNINGS

Part 1: Beginnings

Knud Rasmussen and the Inuit

Knud Rasmussen was born in Ilulissat (then called Jakobshavn), Greenland, in 1879. His father was a Danish priest, his mother a housewife of part-Inuit ancestry. Rasmussen grew up as part of an Inuit community, speaking *Kalaallisut*, a dialect of the widely spread Inuit language, as his mother tongue. He first drove a dog team at the age of eight. During his childhood he revelled in hearing the stories of Inuit Elders, especially about lesser-known groups of Inuit far to the north. But at the age of twelve this idyllic existence came to an end when he was sent to Denmark for his formal education.

In 1902 he returned to Greenland as part of a cultural expedition to the far northwest of the country. It was there he first encountered the *Inughuit*, then known as the Polar Eskimos.[1] Theirs was a small population quite distinct in language and culture from the *Kalaallit* (usually translated as simply "Greenlanders" or "Greenlandic Inuit") who lived all along the west coast south of Melville Bay. In 1909 he returned to that district to help the Greenlandic church establish its North Star Mission.

The Inughuit were at that time in a precarious position. Over the preceding decades they had become dependent on, first, whalers, and then the American explorer Robert Peary for a supply of trade goods. But Peary had claimed to reach the North Pole in 1909 and would be coming to Greenland no more. The Danish government expressed no interest in administering the northwestern part of Greenland. It was in effect a no man's land. So the following year Rasmussen and his friend Peter Freuchen established a trading post there, the Thule Station, to provide for the needs of the population.

---

1 The word "Eskimo" is not generally used today. I use it if it is appropriate to do so in a historical context, and in direct quotations.

Rasmussen conducted a number of geographic and ethnographic expeditions, some using Thule as his base. He called these the Thule Expeditions. And he wrote extensively about his travels and about what he learned from Inuit, documenting their lifeways. Throughout that decade he held fast to a dream—to visit the most isolated Inuit in North America and document their beliefs and experiences before their lives were irrevocably changed by an influx of missionaries, traders, and adventurers. In 1921 he was ready to realize that dream. With four Danes, one *Kalaaleq* ("West Greenlander"), and six Inughuit, he embarked on the Fifth Thule Expedition to the *Akilinirmiut* ("the people on the other side of the water"). Among many goals, Rasmussen wanted to investigate what he called "the great primary problem of the origin of the Eskimo race":[2] to test certain theories about whether Inuit culture had originated and evolved from an inland culture, or whether it was always a maritime culture. In the process of doing this, he and some of his colleagues would investigate and document the folklore and religion of Inuit they encountered—what he called their "intellectual culture."

They established their headquarters on an island they named Danish Island, near Nagjuktuuq (then called Vansittart Island), which is southeast of Naujaat ("the place where seagulls nest," then called Repulse Bay[3]). From there he and the scientists who accompanied him visited Inuit as far north as Iglulik and Pond Inlet, and southwest into the interior of the Kivalliq (then Keewatin) region. Because of his fluency in Greenlandic and his basic interest in Inuit language and its many manifestations, Rasmussen was able to understand, and be understood, wherever he went.

In 1923 he and two of the Inughuit, Qaavigarsuaq[4] and Arnarulunnguaq, left Danish Island and embarked on the high point of the expedition: a trip by dogsled across the top of North America, through the territory of the *Nattilingmiut* (people from Nattilik, "a place with seals") and the *Inuinnait* (Copper Inuit), through the Mackenzie Delta, and into Alaska, from where they continued the trip by boat to Nome. Rasmussen and Qaavigarsuaq even managed to cross Bering Strait to Siberia in an attempt to visit Inuit there. This magnificent journey was documented in Rasmussen's popular book *Across Arctic America: Narrative of the Fifth Thule Expedition.*

The knowledge collected by the expedition appeared in English in twenty-six reports published between 1927 and 1952 (and one final volume published only

---

2 Rasmussen, *Across Arctic America*, vii.

3 Naujaat is today's name for the community. I use Repulse Bay when referring to the historic Hudson's Bay Company trading post, to avoid confusion with the archaeological site Naujaat (also historically spelled Naujan) a few kilometres east of the trading station.

4 For ease of reading by Canadian Inuit, I have generally written Canadian and Greenlandic Inuit personal names in the Canadian Inuktitut standard roman orthography ratified by the Inuit Language Commission in 1976. A few exceptions are made for people recently living who were well-known to Inuit and others by a non-standard spelling of their names; coincidentally, some of these are authors whose names in non-standard orthography are also necessary for the bibliographic record. Note that I have not changed the spelling of the name Qaavigarsuaq; although this is a Greenlandic spelling, he was well-known to Canadian Inuit, many of whom pronounce his name in the Greenlandic way. The same exception is made for the name Qillarsuaq, for the same reason. I have also written Canadian Inuktitut place names and Inuktitut words that appear in the text, including those in direct quotations, in the same standard orthography.

in 1988). The thickest and most interesting of these volumes to readers interested in culture and folklore are Rasmussen's *Intellectual Culture of the Iglulik Eskimos* (1929), *Observations on the Intellectual Culture of the Caribou Eskimos* (1930), *Iglulik and Caribou Eskimo Texts* (1930), *The Netsilik Eskimos* (1931), and *Intellectual Life of the Copper Eskimos* (1932). The other scientists of the expedition also published impressive works on archaeology and ethnography.

Inuit in Canada knew Knud Rasmussen as Kunu, Kunut, or Kunuuti. (Kalaallit called him Kununnguaq, while Inughuit called him Kunupaluk.) Stories of the Fifth Thule Expedition are still told by the descendants of Inuit who knew Rasmussen in the Kivalliq region, as well as among the Nattilingmiut and Inuinnait, and Peter Freuchen is remembered by those in the Kivalliq, including his descendants.

Rasmussen always acknowledged his humble beginnings. "From my heart I bless the fate that allowed me to be born at a time when Arctic exploration by dog sledge was not yet a thing of the past,"[5] he wrote. "It was my privilege, as one born in Greenland, and speaking the Eskimo language as my native tongue, to know these people in an intimate way."[6]

In the introduction to *Across Arctic America*, he wrote, "The Eskimo is the hero of this book."[7] At one point, he claimed that "it is the Eskimos that own my heart."[8]

Thule

In 1909 Knud Rasmussen assisted the Greenlandic Church Cause in establishing the North Star Mission in North Star Bay in Wolstenholme Fiord in the shadow of Mount Dundas, later known as Thule Mountain. The first priest there, Gustav Olsen, was a native Greenlander from Disko Bay and had been Rasmussen's childhood friend. On the voyage to Thule that summer to establish the mission, Rasmussen met the Danish academic Hans Peder Steensby, whose ideas had already influenced him greatly and would continue to do so.

Steensby was a Danish ethnologist and geographer, born in 1875 as Hans Peder Jensen. When a young man, he changed his surname to Steensby, after the parish where he was born. Professionally, he developed an intense interest in the origins of Inuit culture.

Steensby never visited northern Canada—his Arctic experience was confined to Greenland—but he was well-read on Arctic exploration and ethnography. As a

5 Rasmussen, *Across Arctic America*, v.

6 Ibid., vi.

7 Ibid., vii.

8 Hansen, *I Knuds Slædespor*, 177.

scholar, he knew that the Inuit of Greenland had migrated eastward from the lands that are now northern Canada. And so he developed a theory as to where their unique Arctic culture had developed. It was, he theorized, originally not a maritime culture at all, but had developed in the interior of northern Canada near Great Slave Lake. Only later, he thought, had it spread to the coast and adopted its unique adaptation to maritime conditions.

He expressed all these ideas in his PhD thesis at the University of Copenhagen in 1905; it was published as a book that same year under the title *Om Eskimokulturens Oprindelse* (On the Origin of Eskimo Culture). Somewhat revised, it was eventually published for a wider audience in 1916.[9]

Steensby's book left its mark on young Knud Rasmussen. It is no coincidence that in 1905 an article appeared in the Danish newspaper *Politiken* about Rasmussen's plans for a multi-year expedition to the Inuit of North America. "It will be a journey that in distances and duration exceeds most previous polar expeditions," the article informed. "Rasmussen will go north of America by sledge. He starts next spring in Greenland, crosses the Ellesmere Island in the summer and continues further over the islands in the polar sea to Alaska and crosses the Bering Strait to Siberia."[10] That journey never took place, but the seed for a major expedition had been planted, and grew.

When Steensby and Rasmussen met in the summer of 1909, the scientist quickly realized that Rasmussen, with his fluency in Kalaallisut, was completely at home in the Arctic. The younger man was interested in all aspects of Inuit history and culture. He listened to Steensby and became convinced that his theories were correct. And in his mind a plan developed to investigate Inuit origins and prove the truth of the scholar's ideas.

Rasmussen formulated a plan for an expedition to Arctic America, an expedition on which he would visit as many isolated Inuit groups as possible. He believed, following Steensby, that in the Inuit migration to the seacoast, one group had remained inland—the Caribou Inuit. A visit to their isolated homeland would be crucial to proving Steensby's theory. He intended to investigate them, along with as many other Inuit groups as possible.

In 1909 he outlined his plans for a major expedition to Canada in the Danish journal *Geografisk Tidsskrift*.[11] But it would take over a decade for him to actually carry this ambitious plan through to fruition, a decade in which his plans were changed and refined many times.

From the outset, it would be an expedition unlike any that had ventured into Arctic North America before. It would not be an expedition to discover and claim new lands, for it was well-known that the lands he wanted to visit belonged to Canada and the United States. Their sovereignty was not in question, at least not by him. No, this

---

9 Steensby, "Anthropogeographical Study."

10 Quoted in Michelsen, "Plans for the Fifth Thule Expedition," 25.

11 Rasmussen, "Forslag."

venture was to visit people, Inuit, whose lifestyles were on the cusp of change through advancing commerce, government administration, and missionary work. Rasmussen wanted to record legends and beliefs, and in the process investigate the origins of Inuit culture. In simplest terms, he would find out if Steensby's theories held water.

Throughout the evolution of his plan to visit the Inuit of North America, one thing remained constant—that the expedition must be conducted by dogsled. "From the earliest boyhood," he later wrote, "I played and worked with the hunters, so that even the hardships of the most strenuous sledge-trips became pleasant routine for me."[12] Dogs and the sled would be the keys to his success. In his earliest plans in 1905, he wrote, "We must come to the Eskimos by the same means that they themselves use, to meet them as comrades. If we arrive in another way, they will look at us, if not as enemies, then as strangers."[13]

A year after the establishment of the North Star Mission, Rasmussen built a trading station—the world's most northerly—at the same location. He gave it the name Thule, a word used in classical Greek mythology to refer to the extreme north. The Inughuit had their own name for the place; they called it Uummannaq ("the one shaped like a heart").

When Rasmussen established his trading post, he created the Kap York Committee to oversee its running. A number of influential Danes, including his father Christian Rasmussen, sat on the committee, which was headed by Marius Ib Nyeboe. Nyeboe, born in 1867, was an engineer with mining interests in Denmark, Russia, and Greenland. He had been introduced to Rasmussen through his friend Dagmar Andersen, who married Rasmussen on November 11, 1908.

Rasmussen installed his Danish friend, Peter Freuchen, as manager of the station itself. The goal of the trading post was to make a profit from the trade in fur and ivory brought in by the Inughuit. Of course, official financial support for some of the expeditions Rasmussen conducted from his station at Thule was provided later. But nonetheless, the expeditions were subsidized by the trading post. As anthropologist Jean Malaurie put it, "Something truly exceptional came to pass: an archaic society itself subventioned research into its own history. . . . the Polar Eskimos of Thule became the first patrons of Eskimology concerned with an area that ranges from Alaska to the eastern coast of Greenland." In effect, the Inughuit—numbering about 250 at the time—themselves subsidized scientific research into Inuit culture; it is to them, Malaurie wrote, "that Denmark owes its status as an important scientific nation in the Arctic."[14]

From his base at Thule, in addition to trading in furs and ivory, Rasmussen

12 Rasmussen, *Across Arctic America*, vi.

13 Michelsen, "Plans for the Fifth Thule Expedition," 25. (Translation by Michelsen.)

14 Malaurie, *The Last Kings*, 122.

conducted a number of exploratory and scientific expeditions, what he called his "Thule" expeditions. The First Thule Expedition, in 1912, was led by Rasmussen, who was accompanied by Peter Freuchen and two Inughuit dog-drivers, Ulluriaq and Inukittuq. They travelled over the inland ice to northeastern Greenland and proved that Peary Channel, mapped by Robert Peary, in fact did not exist. Rasmussen published the results of that expedition in Danish in *Grønland langs Polhavet* (1919), and in English as *Greenland by the Polar Sea* (1921). The Second Thule Expedition, from 1916 to 1918, was primarily cartographic and also led by Rasmussen. He was accompanied by Danish geologist and cartographer Lauge Koch, Swedish botanist Thorild Wulff, three Inughuit, and a Kalaaleq, Hendrik Olsen. The results were disastrous, with Wulff and Olsen perishing. Rasmussen did not participate in the next Thule expedition in 1919, which simply laid out depots for a polar drift planned by Norwegian Roald Amundsen. In 1919 Rasmussen made a trip to Ammassalik on Greenland's east coast, from there to Thule, and then to Aasiaat (then called Egedesminde) in Disko Bay to study and collect myths and legends. This, the Fourth Thule Expedition, was documented in a three-volume work in Danish, *Myter og Sagn fra Grønland* (1921-1925), and partly in English as *Eskimo Folk-Tales* (1921).

An Inauspicious Start

The expedition Rasmussen planned to northern Canada would be his fifth Thule expedition. In planning, Rasmussen strove to keep the Canadian government informed of his plans. But in the early 1900s Canada was concerned over the possibility of American claims to certain portions of the High Arctic because of the explorations of Robert Peary and his successor Donald MacMillan, as well as the possibility of claims by Norway as a result of Otto Sverdrup's explorations. What resulted was a huge misunderstanding between the governments of Denmark and Canada, and Knud Rasmussen found himself in the middle of it.

The Inughuit knew there was land to the west of the territory they occupied in northwestern Greenland. The ancestors of many of them had immigrated from Canada, led by the shaman Qillarsuaq, a scant few generations earlier. Unlike Greenlanders to the south on the west Greenland coast, the Inughuit could see across to Ellesmere Island. Moreover, Peary and MacMillan had moved many families from Greenland to Ellesmere Island to support their expeditions. Those Inuit knew very well the land and resources on the Canadian side. By 1919, then, when Rasmussen was actively planning his Fifth Thule Expedition, Inughuit were hunting freely on Ellesmere Island, which they regarded rightly as their traditional hunting territory. Rasmussen raised no objection to this.

But the Canadian government did. On July 31, 1919, Canada, through the British Foreign Office, sent a request to the Danish government formally asking them to prevent the Inughuit from killing muskoxen on Ellesmere Island. The Canadian government even offered to station its own personnel, in the form of Royal North-West Mounted Police officers, on the Greenland side of Smith Sound to control the movements of the Inughuit.[15]

The Canadian request was written by James Harkin, Commissioner of Dominion Parks in the Department of the Interior, who was the Canadian civil servant most concerned with Arctic sovereignty, and signed by his Deputy Minister, William Wallace Cory. It passed through a number of hands, including the Colonial Office in London and the Danish Foreign Office, before it eventually reached the Greenland office. The Danes, having no official administration dealing with northern Greenland, sent the request on to Rasmussen. Eventually, in 1920, Rasmussen responded in Danish. His response was translated into English in Denmark, and completely misunderstood when it reached Ottawa.

He talked about the conditions in northern Greenland, and that he believed strongly in muskox conservation and would do whatever possible to comply with the Canadian request.

But it was the following words that upset James Harkin:

> It is well known that the territory of the polar esquimaux falls within the region designated as "no man's land" and there is therefore no authority in the district except that which I exercise through my station—an authority which I've hitherto had no difficulty in maintaining. . . . I venture to close with the observation that, in order to carry out the protective measures indicated in this statement, I shall need no assistance whatever from the Canadian Government.[16]

The Danish government agreed with Rasmussen and advised Canada accordingly.

In saying that the territory of the Inughuit was a "no man's land," Rasmussen was simply referring to the fact that Denmark had not yet established any formal administration in northwestern Greenland. His statements were true; he was the sole authority in the region—an authority that he had unilaterally assumed. His reference to needing no help from the Canadian government is simply a rejection of the Canadian suggestion that Canada station its own personnel in Greenland. But James Harkin viewed the reply in a different light.

---

15 The offer was made on August 27, 1919. See Note from Acting Secretary of State for Foreign Affairs (Curzon) to Minister of Denmark in United Kingdom (H. de Grevenkop-Castenskiold). Foreign Office, London. August 27, 1919, in Cavell, *Canadian External Relations*, 325 (item 214). The Royal North-West Mounted Police merged with the Dominion Police on February 1, 1920, to become the Royal Canadian Mounted Police.

16 Letter from Knud Rasmussen to Greenland Administration, enclosed with note from Minister of Denmark in United Kingdom to Secretary of State for Foreign Affairs, in Cavell, *Canadian External Relations*, 326 (item 215).

Harkin was helped in his misunderstanding by two meddlesome men, neither of them Canadian. Both of them knew better but chose, each for reasons of his own, to be mendacious. A fur trader, Henry Toke Munn, had told the explorer Vilhjalmur Stefansson in the spring of 1920 that Rasmussen was doing a brisk trade in muskox skins taken from Ellesmere Island. Stefansson, who was actually corresponding with Rasmussen at the time—as one explorer to another—double-crossed his fellow explorer and convinced Harkin that "no man's land" referred to Ellesmere Island. Alarmed, Harkin wrote to his deputy minister, stating that Rasmussen and the Danish government disputed Canada's sovereignty over Ellesmere.

Stefansson continued to fuel concern in Ottawa, spreading lies about Rasmussen to the Advisory Technical Board on Canadian Sovereignty, eventually writing to the prime minister himself, telling him that the Danes were thinking of colonizing the islands north of Lancaster Sound. "There is still time for us to do something about this,"[17] he said ominously.

The legal advisor to the Department of External Affairs did a superficial analysis of the situation and submitted a report to the prime minister, in which he claimed that the Danes had already sent an expedition to occupy Ellesmere Island.

This was all nonsense. The Danes had not invaded Ellesmere Island. Any comment Rasmussen may have made to Stefansson or others about a forthcoming expedition into Canadian territory could only have been a reference to his long-planned and not-yet-commenced Fifth Thule Expedition.

But Stefansson had done his damage, and Rasmussen's plans were treated with great suspicion in Ottawa.

Eventually saner heads prevailed there, and the government, even James Harkin, came to the realization that Vilhjalmur Stefansson had his own selfish motives, and was no friend to Rasmussen.

The meddling by Stefansson and Munn had been a nuisance, but had not delayed or scuttled the expedition. But it came close. It lasted well into 1921, the year the expedition left for Canada.

On June 18, 1921, Knud Rasmussen and two Danish scientists, Therkel Mathiassen and Kaj Birket-Smith, left Denmark on the Swedish ship the *Bele*, bound for Nuuk (then called Godthaab), Greenland. The Greenland administration had chartered the ship—at that time the largest vessel ever to go to Greenland—to take dignitaries to Nuuk to celebrate the bicentenary of the first missionary's arrival in Greenland and to carry supplies. Most of the Fifth Thule Expedition's materials were aboard that ship, including their winter house, guns, ammunition, and photographic material.

17 Stefansson to Meighen, September 16, 1920, quoted in Cavell, *Canadian External Relations*, 337 (item 220).

Captain Peder Pedersen had left earlier with the Thule trading station's small ship the *Søkongen* ("Sea King") for Thule to pick up Inughuit to work for the expedition. Helge Bangsted, a Dane, had wintered in Greenland. Peter Freuchen was already there with a film expedition and would arrive in Nuuk at the end of June.

The *Bele* arrived in Nuuk on June 28 and deposited its dignitaries there to await the festivities that would begin five days later. It then continued north with Mathiassen and Birket-Smith. But on July 14, the ship struck a rock near the island of Tukingasoq[18] between Uummannaq[19] (often spelled Umanak) and Upernavik. Its forty-two passengers had to take refuge ashore and sleep under tarpaulins. In the meantime, King Christian X, who coincidentally was to be the patron of Rasmussen's expedition, had arrived in Nuuk aboard the steam ship *Island*. The *Bele*'s wireless operator sent an SOS message, hoping it would be picked up by the king's ship—these two ships carried the only wireless equipment in Greenland at the time.

Rasmussen and Freuchen, meanwhile, had left Nuuk on the *Søkongen* a day before the wreck of the *Bele*. Four days later at Ilulissat, they learned of the accident. The *Island* had received the SOS from the *Bele*, steamed north, and picked up the stranded passengers. It then rendezvoused with the *Søkongen*. Rasmussen feared that his expedition might be doomed because of the loss of critical supplies that had been in the hold of the *Bele*, especially the material for the expedition's headquarters building. Fortunately, the director of the Greenland Administration, Jens Daugaard-Jensen, was aboard the *Island*, accompanying the king. Daugaard-Jensen telegraphed to Denmark a list of the most urgent supplies that the expedition would need in order to go ahead, asking that they be mustered and sent out immediately to Nuuk on the next ship, the *Hans Egede*. Attempts were made to salvage items from the *Bele*, but little was usable.

Human tragedies also put the expedition in jeopardy. Peter Freuchen's wife, Navarana, who was to be a housekeeper at the expedition's base, had been staying at Uummannaq. One account says that she then joined the expedition at the *Bele* salvage site, but Freuchen's own account says that she was already in Ilulissat, having travelled down by sled after preparing the skin clothes needed for the expedition. Ominously, Freuchen said that "she was not very well. . . . She had fallen victim to a cold germ that had been carried north by a ship which had stopped at Umanak [Uummannaq], and was in such poor health."[20]

The *Søkongen* proceeded north to Upernavik, where Navarana's condition suddenly worsened. She was taken to a house in the settlement to rest. "I did not leave her side," wrote Freuchen, "and got our good friend Fat Sofie to help nurse her."[21]

---

18 I have spelled Greenlandic place names in the orthography used in Greenland today. All those used in the text are officially recognized place names.

19 This is not the Uummannaq in North Star Bay in the Thule District. Uummannaq is a common place name in the North.

20 Freuchen, *Arctic Adventure*, 323.

21 Ibid., 325.

When the *Søkongen* continued farther north to pick up the Inughuit whom Rasmussen had recruited to accompany the expedition, Freuchen remained in Upernavik with his wife. The following day, she died. "In the evening she asked me what I thought was the matter," Freuchen recalled. "Her head was buzzing with thoughts which came unsummoned, she said. It was ghastly to sit helpless and watch her fade away. I told her to try to sleep but she could not. I went into the kitchen to brew tea for her. . . . Navarana was so quiet that I tiptoed in to look at her. As I watched her, her lip just quivered. Then she was dead."[22]

Sofie and another friend made arrangements for a coffin. But then the Lutheran Church had a surprise for Freuchen; because Navarana was not baptized, she could not be buried in the graveyard. Freuchen later described the local minister as "an undersized, native imbecile" who told him that "no bell might toll over her funeral and, he was sorry, he could not deliver a sermon."[23] Seething with rage, Freuchen buried his wife himself. Freuchen was now a widower; his two children, Pipaluk and Miqqusaaq, were motherless.

The *Søkongen* returned from Thule with seven Inughuit who had agreed to leave home and accompany the expedition for three years. It had been intended that an additional man, Aajaku, a favourite of Rasmussen, would also accompany him. He had travelled with the explorer on an earlier expedition and had also spent a few years in Denmark. But, tragically, he had committed suicide in Greenland earlier that year.

One more person was needed. Rasmussen recruited an old friend, Jacob Olsen, minister at Ujarasussuk, as interpreter, secretary, dog-driver, and hunter. Olsen was a native Kalaaleq, and a brother to Gustav Olsen, who had served as the first priest at the North Star Mission in Thule in 1909.

The little vessel continued down the coast and reached Nuuk on August 24. But a vicious flu was ravaging Greenland that summer, and all the Inughuit came down with it. They were all admitted to the local hospital, where six out of seven were diagnosed with pneumonia. On September 6 tragedy struck again with the death of Iggiannguaq. The expedition had not even left Greenland and already three Inughuit were dead. A day after Iggiannguaq's death, all the Inughuit were baptized; that evening the expedition left for Canada.

Rasmussen had intended to base his expedition on the mainland near Lyon Inlet. But by mid-September, the lateness of the departure from Greenland and the need to hurry because of ice making in Foxe Basin dictated a different location. Time was running out before winter would set in. The *Søkongen* made land at a small island that Rasmussen later learned was known to local Inuit as Uglirjuaq ("the walrus hauling-out place") near Repulse Bay. Not knowing exactly where they were, Rasmussen called the place Danske Ø (Danish Island). He thought they were between Lyon Inlet and Gore Bay, but later learned that what they thought was main-

22 Freuchen, *Arctic Adventure,* 325-6.

23 Ibid., 326.

land behind them was in fact another larger island, Nagjuktuuq, separated from the mainland by Hurd Channel. It was larger and had a different shape than recorded a century earlier by William Edward Parry. Because of the swift current running through Hurd Channel, this was not an ideal place to base their operations, but they had to make the best of it. This would be the expedition's headquarters for the next three years.

The ship departed on September 24. Snow covered the ground and the bay was freezing over. The house, built out of material originally intended for a provisions shed, was up, and after four days of feverish activity they were able to move into the house. The Inughuit were still too weak from their illnesses to be of much help in the construction, but they were able to pitch the tents and look after the dogs. They quickly recovered after a few days ashore. The Danes named their new home Blæsebælgen ("the bellows"), so named because of a wind that was all too common on the island.

The Fifth Thule Expedition had begun.

Inughuit on the Expedition

When Knud Rasmussen embarked on the Fifth Thule Expedition in 1921, he did something quite different than previous expeditions to the Arctic had done. Other explorers had usually recruited guides, hunters, and seamstresses once they arrived. Rasmussen, of course, did that too. But he also brought his own assistants with him: six Inughuit from the Thule District of northwestern Greenland, people whom he knew well, had worked with before, and trusted.

These Inughuit, and the Kalaaleq Jacob Olsen, became well-known to the Canadian Inuit in the districts where the Fifth Thule Expedition worked and travelled, particularly the Naujaat and Iglulik areas, but also, depending on where various members travelled, in Pond Inlet and Arctic Bay, on Southampton Island, and in the Chesterfield Inlet and Baker Lake areas.

Who were these people?

The two most well-known, through the writings of Rasmussen and the other scientists, were a young man, Qaavigarsuaq, and a young woman, Arnarulunnguaq.

Qaavigarsuaq was born in northern Greenland about 1900. Family lore says that he was born aboard a ship on one of Robert Peary's expeditions. It is also suggested that he had a *Qallunaaq* ("white person") father, probably Bob Bartlett, a Newfoundlander who participated in some of Peary's expeditions. Qaavigarsuaq was a young man in 1923, and an excellent hunter. Moreover, he was unmarried and so would be an excellent choice to accompany Rasmussen on the highlight of his expedition, the long dogsled trip from the Repulse Bay area across the top of North America to Alaska. He would also accompany Rasmussen to Chesterfield Inlet and to the inland Inuit south of Baker Lake. Handsome and outgoing, he was popular with Inuit he met everywhere on his journeys. In some of Rasmussen's writings, he is known as Mitiq.

Arnarulunnguaq was Qaavigarsuaq's cousin. She was born about 1895. Her father died when she was seven, leaving her mother with four children. Unable to provide for her daughter, the mother, following the custom of the time, decided to put the little girl to death. But her brother Aajaku pleaded for her life, and she was spared. As a young girl growing into adulthood, she learned the skills of sewing and managing a household, and married Iggiannguaq, a skilled young hunter whom Rasmussen had met in 1903. Rasmussen recruited the couple for his expedition, but Iggiannguaq died of influenza in Nuuk the day before the expedition was to leave Greenland. Although grieving, Arnarulunnguaq decided to continue with the expedition. Had she returned to Thule, with her husband and brother both dead, she would have had no means of support. She told Rasmussen at the time, "Before it was you who needed me; now it's me who needs you."[24]

Rasmussen described her as "the most skilled of the women we have with us." He described her role: "It was her duty, as that of the other women, to keep the fur clothing mended, to cook, and, on the journey, to help drive the dogs."[25] Because she was widowed, it was decided that she too should accompany Rasmussen on the long sled journey, along with Qaavigarsuaq.

The other four Inuit were two married couples.

Aaqqiuq was the oldest of the group, having been born about 1891. He had worked for several expeditions in northern Greenland, and had travelled extensively in far northern Canada. Between 1913 and 1917 he had been a guide for Donald MacMillan's Crocker Land Expedition. He had crossed Ellesmere Island a number of times, in addition to sledding the east coast of the island for most of its north-south distance; in 1916 he accompanied MacMillan as far west as King Christian Island.

His wife was Arnannguaq, born about 1896. As a teenager in 1911 she had been married for a time to Minik, an Inuk who had been taken to New York as a young boy and remained there for twelve years before returning north.[26] The young couple had lived in the home of Knud Rasmussen and Peter Freuchen at their Thule station. But the marriage failed because Arnannguaq, although an excellent seamstress, was extremely lazy and spent most of her time sleeping. Freuchen described her at the time as the most resourceless girl he had ever met. Later she married a hunter, Ittullak, with whom she had two children, but that marriage too failed. Eventually she married Aaqqiuq. In the meantime she must have outgrown her laziness, otherwise Rasmussen would probably not have chosen the couple to accompany his expedition.

---

24 Lidegaard, "Arnarulunnguaq," unpaginated.

25 Rasmussen, *Across Arctic America*, ix.

26 For the story of Minik, including his short-lived marriage to Arnannguaq, see Harper, *Minik*, 169-173.

The other couple was a young man, Nasaitsurluarsuk, born about 1897, and his young wife, Aqattaq, only sixteen years old. Nasaitsurluarsuk, when he was about nineteen, had participated in the disastrous Second Thule Expedition into farthest northern Greenland. The young guide's name was a mouthful, and he was usually known in Danish as Bådsmand (Boatman) and in English as "The Bosun." In *Inuktun*, the language of the Thule district, this became Puursimaat, the name by which he is remembered in Canada. He was a good marksman and an excellent seal hunter. In a letter to Mathiassen in 1924, Peter Freuchen claimed that Puursimaat was the best hunter of the group and the most skilled in travelling by dogsled. Although he was often the last to get up in the morning, he made up for it by working late into the evenings, even after the others had gone to bed.[27] His wife, Aqattaq, was the youngest member of the expedition. Perhaps because she was less experienced in travel than the other women of the expedition, she was often left in charge of Blæsebælgen while the others were away. This couple became especially well-known to the people of the Uluksan camp just outside Arctic Bay, where they spent time in 1924 during their return to Greenland via north Baffin Island.

These were the Inughuit, the largely unsung heroes and aides who helped to make Rasmussen's expedition a success.

27 Kleist, "The Fifth Thule Expedition," 44-45.

Part 2:
DANISH ISLAND

Part 2: Danish Island

Akilinirmiut: Meeting New People

Danish Island would be the base from which the expedition members would conduct their scientific explorations and pursue Rasmussen's dream of meeting as many Canadian Inuit as possible. Blæsebælgen was their Canadian home.

Therkel Mathiassen, the expedition's archaeologist, described the building as "neither a large nor a comfortable erection, but it fulfilled its purpose in every way."[1] Two thicknesses of timber were separated by a layer of insulation, and the exterior was covered with roofing felt. In the middle of a large central room stood a cooking range. The rear half of the room had a large traditional sleeping platform where the six Inughuit, the West Greenlander Jacob Olsen, and the Dane Peter Freuchen slept by night and worked by day. At the west end of the house, Knud Rasmussen had his own room with a storeroom behind it. At the opposite end was a room where the other three Danes slept, and behind it another storeroom for scientific equipment. Three windows all faced south.

It was a little over two months before Rasmussen first encountered Akilinirmiut, Canadian Inuit, the object of his quest. On December 4, he, Peter Freuchen, and one of the Inughuit hunters brought from Greenland, Puursimaat, were travelling by dogsled en route to the Hudson's Bay Company (HBC) post at Repulse Bay when they met a group of Inuit returning to their camp at Lyon Inlet from a trading trip. Rasmussen described the unexpected encounter:

> It was about noon; the red of the sun tinged the horizon. . . . I perceived some four km distant, a black line extending across the ice midway out in the bay. . . . I stopped the team at once and got out my glass; and now I could plainly distinguish a whole line of

1 Mathiassen, "Report on the Expedition," 23.

> sledges with a great number of dogs. . . . One man broke away from the rest, and came running across the ice at right angles to the line I was following. I realized that he was making for me, and with the excitement natural to a first meeting with human beings in these wilds, I at once jumped on the sledge and gave my dogs the signal for full speed. . . .
>
> In a few minutes I had come up with him, and the dogs, themselves excited by the strange smell of him, and his unfamiliar dress, would have attacked him had I not shouted to him to stand still. I stopped the team at the same moment, cracked my whip over their heads, and leapt clear of the sledge in front of the dogs, so as to place myself between them and the stranger. I had made a long jump, and with such impetus that to avoid knocking him over I was obliged to throw my arms around his neck. So there we stood, laughing and shaking each other, while the dogs, crestfallen, lay down on the ice, as if ashamed at having mistaken a friend for an enemy.[2]

Many years later, one of the Canadian Inuit, Amiimiarjuk, recalled that same fortuitous encounter:

> That year we camped up at Tasirjuaq, where we had spent the summer hunting caribou. From there we had come to visit the white man at Naujaat, when there was beginning to be snow on the ice. It was when we were on the way back that the meeting took place on the other side of Pitiktarvik, close to Ikartalik.
>
> We saw three sleds coming from the direction of Uglirjuaq, and we stopped to wait for them.
>
> They were strangers.
>
> Kunut [Knud Rasmussen] came first. Puursimaat followed him. Distrustful, the men of our group had prepared themselves for any eventuality. But lo and behold they weren't dangerous people at all. Piita [Peter Freuchen] came too. His sled was broken. We approached them.
>
> At Kunut's request we made camp. Kunut slept in our *iglu* [snow house]. . . . He asked us all . . . to go see him (at Danish Island): he wanted to learn more about us. . . . Later, since we were the first people he had met, and he often saw us again, each time we met him he stayed with us. . . . He was very nice, very appealing and he liked young people a lot.[3]

---

2 Rasmussen, "Iglulik Eskimos," 12-13.

3 Mary-Rousselière, "The Fifth Thule Expedition," 23-24.

The Thule hunter Puursimaat, in old age, also gave a detailed account of that first meeting:

> It was at Sirluaq (Haviland Bay) that we met the Inuit.
>
> There were three of us, each one with his sled: Kunut (Knud Rasmussen), Piita (Peter Freuchen) and me. We were coming from Nagjuktuuq (Vansittart Island). Aaqqiuq and Qaavigarsuaq had accompanied us for a long way but they had just left us to return and there were only the three of us.
>
> Since Piita had broken his sled whose wood was split, we had had to stop to fix it, so that we had stayed behind while Kunut went ahead.
>
> Suddenly, towards the land, we saw something in the distance which we first took to be caribou. Piita and I asked ourselves: "Caribou, maybe?. . . Sleds, maybe?"
>
> Actually it was sleds, those of Itirjuaq, Papik and Pilakapsik. They were coming home from the white man's place [Repulse Bay].
>
> Up until then we hadn't seen any Inuit. We went up to them and invited them to camp close by on the land. While we went ahead I could hear the Canadians call "We are going to have a good time!" because we were going to camp together. . . .
>
> After testing the snow with the shaft of their seal harpoons, they started building iglus. They built three: Papik on one side, Itirjuaq in the middle, and Pilakapsik on the other side. Meanwhile I was heating coffee. Kunut had told me to make the coffee. He was giving them tobacco.
>
> The women banked the iglus with their snow shovels. Then when the iglus were finished, they lit their oil lamps inside.
>
> We prepared a place for our sleds and staked out our dogs. Then we built lean-tos next to the iglus in which to put our things.
>
> I stayed with Papik. In the middle was Piita with Itirjuaq. Kunut was in Pilakapsik's iglu.
>
> We really enjoyed ourselves. We chatted and laughed a lot that we could understand each other. Everything was so new for us. They told us: "You didn't have to make camp for you are almost there [Repulse Bay]. We camped because we are very slow."[4]

This was an auspicious start to Rasmussen's expedition and boded well for its success. The man into whose arms Rasmussen had leapt from his sled was Papik, and he was a *Nattilingmiutaq*—a member of a group of Inuit who had moved into the area from the northwest in the previous fifty years, attracted by the presence of

4 Ibid., 21-22.

whalers with whom they could trade. Rasmussen was pleased that he and his new friend could understand each other. He was even more pleased to learn that in the immediate area were camps of Nattilingmiut, *Aivilingmiut* (people from Aivilik, "a place with walrus"), and *Iglulingmiut* (people from Iglulik, "a place with houses").

As explorers' and anthropologists' knowledge of Canadian Inuit groupings developed, scientists generally called all Canadian Inuit "The Central Eskimos," because they occupied a central position in the Inuit circumpolar world. (That classification often excluded the Inuit of the Mackenzie Delta, the majority of whom were immigrant Alaskans.)

Smaller Canadian Inuit cultural and linguistic groups are generally described by a geographic name with the Inuktitut suffix "-miut" appended. The name thus created denotes the people of a specific place or a general region, and the people so described are "discrete cultural-linguistic units."[5] They can be thought of as regional bands. One definition of a regional band describes it as "the largest discrete socio-territorial group occupying a territory with sufficient resources to support its members over many generations, and . . . sharing a recognized genetic or affinal kinship."[6] Each was a group small enough to self-identify "in terms of a specific feature of the territory it occupied."[7] The scholar Renée Fossett Jones wrote, "Members of a miut recognized a common genetic inheritance and had kinship ties with nearly all other members of the group, although temporary residents from other miuts . . . were common. The marriage universe was almost entirely contained within the regional band."[8]

Rasmussen and Mathiassen distinguished between the Iglulingmiut and Aivilingmiut, but recognized that they were both branches of an overarching group, the "Iglulik Eskimos," sometimes also confusingly called the Iglulingmiut. Using this term collectively comprised the *Tununirmiut* of north Baffin Island, the Iglulingmiut (proper) of the northeast coast of Melville Peninsula, and the Aivilingmiut of the southern part of that peninsula and extending as far south as Cape Fullerton.

On the day following his fortuitous first meeting with local Inuit, Rasmussen and his party continued on to Repulse Bay, established as a trading post by the Hudson's Bay Company in 1920.[9] There they made the acquaintance of the trading post manager, George Cleveland, an American who had been shanghaied onto a whaling ship as a young man. He was known to Inuit as Sakkuaqtirungniq ("the harpooner"). Northern

5 Jones, "The Keewatin Inuit," 23.

6 Ibid., 26.

7 Ibid., 27.

8 Ibid., 29.

9 A post was established farther south at Bury Cove in 1919. The following year its building was moved to Repulse Bay.

literature often calls him Captain Cleveland, although he had never been a ship's captain. He also called himself George Washington Cleveland, although his true middle name was "Grover," not "Washington." Eccentric and outrageous, he was already famous in the eastern Arctic as a man who had fathered a number of children with the wives of numerous Inuit men. Rasmussen and Cleveland would have problems over the next two years over matters of trade, with Cleveland accusing the Danes of siphoning Inuit trade away from his post. Yet through it all, relations remained cordial, with Cleveland extending generous hospitality to the Danes whenever they visited his lonely post.

Some months later Rasmussen told Father Lionel Ducharme, a young Catholic priest known to Inuit as Mikilaaq ("the smallest one"), an amusing account of his first encounter with Cleveland. Decades later, Ducharme committed it to paper:

> So Rasmussen arrives with his fellow travellers. What an event! Cleveland is everywhere, giving voluble commands to the Eskimos. He invites Rasmussen and his party to come warm themselves at his house. Some Eskimos come in at the same time. Cleveland spouts words and gestures. Rasmussen asks what language they are speaking whereupon his host answers:
>
> "These Eskimos here on the west coast speak a language that I am the only white man to know and understand. For the success of your project, it is imperative that I accompany you—which I will consent to do, provided I am furnished a generous recompense for losses to be incurred during my absence."
>
> Rasmussen said this felt like a cold shower on him and his companions. They recognized an obstacle to their project so serious as to make them start thinking of their voyage to the south, to Sikuligjuaq in particular, as a waste of money and energy.
>
> However, seizing an opportunity, Rasmussen went out to talk with the *Naujaarmiut* [people from Naujaat], particularly with Cleveland's right hand man.
>
> "Listen," he said, "I speak like people at home. Do you understand me well?" "Of course," answered the man, then the conversation started—in Eskimo of course. It was a revelation. "But what language does your boss speak?" "I don't know." "But you seem to understand him." "Listen. I'm so used to my boss that I understand his facial expressions and gestures. Me, and the rest of us, we imitate the dogs: we obey. . . ."
>
> Rasmussen was relieved. He decided to follow through on the southern adventure, after having thanked Sakkuaqtirungniq for his services.[10]

10 Ducharme, "Knud Rasmussen and his visit," 6.

Cleveland succeeded in doing what few *Qallunaat* ("white people") ever accomplished in the "old days"—he lived intimately with Inuit for years, often as the only Qallunaaq among them, and yet failed to learn their language, relying instead on a clumsy substitute of words out of context, facial expressions, and gestures.

In December of 1921 Therkel Mathiassen and Kaj Birket-Smith arrived at Repulse Bay and stayed with Cleveland; they were tremendously impressed with the whaler's knowledge and assistance. The expedition's summary report, written by Mathiassen, says that "in rich measure [Cleveland] gave them the benefit of his knowledge of the land and its people."[11]

Peter Freuchen's account of this meeting adds some colour to the event. He wrote that both scientists were "overcome with joy as they met him. 'He is the most amazing man!' they said. 'He knows everything! He's worth his weight in gold!' They had their notebooks in hand and jotted down every remark he made."[12]

Freuchen wrote that Mathiassen and Birket-Smith were both great scientists and suspicion was not in their souls, but, "unfortunately I have never been a saint, but I was saved by experience from believing in the old man, and I told them that he was a damned liar, and nothing else. I recognized the stories he told as the same old ones that were always used in the North to impress greenhorns."[13]

Freuchen was right, for Mathiassen had to note that "afterwards his information proved not to be wholly reliable."[14]

Ducharme summed up his impressions of Cleveland's linguistic ability: "Knowing only a few words of Eskimo, he spoke a marvellous language that nobody understood, however everyone got along with him!"[15]

While at Repulse Bay Rasmussen met a man, Ivaluarjuk, whom he described as the geographer of the tribe. He sported a long white beard and "red, rheumy eyes"[16] that had become dimmed by exposure to too many blizzards. The old man had travelled extensively throughout his life and drew for Rasmussen a map of the entire coastline from Repulse Bay to Pond Inlet. Rasmussen received his introduction to the folklore of the Iglulingmiut from this man. He had a "worn look" but narrated his stories in a "quiet, steady manner"[17] that created a deep impression on his listeners. At first Ivaluarjuk was reserved when Rasmussen encouraged him to tell the stories

11 Mathiassen, "Report on the Expedition," 30.

12 Freuchen, *Arctic Adventure*, 337.

13 Ibid.

14 Mathiassen, "Report on the Expedition," 30.

15 Ducharme, "Knud Rasmussen and his visit," 6.

16 Rasmussen, "Iglulik Eskimos," 16.

17 Ibid., 17.

of his people. In fact, Rasmussen's impression was that the Inuit of this area were extremely cautious in expressing their views to white men. Rasmussen thought it was a "kind of spiritual shyness" mixed with "a certain sense of dignity"[18] that made them reticent to speak about their beliefs. He then determined that he would make it clear that he was not there to condemn or ridicule their beliefs, as visiting white men had done in the past, but had come "expressly for the purpose of learning what they could teach."[19]

Rasmussen won Ivaluarjuk's confidence, and in a quiet and steady tone, the old man narrated the traditional tales and songs of his people and told of his own eventful life.

Rasmussen recorded a song that the old man shared with him:

Cold and mosquitoes,
These two pests
Come never together.
I lay me down on the ice.
Lay me down on the snow and ice,
Till my teeth fall chattering.
It is I,
Aja - aja - ja.

Memories are they,
From those days,
From those days,
Mosquitoes swarming
From those days,
The cold is bitter,
The mind grows dizzy
As I stretch my limbs
Out on the ice.
It is I,
Aja - aja - ja.

Ai! But songs
Call for strength
And I seek after words,
I, aja - aja - ja."[20]

Ivaluarjuk concluded a session of his storytelling with a statement that embodies

18 Ibid., 20.

19 Ibid.

20 Ibid., 18-19.

the beautifully poetic narrative techniques of the traditional Inuit storyteller:

> But when I chance to think of my childhood and recall all the old memories from those days, then youth seems a time when all meat was juicy and tender, and no game too swift for a hunter. When I was young, every day was as a beginning of some new thing, and every evening ended with the glow of the next day's dawn. Now, I have only the old stories and songs to fall back upon, the songs that I sang myself in the days when I delighted to challenge my comrades to a song-contest in the feasting house.[21]

This was a fortuitous meeting. Rasmussen had met Inuit little touched by outside influences, and their Inuktitut dialects and his Kalaallisut speech from Greenland were mutually intelligible. He felt the expedition was off to a good start.

Tagurnaaq and Palluq

On the way back to Blæsebælgen, Rasmussen and his party chanced upon an old woman jigging for trout. She had heard nothing of the arrival of Rasmussen's party in the district and so she was naturally frightened at the encounter. The cut of the strangers' clothes, their sleds, the harnesses of their dogs, and even their speech was different from what she was familiar with. But her apprehension disappeared when Rasmussen explained that he came from a land beyond Tununiq (the name by which she knew far-off Pond Inlet), from a country "beyond the great sea that washed the shores of Baffin Land."[22]

She had been to Tununiq and had met Scottish whalers there. From them she had heard of Greenland and of the people there who spoke her language. By then unafraid, she warmed to her visitors, and invited them to make themselves at home in her iglu, one of three in a village nearby. She told the strangers that she and her husband had moved from Iglulik to the Naujaat area to be nearer to white men and the goods one could acquire through barter with them.

The old lady's name was Tagurnaaq. It means "the one who is shy of strangers," but, she informed her new friends, she was just the opposite; indeed, the woman chattered incessantly. She told Rasmussen that she would much rather talk than listen. Rasmussen was happy to hear it; he would much rather listen, especially as Tagurnaaq was a true *Iglulingmiutaq* (a person from Iglulik). Her people, of all the

21 Rasmussen, "Iglulik Eskimos," 17.

22 Ibid., 21.

Inuit on the west coast of Hudson Bay and Foxe Basin, had had the least interaction with non-Inuit. Rasmussen later wrote that she was the first of all the Inuit he met whose confidence he felt he truly gained.

So pleased was Tagurnaaq at her discovery of these strangers in her land that she immediately composed a song in their honour:

Ajaja - aja - ja ja
The lands around my dwelling
Are more beautiful
From the day
When it is given me to see
Faces I've never seen before.
All is more beautiful.
All is more beautiful.
And life is thankfulness.
These guests of mine
Make my house grand,
Ajaja - aja - ja ja[23]

Tagurnaaq recounted the story of her life for Rasmussen. It was a tale filled with the joys of summer, the privations of winter, starvation, shamanic ritual, births and deaths, marriages happy and miserable, and bereavements.

Tagurnaaq's husband, Palluq, was the opposite of his wife; in Peter Freuchen's humorous words, he was "not a great man for talking and working, but he was a terrible man for thinking, and he took his time when he indulged in his specialty."[24] Rasmussen described him, more seriously, as "a quiet and persevering hunter and a good traveller."[25] Palluq was a shaman, as was his wife, and Rasmussen learned much from the couple about traditional beliefs. In modern parlance we might say that, for an ethnographer like Rasmussen, Tagurnaaq and Palluq were pure gold.

The couple soon relocated to Danish Island and remained with Rasmussen through the rest of the winter. The ethnographer hunted often with Palluq and came to know and understand him well. He thought the man to be of a "humble, religious turn of mind."[26] A fatalist, Palluq felt that "only by the most ingenious system of taboo, with propitiatory rites and sacrifices, could the balance of life be maintained."[27]

From their intimacy, the ethnographer formed some conclusions about the inner philosophy of the people and the qualities inherent in their legends and beliefs:

---

23 Ibid., 27.

24 Freuchen, *Arctic Adventure*, 348.

25 Rasmussen, "Iglulik Eskimos," 32.

26 Ibid.

27 Ibid.

> I could not but think, many a time, how unjust it is to accuse "primitive peoples" of being only concerned with their food and how to get it with the least trouble. True, they say themselves that a man's only business is to procure food and clothing, and while fulfilling his duties in this respect he finds, in his hunting and adventures, the most wonderful experiences of his life. Nevertheless, men may be to the highest degree interested in spiritual things; and I am thinking here not only of their songs and poems, their festivals when strangers come to their place, but also of the manner in which they regard religious questions, wherein they evince great adaptability and versatility.
>
> This it is which always gives their accounts that delightful originality which is the peculiar property of those whose theories are based on experience of life itself. Their naturalness makes of them philosophers and poets unawares, and their simple . . . orthodoxy gives to their presentment of a subject the childlike charm which makes even the mystic element seem credible.[28]

These were among the lessons that Rasmussen learned from Palluq and Tagurnaaq.

It was not only Rasmussen whom Palluq assisted. In 1923, accompanied by Tagurnaaq, Palluq acted as guide for the expedition's archaeologist, Therkel Mathiassen, when he left Blæsebælgen for the final time and travelled over northern Baffin Island to Pond Inlet to continue his own research into what came to be known as the Thule Culture.

In 1972, Kivalliq Elder Louis Tapatai told *Inuktitut* magazine about Palluq and Tagurnaaq. Tapatai, born in 1905, was married to Palluq's daughter by a former wife. He remembered his father-in-law as a powerful shaman, yet a "very lovable, and a very interesting man"[29] with strong dogs able to haul heavy loads. He described the couple, Palluq and Tagurnaaq, as "fun to be with. . . . They had no enemies and were always very happy."[30]

Tapatai remembered: "Palluq used to play with polar bears because he was so brave and powerful. One day while he was playing with the bears, he slipped and fell on the ice. He received three large scratches on his arm. He used to show us the scars to prove it."[31]

---

28 Rasmussen, "Iglulik Eskimos," 33.

29 Tapatai, "Akulak," 10.

30 Ibid., 12.

31 Ibid.

Rasmussen was fortunate in meeting Tagurnaaq because the elderly woman loved to talk. Among the many stories she told her eager listener was one that she described as "the worst thing I remember." It is the tragic story of Ataguttaaluk, a woman still living at that time among the Iglulingmiut. It is illustrative of the living conditions of the isolated Iglulingmiut and the hardships they endured at a time almost two decades before Rasmussen's arrival.

> In the course of my life, from childhood to old age. I have seen many lands, and lived in many different ways. There were times of abundance, and times of dearth and want. The worst thing I remember was when I found a woman who had eaten her husband and her children to save herself from starvation.
>
> Uumaga [the pet name for her husband] and I were travelling from Iglulik to Tununiq when he dreamed one night that a friend of his had been eaten by his nearest kin. Uumaga has the gift of second sight, and always knows when anything remarkable is going to happen.
>
> Next day we started off, and there was something remarkable about our journey from the start. Again and again the sledge stuck fast, but when we came to look, there was nothing to show what had stopped it. This went on all day, and in the evening we halted at Aunirit ("the melted place," in the interior of Cockburn Land) [an old name for northern Baffin Island]. Next morning a ptarmigan flew over our tent. I threw a walrus tusk at it, but missed. Then I threw an axe, and again missed. And it seemed as if this also was to show that other strange tidings were to happen that day. We started off, and the snow was so deep that we had to help pull the sledge ourselves.
>
> Then we heard a noise. We could not make out what it was; sometimes it sounded like a dying animal in pain, and then again like human voices in the distance. As we came nearer, we could hear human words, but could not at first make out the meaning, for the voice seemed to come from a great way off. Words that did not sound like real words, and a voice that was powerless and cracked. We listened and kept on listening, trying to make out one word from another, and at last we understood what it was that was being said. The voice broke down between the words, but what it was trying to say was this: "I am not one who can live any longer among my fellows; for I have eaten my nearest of kin."
>
> Now we knew that there should properly be no one else in this part of the country but ourselves, but all the same we could distinctly hear that this was a woman speaking, and we looked at each other, and it was as if we hardly dared speak out loud, and we whispered: "An eater of men! What is this we have come upon here!"

We looked about us, and at last caught sight of a little shelter, built of snow with a piece of skin rug. It lay half hidden in a drift and was hardly to be noticed in the snow all round, which was why we had not made it out before. And now that we could see where it was the voice came from, it sounded more distinctly, but still went on in the same broken fashion.

We went slowly up to the spot, and when we looked in, there lay a human skull with the flesh gnawed from the bones. Yes, we came to that shelter, and looking in, we saw a human being squatting down inside, a poor woman, her face turned piteously towards us. Her eyes were all bloodshot, from weeping, so greatly had she suffered.

"Kikkaq," she said (literally, "you my gnawed bone," which was her pet name for Palluq, whom she knew well). "Kikkaq, I have eaten my elder brother and my children." "My elder brother" was her pet name for her husband. Palluq and I looked at each other, and could not understand that she was still alive and breathing. There was nothing of her but bones and dry skin, there seemed indeed hardly to be a drop of blood in all her body, and she had not even much clothing left, having eaten a great deal of that, both the sleeves and all the lower part of her outer furs. Palluq bent down quite close to hear better, and Ataguttaaluk—for we knew her now, and could see who it was—said once more:

"Kikkaq, I have eaten your fellow-singer from the feasting, him with whom you used to sing when we were gathered in the great house at a feast."

My husband was so moved at the sight of this living skeleton, which had once been a young woman, that it was long before he knew what to answer. At last he said: "You had the will to live, therefore you live."

We now put up our tent close by, and cut away a piece of the fore curtain to make a little tent for her. She could not come into the tent with us, for she was unclean, having eaten dead bodies. When we went to move her, she tried to get up, but fell back in the snow. Then we tried to feed her with a little meat, but after she had swallowed a couple of mouthfuls, she fell to trembling all over, and could eat no more. Then we gave her a little hot soup, and when she was a little quieter, we looked round the shelter and found the skull of her husband and those of her children; but the brains were gone. We found the gnawed bone, too. The only part she had not been able to eat was the entrails. We gave up our journey then, and decided to drive back to Iglulik as soon as she felt a little stronger.

And when she was once more able to speak, she told us how

it had come about. They had gone up country hunting caribou, but had not been able to find any; they then tried fishing in the lakes but there were no fish. Her husband wandered all about in search of food, but always without success, and they grew weaker and weaker. Then they decided to turn back towards Iglulik, but were overtaken by heavy snowfalls. The snow kept on. It grew deeper and deeper, and they themselves were growing weaker and weaker every day. They lay in their snow hut and could get nothing to eat. Then, after the snow had fallen steadily for some time, there came fierce blizzards, and at last her husband was so exhausted that he could not stand.

They kept themselves alive for some time by eating the dogs, but these also were wasted away and there was little strength in them as food. It simply kept them alive, so that they could not even die. At last the husband and all the children were frozen to death; having no food, they could not endure the cold. Ataguttaaluk had been the strongest of them all, though she had no more to eat than the others. As long as the children were alive they had most. She had tried at first to start off by herself and get through to Iglulik, for she knew the way, but the snow came up to her waist, and she had no strength; she could not go on. She was too weak even to build a snow hut for herself, and the end of it was she turned back in her tracks and lay down beside her dead husband and the dead children. Here at least there was shelter from the wind in the snow hut and there were still a few skins she could use for covering.

She ate these skins to begin with. But at last there was no more left, and she was only waiting for the death to come and release her. She seemed to grow more and more dull and careless of what happened. But one morning, waking up to sunshine and a fine clear sky, she realized that the worst of the winter was over now, and it could not be long till the spring. Her snow hut was right on the road to Tununiq, the very road that all would take when going from Iglulik to trade there. The sun was so warm that for the first time she felt thawed a little, but the snow all about her was as deep and impassable as ever.

Then suddenly it seemed as if the warm spring air about her had given her a great desire to go on living, and thus it was that she fell to eating of the dead bodies that lay beside her. It was painful, it was much worse than dying, and at first she threw up all she ate, but she kept on, once she had begun. It could not hurt the dead, she knew, for their souls were long since in the land of the dead. Thus she thought, and thus it came about that she became an *inuktuumajuq*, an eater of human kind.

> All this she told us, weeping; and Palluq and I, realizing that after all these sufferings she deserved to live, drove her into Iglulik, where she had a brother living. Here she soon recovered her strength, but it was long before she could bear to be among her fellows. It is many years now since all this happened, and she is married now, to one of the most skilful walrus hunters at Iglulik, named Ittuksaarjuat, who had one wife already; she is his favourite wife and has had several more children.
>
> That is the most dreadful thing in all my life, and whenever I tell the story, I feel I can tell no more.[32]

The terrible events that Tagurnaaq described took place in the spring of 1905. Although it is rare that an event that forms part of Inuit traditional lore can be accurately dated, this tragic story is an exception. Atuat, the adoptive daughter of Tagurnaaq and Palluq, had accompanied her parents on the trip on which they had found Ataguttaaluk. Scottish Captain James Mutch had wintered his whaling and trading vessel at Erik Harbour, just to the east of Pond Inlet, in the winter of 1903-04, and the news of his arrival had spread quickly among the Inuit, for Mutch had trade goods and was the first whaler to winter in the area. In her old age, Atuat retold the story of Ataguttaaluk's ordeal. The tragic events, she said, took place during the winter and spring following Mutch's first wintering.[33]

Peter Freuchen would refer to Ataguttaaluk as the "foremost lady of Fury and Hecla Straits."[34] White people in the region would later call Ataguttaaluk and her husband the king and queen of Iglulik. Ataguttaaluk was one of the first to be baptized in 1931 when Father Etienne Bazin established the first mission in the area, on the island of Avvajja. Her husband was finally baptized nine years later. In June of 1948, Ataguttaaluk fell ill when an influenza epidemic hit Iglulik. Father Guy Mary-Rousselière visited her and she began to complain about her illness. Then her tone suddenly changed. "Come, come," she said, "it's your turn to say beautiful things to me." The priest spoke to her about her impending death, but she, who had lived with death, cut him off. "I am not afraid,"[35] she told him. In early July she was moved to a camp, Kangiq, on Melville Peninsula. Refusing to stay inside her son's tent, she awaited death outside. On July 16, having outlived her husband by almost four years, Ataguttaaluk passed away peacefully. She was buried on a hilltop overlooking the shore. In memory of her, a school in Iglulik bears her name.

---

32 Rasmussen, "Iglulik Eskimos," 29-32.

33 There are also other sources for this story, some more reliable than others. Among them are: Freuchen, *Arctic Adventure*, 374-5; Mary-Rousselière, "History of a Case of Cannibalism," 6-23; Tremblay, *Cruise of the Minnie Maud*, 232-233; Niviatiaq, "Ananaga," 6-10.

34 Freuchen, *Arctic Adventure*, 374.

35 Mary-Rousselière, "Monica Ataguvtaluk," 14.

The Caribou Inuit and the Origins of Inuit Culture

One of the main goals of Rasmussen's Fifth Thule Expedition was to investigate the origins of the "Eskimo race."[36] He had been influenced by the theories of Hans Peder Steensby, an ethnologist who believed that Inuit culture had originated and evolved from an inland culture, and that only later had it become a maritime society. One of Rasmussen's plans was that he and Kaj Birket-Smith, an ethnologist, would travel to the Inuit in the inland of the Kivalliq region, to test and hopefully prove Steensby's theory. Leaving from Repulse Bay, they would travel with Inuit guides south to Chesterfield Inlet, then westward to Baker Lake, and then south into the interior.

Birket-Smith, whom Inuit had nicknamed Qakulluk ("the fulmar"), allegedly because of his bird-like appearance, set off first with the Greenlandic interpreter and assistant Jacob Olsen and two Canadian Inuit, Pilakapsik and Mauniq. It was mid-January, the temperature hovered below minus-forty degrees Celsius, and they faced blizzards. At Bury Cove (then called Berthie Harbour, or Mattuq to the Inuit), near the northern entrance to Wager Bay, they met the trader Jean Berthie of the Hudson's Bay Company, who was wintering on the motor schooner the *Fort Chesterfield.*

The schooner was a floating trading post, and Birket-Smith and Olsen restocked their provisions there before heading overland along the northern coast of the inlet in search of a safe place to cross, the mouth of Wager Bay being almost always open because of a strong current. Having crossed safely, they continued south past Cape Fullerton (Qatiktalik to the Inuit), with its abandoned police buildings,[37] and finally reached Chesterfield Inlet on February 11.

A peculiarity of a northern "settlement" in those long-ago days was that its population included very few Inuit. Chesterfield was no exception. It comprised a Hudson's Bay Company trading post, a Royal Canadian Mounted Police (RCMP) detachment, and a Roman Catholic mission. A few Inuit were employed by these institutions and lived at the settlement, but the vast majority were dispersed in numerous camps—living on the land. Some Inuit at the settlement were *Qairnirmiut* ("people of the flat land or bedrock"), an inland group that had been enticed to the coast for employment and trade.

At the HBC post the travellers were hospitably received by the long-time trader there, Solomon Ford. He had been born at Nachvak on the northern coast of Labrador. The Ford family had originally come from England, but made Labrador their home. Ford spoke Inuktitut and was at home anywhere in the north. He had been at Chesterfield Inlet for a decade. A young clerk, Bill Phillips, worked with him.

The police detachment was manned by Sergeant William Osborn Douglas—in another year he would leave the force and join the HBC as a trader. Douglas was assisted by Constable Packett.

---

36 Rasmussen, *Across Arctic America*, vii.

37 The Royal North-West Mounted Police established a post there in 1903 to issue licenses to foreign whalers, collect customs duties, and enforce the law. It closed about 1914.

The mission was staffed by Father Arsène Turquetil, who had founded it a decade earlier, and the young priest, Lionel Ducharme.

After a month at Chesterfield, Birket-Smith left for Baker Lake with Sergeant Douglas, who was on patrol. Jacob Olsen remained at Chesterfield.

Rasmussen, meanwhile, had been spending his time productively with the great Iglulingmiutaq shaman, Aua, at his camp at Cape Elizabeth, north of Danish Island. Finally he left his headquarters on March 24 and joined Helge Bangsted, Qaavigarsuaq, and Arnarulunnguaq at Repulse Bay, where they stayed with the always-hospitable Captain Cleveland. They left at the end of the month for Chesterfield, accompanied by a young guide, Inuujaq, described as "not a very competent man but inoffensive and hard-working when put to a job."[38] Inuujaq would remain an employee of the expedition until its end.

Before leaving Repulse Bay they encountered an unpleasant reality: the iron runners of their sleds slid very poorly through the snow in severe cold. They had learned the ingenious method of Inuit to cover the bottom of the runners with mud, but mud proved unavailable in the extreme cold, so they modified the Inuit adaptation by coating the runners with a paste of flour moistened and kneaded to a porridge-like consistency. That solved their problem.

Rasmussen's party followed the route that Birket-Smith and Olsen had earlier taken, and enjoyed a pleasant visit with Captain Berthie on his schooner.

At Depot Island south of Cape Fullerton, Rasmussen was surprised that the first person they met was the daughter of a liaison between a Black cook on a whaling vessel and an Inuk woman. He later learned that this woman was not the only result of such liaisons, which had been common in the heyday of whaling. Captain George Comer, who sometimes wintered his ship the *Era* at Fullerton, employed Black crew members. Inuit called them *Puatugi*, meaning Portuguese, because many originated in the Cape Verde Islands, a Portuguese territory.

Rasmussen and his companions camped on the sea ice near Chesterfield Inlet the night before their arrival, not realizing the settlement was only a short distance away. Father Ducharme wrote a description of their arrival:

> The bell rings just as Knud Rasmussen and his companions see the bell tower, then the houses and iglus. As they approach they see the populace becoming more and more animated. Rasmussen leads his group towards the mission, shakes hands with Father Turquetil . . . thanking him effusively for the warm welcome.
>
> As we have seen, the ringing of the bell was but a coincidence though a happy one, for the visitors immediately felt at home. Later Rasmussen said that he and his friends had felt such joy that instantly they had all forgotten the fatigues of their long trip from their little island. . . . They had never dreamed of such a meeting. . . .

38 Mathiassen, "Report on the Expedition," 36.

The pealing of the bell was a good omen."[39]

A church service had been scheduled for 10:00 a.m., and Rasmussen asked if he could assist at it. The service was, of course, in Inuktitut, and the visitors followed the prayer book attentively. Rasmussen was relieved that the differences between the Qairnirmiut dialect and his Greenlandic language, coupled with what he had already learned of the Iglulingmiut dialect, were minor—language would not pose a problem in the work he hoped to do.

He talked at length with Father Turquetil, who had lived with inland Inuit before moving to Chesterfield. Ducharme thought that Rasmussen "was observant and had an open and inquisitive mind."[40] This would allow him, in Ducharme's poetic opinion, to leap more than a hundred years into the past in search of his ancestors when he reached the inland Inuit.

On May 3, Jacob Olsen and Arnarulunnguaq left with Inuujaq to return to Danish Island. That same day, Rasmussen, Bangsted, and Qaavigarsuaq left for Baker Lake. The weather was milder now, and they camped in tents instead of snowhouses. Nine days later they reached the trading post on Uqpiktujuq Island in Baker Lake, where they were met by Birket-Smith and the local trader Henry Thomas Ford (Uqallujujuq to Inuit), who was Solomon Ford's older brother. He had been an Inuktitut interpreter on the official Canadian voyage of William Wakeham on the *Diana* in 1897, and on the Canadian Arctic patrol the *Neptune* in 1903, before serving the Royal North-West Mounted Police as a special constable from 1904 until 1911.

Rasmussen and his companions remained at Baker Lake for three days, learning about local conditions from Henry Ford and Inuit who lived near the post. Finally, Rasmussen and Birket-Smith were ready to meet the true inland Inuit.

They learned that there were four groups of Inuit living inland. They had already met some Qairnirmiut at Chesterfield Inlet. The others were the *Harvaqtuurmiut* ("the people of the rapids or whirlpools"), who lived in various settlements on the middle and lower course of the Kazan River; the *Paallirmiut* ("the people of the willow thicket"), who lived at Hikuligjuaq and were purely inland people; and the *Hauniqtuurmiut* ("the people of the place with bones") west of Rankin Inlet. Rasmussen called them collectively the "Caribou Eskimos," a term that had not previously been used.[41]

The anthropologist Tiger Burch has pointed out that both Rasmussen and Birket-Smith failed to mention another group, the people of the upper Kazan River, in the far southwest of present-day Nunavut, living along the treeline from Nueltin

---

39 Ducharme, "Knud Rasmussen and his visit," 4.

40 Ibid., 7.

41 There is confusion over the use of the term Paallirmiut. Rasmussen distinguishes between two groups whose names are confusingly similar, the Paallirmiut ("the people of the willow thicket"), whom he visited, and Paallimiut or Paadlimiut ("the people at the river mouth out by the sea"), coastal people whom he did not visit. See Rasmussen, "Observations on the Intellectual Culture," footnote on pages 5-6. Rasmussen disagreed with Birket-Smith in this. Birket-Smith used the term Paallimiut for both groups, considering them two branches of the same group.

Lake to Dubawnt Lake. They traded to the south and did not have much to do with the other inlanders. They came to be known as the *Ahiarmiut*. This was an odd omission, since Father Turquetil, with whom both travellers had discussed inland Inuit cultures at length while at Chesterfield Inlet, had ministered to the Ahiarmiut when they came to trade at his first posting, Brochet, on Reindeer Lake in northern Saskatchewan, and had visited them in their own territory on a foray in 1901.[42]

On May 15 Rasmussen and his party headed south in search of the inlanders. It was already late in the season. Soon they reached a Paallirmiut settlement of three tents at the north end of the lake known as Hikuligjuaq ("the place with much ice"). This great lake is often marked on maps as Lake Yathkyed; the name is testament to the fact that this area was previously frequented by Chipewyans who now lived farther south below the treeline. There Rasmussen met the head man of the camp, Igjugaarjuk (which means "the little testicle"), a man held in high esteem by his countrymen. His camp had an abundance of caribou meat.

Rasmussen was most impressed by Igjugaarjuk. He thought him wise, independent, and intelligent. Given the number of Inuit that Rasmussen met before the expedition's end, it is high praise indeed that he wrote, "of all the people I have met on the long stretch between Greenland and Siberia, he occupies an outstanding place among all the prominent Eskimos."[43]

As if to prove his worth, Igjugaarjuk showed Rasmussen a document issued to him by Alfred E. Reames of the RCMP, who had been at his camp a year earlier on a manhunt for a young Inuk murder suspect. Reames had asked for Igjugaarjuk's assistance and deputized him with an "Appointment as Special Constable."

Despite his admiration for the man, Rasmussen found this an amazing circumstance, for he already knew that Igjugaarjuk was himself guilty of a mass murder. Despite the scarcity of women in the camps—a result of infanticide of female babies—Igjugaarjuk had two wives. How he had acquired one of them was the source of Rasmussen's astonishment; he told the tale succinctly: "As a young man Igjugaarjuk had been in love with a woman named Kibgarjuk, but her family were opposed to the match. When he heard later that they thought of giving her to another man, he turned up unexpectedly one day, with his eldest brother, Harpik, at the entrance to the snow house where Kibgarjuk lived, and from there shot down her father, mother, two brothers with their respective wives, and finally, when Kibgarjuk had become alone, sprang in, carried her off and married her."[44]

The policeman, not knowing Inuktitut, had probably known nothing of Igjugaarjuk's past. It is also probable that Igjugaarjuk put little effort into bringing the accused into custody.

Birket-Smith and Bangsted busied themselves collecting ethnographic specimens, but Rasmussen's agenda was different. He craved stories, legends, and

42 See Mary-Rousselière, "Father Gasté," 3-15; and Clabaut, "Bishop Turquetil," 3-11.

43 Rasmussen, *Across Arctic America*, 62.

44 Rasmussen, "Caribou Eskimos," 32.

language. When leaving a Qairnirmiut camp earlier, a man named Pukirluk had told him, "Your tongue is not so frozen as when you came,"[45] a tribute to his progress in adapting to the local dialect. He also had no difficulty in communicating with Igjugaarjuk. So on June 14, leaving the other two men at Igjugaarjuk's camp, Rasmussen and Qaavigarsuaq continued south over the still-frozen lake to a camp on its south shore presided over by Uningujaaq. Their time there was brief. They returned to Igjugaarjuk's camp on June 22.

Three days later Birket-Smith and Bangsted left for Baker Lake with a guide by canoe. They reached the trading post on July 5 "in an extreme state of starvation."[46] The day after their departure from Hikuligjuaq, Rasmussen and Qaavigarsuaq headed north for Baker Lake by sled, assisted for part of the way by Igjugaarjuk himself. Summer was coming on quickly now, and they were hampered by an absence of snow on the land. They reached the post on July 9, four days after their compatriots. A day later they left for Chesterfield Inlet, which they reached on July 30. Birket-Smith and Bangsted arrived there on August 7. A few weeks later, they all took passage with Captain Berthie on the HBC vessel the *Fort Chesterfield* to Repulse Bay, and returned to their home at Danish Island.

The inland adventure was over. It had been all too brief. To read Rasmussen's earlier plans, the investigations of the culture of the inlanders would be the main focus of his expedition, the means by which he and Birket-Smith would test the theories of his mentor, Steensby, on the origins of the entire Inuit people. One wonders, then, why the trip was left to so late in the season. Alternatively, why did not Rasmussen pass a summer inland, and explore the unique cultures he found there in even greater detail? Mathiassen, Freuchen, and Olsen all had their own work plans and agendas, so their work would not have suffered by Rasmussen's absence. He could even have remained with Qaavigarsuaq, and sent Birket-Smith and Bangsted back. As it was, he documented a unique culture extremely well in the short time at his disposal, but a lack of time constraints would have allowed him to learn so much more.

Why didn't he stay longer in such a culturally rich area? There are two possible reasons.

One is that, in planning his expedition with its intended focus on the Caribou Inuit, he had not anticipated the rich store of information he would discover so close to his headquarters at Danish Island in the great shaman and storyteller Aua, not to mention Aua's wife, Urulu, and the other major Iglulingmiut storytellers, especially Tagurnaaq and Aua's brother, Ivaluarjuk. This unexpected wealth of information was on his doorstep and he had mined it extensively, especially on his first visit to Aua's camp. Indeed, his winter visit to Aua was likely the reason for his late start to visit the inlanders. And, as rich as its results were, it was but a portent of what was yet to come the following year, when Rasmussen would again visit the Iglulik shaman. Perhaps

45 Ibid., 30.

46 Mathiassen, "Report on the Expedition," 40.

Rasmussen had decided that an early return to Danish Island would maximize the time he would subsequently be able to spend with Aua.

The other possible reason is starvation.

Knud Rasmussen and Kaj Birket-Smith believed, following Steensby, that Inuit culture had developed inland and only later expanded to the coast to become a maritime culture. It was to prove this theory that Rasmussen had wanted to visit the Inuit of the Kivalliq interior. Ultimately, their theory would be proven wrong by none other than their archaeologist colleague Therkel Mathiassen, who would show that Inuit culture had originated in Alaska and spread eastward across Canada and Greenland.

So why were Inuit living inland in the Kivalliq region? Modern ethnographers have shown that Chipewyans from the forests of northern Manitoba travelled regularly into the treeless lands west of Hudson Bay in the 1700s. The nearest Inuit were around Chesterfield Inlet. Despite occasional hostilities, when Chipewyans and Inuit met, relations were usually friendly. The establishment of a Hudson's Bay Company trading post at Churchill in 1717 eventually drew Inuit south along the coast to trade. Then, in 1781-82, a smallpox epidemic among the Chipewyans decimated that population and left the interior almost unpopulated. Traders also encouraged the Chipewyans to remain in the forest, where valuable furs could be had. The result was a much smaller Chipewyan presence in the barren lands, followed by a migration of Inuit from the coast inland during the 1800s to what had been the traditional hunting grounds of the Chipewyan Dene. From that time on there was an overlap in use of the territory. Relations between the two groups continued to be generally harmonious, though marred by occasional acts of violence.

By 1881, 217 Inuit, all from the inland Kivalliq (most from the southwestern part) traded regularly at the HBC post at Brochet on Reindeer Lake, Manitoba; this compares with 515 mostly coastal Inuit trading into Churchill.

The Caribou Inuit expanded west and south until approximately 1920—that is, until approximately the time that Rasmussen visited them.

Since this trip to the inland Inuit was so critical to Rasmussen's research, the other reason why the trip was so abbreviated may have been the possibility of starvation—his own.

Serious episodes of starvation had occurred among the inland Inuit numerous times since the mid-1800s. But the most serious episodes began about 1916 and continued for a decade—a period some scholars have called the Great Famine.

Solomon Ford, the HBC manager at Chesterfield Inlet, compiled a census of the "Southern Keewatin" in 1918. When it is compared with figures reported by Rasmussen and Birket-Smith in 1922 and 1923, it shows that the population of Harvaqtuurmiut dropped from 186 in 1918 to 74 in 1923. In the same period the

Hauniqtuurmiut population dropped from 96 to 54, the Qairnirmiut population from 214 to 101 or less, and a portion of the Paallirmiut from 304 to 107. On the upper Kazan River, in the territory of the Ahiarmiut, the population dropped from an estimated 600 people to about 100 shortly before the arrival of the expedition.

Rasmussen was told of another Inuit sub-group, the *Tahiujarmiut* (people from Tahiujaq), who had almost all died out through starvation only three years earlier. Birket-Smith reported that over one hundred Tahiujarmiut had died during the winter of 1919. Scholar Tiger Burch noted cryptically, "Despite their professed concern with Inuit history, neither Rasmussen nor Birket-Smith seem to have been interested in anything that happened prior to their visit, even something as momentous as the extinction of an entire society. The Tahiujarmiut received no further notice in their reports."[47]

The Caribou Inuit population therefore had declined by more than half in the years just prior to the Fifth Thule Expedition. In fact, people were dying of starvation while Rasmussen and Birket-Smith were there. Burch stated quite starkly, "What the Fifth Thule Expedition encountered in southern Keewatin was a group of societies on the verge of extinction."[48] Burch went on to suggest that, when Rasmussen wrote about the "careless mind and great capacity for resignation"[49] of the Caribou Inuit, he may have been noting the attitudes of people in despair.

Two years later, Rasmussen was at Herschel Island in the western Canadian Arctic, where he reported to RCMP Inspector Stuart Taylor Wood on the progress of his expedition to date. Among other information, Rasmussen told the inspector of his visit to the inland Caribou Inuit.

Wood wrote a report to police headquarters, summarizing what Rasmussen had told him. He wrote: "Mr. Rasmussen and Birket-Smith found the Eskimo in [the] vicinity of Yathkyed and Dubawnt Lakes in a deplorable condition, many starving and all suffering untold hardship through lack of any kind of fuel during the winter months."[50]

He noted that J. B. Tyrrell had travelled through the area between 1893 and 1895 and reported that there were four to five hundred Inuit in that area at the time, but that, according to Rasmussen, "there are but 50 families in one place and 3 in another now, the remainder having died from starvation. . . . Absence of the caribou appears to be the prime reason."[51]

Wood described the game conditions as reported to him by Rasmussen, then returned to the condition of the Caribou Inuit: "Regarding the starving people of Yathkyed and Dubawnt and Ennadai Lakes . . . these people and those at Baker Lake, Kazan River have no fuel; they depend entirely on the caribou for food and

---

47 Burch, "Inland Eskimos," 88.

48 Ibid., 91.

49 Ibid.

50 Treude, "The work of Knud Rasmussen," 189.

51 Ibid.

clothing. . . . These people live under deplorable conditions of the greatest hardship and there are many deaths every winter from starvation."[52]

But it is the penultimate sentence that is so shocking: "He [Rasmussen] informed me that he would not make public the starving condition of the natives he met with in vicinity of Yathkyed Lake and Backs River." This no doubt pleased the police inspector. But why did Rasmussen agree to keep such damning information a secret? Years later anthropologist Diamond Jenness wrote that Rasmussen "had been shocked by the deplorable conditions of the Eskimos . . . and that only international courtesy, and the feeling that they had been guests on Canadian soil, prevented him and his colleagues from exposing the situation at the time."[53]

And so it was left to popular writer Farley Mowat, three decades after the Fifth Thule Expedition, to inform the public of the ongoing starvation of Inuit in the area with his books *The People of the Deer* and *The Desperate People*, and finally to create a storm of indignation.

Igjugaarjuk the Shaman

When Igjugaarjuk, the powerful shaman of the inland Paallirmiut, met Knud Rasmussen in 1922, he told him about the spirits that governed the lives of the inland Inuit. The coastal Inuit feared the spirit *Nuliajuq*, who governed access to the animals of the sea. But inland Inuit, who depended almost entirely on the caribou, knew nothing of a spirit by that name, fearing instead one called *Pinga* ("the one up in the sky") who was the guardian of all life, both animal and human. They also feared *Hila*, the spirit of weather.

Rasmussen was interested in how a man became a shaman and asked Igjugaarjuk to describe the training he had undergone. Igjugaarjuk told him that one could only become a shaman through sufferings that are almost enough to kill. Here is his story:

> When I was to be a shaman, I chose suffering through the two things that are most dangerous to us humans, suffering through hunger and suffering through cold. First I hungered five days and was then allowed to drink a mouthful of warm water. The old ones say that only if the water is warm will Pinga and Hila notice the novice and help him. Thereafter I went hungry another fifteen days, and again was given a mouthful of warm water. After that I hungered for ten days, and then could begin to eat, though it only had to be . . . the sort of food

52 Treude, "The work of Knud Rasmussen," 192.

53 Jenness, *Eskimo Administration*, 30.

on which there is never any taboo, preferably fleshy meat, and never intestines, head, heart or other entrails, nor meat that had been touched by wolf or wolverine while it lay in a cache. I was to keep to this diet for five moons, and then the next five moons might eat anything. But after that I was again forced to eat the meat diet that is prescribed for all those who must do penance in order to become clean. . . .

My instructor was my wife's father, Piqannaaq. When I was to be exhibited to Pinga and Hila, he dragged me on a little sledge that was no bigger than I could just sit on. He dragged me far over on the other side of Hikuligjuaq. It was a very long day's journey inland to a place we call Kinngaarjuit—the high hills. . . . It was in winter time and took place at night with the new moon. . . . I was not fetched again until the next moon was of the same size.

Piqannaaq built a small snow hut at the place where I was to be, this snow hut being no bigger than that I could just get under cover and sit down. I was given no sleeping skin to protect me against the cold, only a little piece of caribou skin to sit upon. There I was shut in. . . . The entrance was closed with a block, but no soft snow was thrown over the hut to make it warm. When I had sat there for five days, Piqannaaq came with water, tepid, wrapped in caribou skin, a watertight caribou-skin bag. Not until fifteen days afterwards did he come again and hand me the same, just giving himself time to hand it to me, and then he was gone again, for even the old shaman must not interrupt my solitude. The snow hut in which I sat was built far from the trails of men, and when Piqannaaq had found the spot where he thought it ought to be built, he stopped the little sledge at a distance, and there I had to remain seated until the snow hut was ready. Not even I, who was after all the one to have to stay there, might set my footprints in the vicinity of the hut, and old Piqannaaq had to carry me from the sledge over to the hut so that I could crawl in.

As soon as I had become alone Piqannaaq enjoined me to think of one single thing all the time I was to be there, to want only one single thing, and that was to draw Pinga's attention to the fact that there I sat and wished to be a shaman.

My novitiate took place in the middle of the coldest winter, and I, who never got anything to warm me, and must not move, was very cold, and it was so tiring having to sit without daring to lie down, that sometimes it was as if I died a little. Only towards the end of the thirty days did a helping spirit come to me, a lovely and beautiful helping spirit. It was a white woman. She came to me whilst I had collapsed, exhausted, and was sleeping. But still I saw her lifelike, hovering over me, and from that day I could not close my eyes or

> dream without seeing her. . . . I have never seen her while awake, but only in dreams. She came to me from Pinga and was a sign that Pinga had now noticed me and would give me powers that would make me a shaman.[54]

After Igjugaarjuk had endured his time of privation on the land, his teacher, Piqannaaq, came to fetch him. The older man hauled him home on his sled, for the newly trained shaman was too weak to stand. He had slowly to be nursed back to health.

Igjugaarjuk resumed his story:

> Later, when I had become quite myself again, I understood that I had become the shaman of my village, and it did happen that my neighbours or people from a long distance away called me to heal a sick person, or to inspect a course if they were going to travel. When this happened, the people of my village were called together and I told them what I had been asked to do. Then I left tent or snowhouse and went out into solitude: *ahiarmut*, away from the dwellings of man. . . .
>
> If anything difficult had to be found out, my solitude had to extend over three days and two nights, or three nights and two days. In all that time I had to wander about without rest, and only sit down once in a while on a stone or a snow drift. When I had been out long and had become tired, I could almost doze and dream what I had come out to find and about which I had been thinking all the time. Every morning, however, I could come home and report on what I had so far found, but as soon as I had spoken I had to return again, out into the open, out to places where I could be quite alone. . . .
>
> These days of seeking for knowledge are very tiring, for one must walk all the time, no matter what the weather is like and only rest in short snatches. I am usually quite done up, tired, not only in body but also in head, when I have found what I sought.[55]

He summed up his beliefs: "True wisdom is only to be found far away from people, out in the great solitude, and it is not found in play but only through suffering. Solitude and suffering open the human mind, and therefore a shaman must seek his wisdom there."[56]

---

54 Rasmussen, "Caribou Eskimos," 52-53.

55 Ibid., 53-54.

56 Ibid., 55.

Not all shamans were men.

Kiinaalik was a woman of about thirty years when Rasmussen met her. He described her as intelligent, pleasant, and easy to talk with. Moreover, she was neat and clean, amiable, and trustworthy.

She had a reputation among her people for being a powerful shaman. Like the male shamans in her group, she had a special shaman's belt, to which were attached a number of items used as amulets: a part of a gun butt, a piece of sinew, a piece of ribbon that had been tied around a gift of tobacco, a piece of the cap of her deceased brother, a piece of white caribou skin, a piece of a knitted vest that had belonged to a white man, a caribou tooth, caribou-skin mittens, and part of the skin from a seal flipper. All of these items had been gifts and, as such, imparted magical powers to her.

Kiinaalik was a sister-in-law of Igjugaarjuk. It became apparent to the people of her village that she was destined to become a shaman because of powerful dreams that she had had. She spent five days out in extreme weather, suspended from tent poles above the ground, so that Hila, the spirit of the air, might take notice of her. She felt no cold because of the presence of her helping spirits. Next, the people of her village were called together, and her mother, Abgaarjuk, decided that she should be shot, as this was also a means of acquiring shamanic power.

Kiinaalik sat in an iglu, in a kitchen off the entrance passage. Her brother-in-law Igjugaarjuk shot her with a small round stone, and Kiinaalik fell over dead. The villagers held a song-feast while the woman lay dead the whole night. The next morning she woke up of her own accord. She had been shot through the heart—the stone was removed and her mother preserved it.

This death and resurrection had made Kiinaalik acceptable to the spirits. Hila had noticed her, and helping spirits would henceforth come to her of their own volition. Chief among them was her dead brother, of whom she spoke freely and cheerfully, for among her people there was no prohibition on mentioning the names of the dead, as there was among the coast dwellers. Her brother "used to come to her gliding through the air, legs uppermost, head downwards, but as soon as he had reached the ground he could walk like an ordinary man."[57]

She also had a polar bear as a helping spirit.

Igjugaarjuk trained Kiinaalik in shamanism, but he did not carry her training as far as he might, for he took pity on her suffering. That was because it was necessary to suffer a great deal in order to become a powerful shaman. Rasmussen, who learned all this from Igjugaarjuk, concluded that "the fact is that the more one suffers for one's art, the greater shaman one becomes."[58]

But not all Inuit believed in the power of the shaman.

Igjugaarjuk did not think much of the shamans on the coast, those he called saltwater *angakkut* ("shamans"). "These angakkut never seemed trustworthy to me,"

57 Ibid., 58.

58 Ibid.

he told Rasmussen. "A real shaman does not jump about the floor and do tricks, nor does he seek by the aid of darkness, by putting out the lamps, to make the minds of his neighbours uneasy."[59]

A man named Utahania, who lived at Hikuligjuaq, made a visit to the coast and while there criticized the abilities of one of the "saltwater shamans"—a man who was, however, highly respected among his own people. The offended shaman invited Utahania to attend a performance where he could demonstrate his prowess. Another Inuk who was present recounted what transpired there:

> First the shaman shot himself in the forehead with a gun of heavy calibre. The bullet went in through his brow and came out through one sleeve. He shot himself in the heart in the same manner. Then he went out with the men of his village, while the women had to remain in the house. A shotgun was set up with the muzzle pointing towards him, and then he ran towards it and disappeared into the barrel. He could be heard speaking inside it. Then the shotgun was carried into the house. It was then very heavy to carry. Inside the house they suddenly heard a voice from inside the barrel say "*ipiliqihunga*—I am choking." And so the gun was taken outside and the shaman crept out again.
>
> This shaman had a walrus for an amulet, and he allowed his amulet to come into the entrance passage of the house. It could be heard dragging its heavy body in through the passage, and from the passage it squirted salt water in on to the floor of the house, for the shaman kept the walrus out in the passage and did not allow it to come inside. Later the walrus appeared at the window and the shaman harpooned it from the house through the window, without the window being broken. In this manner he convinced Utahania of his powers as a shaman, and after that Utahania declared himself a believer.[60]

The Inuk who recounted this story in 1922 was a skilled hunter, lively and curious about anything that was a little out of the ordinary. He maintained a healthy scepticism, feeling that there was as much reason to believe in the shamans as to doubt them. "There are certainly angakkut who are frauds," he stated, then added, "but there are others, *qanukiaq*—I wonder. . . ."[61]

One man with whom Rasmussen travelled, a Paallirmiut named Uquutaq, had once been a novice shaman but changed his mind about following that path. It was not the sufferings that dissuaded him but rather that he was quite unable to

---

59 Rasmussen, "Caribou Eskimos," 54.

60 Ibid., 58-59.

61 Ibid., 59.

make any contact with his helping spirits "or see all the remarkable signs that his master asserted were given him." He told Rasmussen candidly that he believed it was all "lies and humbug, and only intended for people who were either born timid or were easily fooled."[62] But he dared not give open expression to his disbelief, telling his fellows that he simply believed his qualifications were lacking.

Rasmussen weighed the various opinions he had heard about the power of the shamans. Recognizing that there were skeptics among the Caribou Inuit, he concluded, "One can only say that on the whole the genuine shamans work with an honest mind and an absolute belief that what they do is done with the help of an inspiration which, in some inexplicable manner, they receive from the guiding spirits of the universe."[63]

Umik's New Religion

Knud Rasmussen and Kaj Birket-Smith were not the only participants on the Fifth Thule Expedition who did major scientific work and achieved noteworthy results. One of those accompanying the expedition was the Danish archaeologist Therkel Mathiassen, who was twenty-nine years of age when the expedition reached Danish Island.

In mid-December 1921, Mathiassen remained at Repulse Bay for over a month, assessing the location's suitability for his later archaeological work there. On February 2, 1922, he left with an Inuit guide, Qillaq, for Itijjariaq, the camp of the shaman Aua, where he would meet up again with Peter Freuchen. From there the two would begin their first major travel, a cartographic, geological, and ethnographic trip north to Baffin Island. They left Aua's camp on the last day of February accompanied by the Inughuit couple Aaqqiuq and Arnannguaq, and the young man Puursimaat. Aua and his wife, Urulu, also accompanied them, intending to introduce them to Inuit they would meet at Iglulik.

But Puursimaat, Aua, and Urulu turned back on March 29 to accompany a group of Iglulingmiut who were southward bound to Repulse Bay to trade. Freuchen and Mathiassen reached Iglulik the following day.

After a number of days to rest and replenish their dog food, Mathiassen, the Inughuit couple, and an Iglulik man, Akuanu, continued on to Baffin Island. They reached Admiralty Inlet, one of the world's longest fjords, and Mathiassen mapped its southern part. He reached as far north as Moffet Inlet. Hunting proved to be terrible, and Mathiassen and his party returned to Iglulik on May 9 "without a scrap

62 Ibid.

63 Ibid., 60.

of food or dog-food left."[64] The scientist was in poor health—he had had difficulty living solely on a meat diet.

Mathiassen was not an expert at dog team travel. Freuchen, skilled at driving dogs, had instructed him and Birket-Smith in travel techniques in the fall of 1921, but Mathiassen never became very good at it. Instead, he adopted an unusual method of travel on this and subsequent trips—he walked. He felt, moreover, that this gave him an advantage. Freuchen wrote: "He started off early in the morning and when we caught up with him he rode for a short distance. Whenever we stopped he walked ahead, and towards evening he dropped behind and caught up with us after we had camped."[65] This gave him plenty of time for detours to examine geological formations and Inuit ruins, and to collect geological and ethnographic samples. It also allowed him time to correct existing maps.

While Mathiassen had been exploring Admiralty Inlet, Freuchen and an incompetent young guide named Qattalik had had a disastrous trip to the south-western reaches of Brodeur Peninsula. They had returned to Iglulik a day before Mathiassen.

After regaining their strength for almost a week, the two Danes with their guides continued south to expedition headquarters at Danish Island, which they reached on May 29 in a raging snowstorm.

This trip unexpectedly gave Mathiassen and Freuchen the opportunity to be the first outsiders to document the coming of Christianity to the Inuit of Melville Peninsula. A prophet, Umik, had arrived on the peninsula with his son Nuqallaq from Pond Inlet in the spring of 1922, and brought a version of Christianity that was being promulgated there by a man named Akumalik. Mathiassen said that the conversion to the new beliefs happened in Melville Peninsula "in a flash." It was easy to tell when one approached a camp of the newly minted Christians because "we saw a white rag on a pole outside the snow house and, when we arrived at the place we were surprised by the inhabitants shaking hands with us; even the tiniest child had to do it."[66] Whenever anyone arrived at or left a settlement, everyone gathered to sing a hymn and there was hand-shaking all round; Mathiassen commented that even the dogs' paws were shaken. An indication of the close relationship between Inuit and man's best friend is that the dogs also wore crucifixes carved from wood![67]

Mathiassen noted that Umik's religion included "abstention from work on Sundays, gathering now and then in his snow house and singing hymns which he

64 Mathiassen, "Report on the Expedition," 49.

65 Freuchen, *Arctic Adventure*, 342.

66 Mathiassen, "Material Culture," 235-6.

67 Rasmussen, *Across Arctic America*, 87.

had taught them, and, what is more, the hunters were to bring their booty to him and he would distribute it."[68]

The prophet, Umik, was a liberal man who permitted polygamy. He offered to lend his wife to Mathiassen's party for their stay—Mathiassen politely declined the offer.

Neither Freuchen nor Rasmussen himself—who never met Umik or Nuqallaq—wrote about the beliefs that Umik promulgated or the ritual of conversion. They wrote about the external manifestations of the new beliefs, but did not document the beliefs themselves. This is a peculiar omission for an expedition the main goal of which was ethnography. The Inuit were adept at keeping their conversion ritual away from the prying eyes of outsiders. Only a few observations on Akumalik's new beliefs, but not the ritual of conversion itself, were recorded in Pond Inlet by the trader Henry Toke Munn.

Adoption of the new religion meant Inuit no longer observed a multitude of taboos they once did, many of which had become meaningless and counterproductive. Freuchen described the effects of adherence to the taboos: "At first they were very strict in abiding by their ancient pagan rules. This made it difficult as we needed a great deal of help, and the women could not sew caribou skins while the sun was on the decline. When they were pregnant they could not eat out of the same pot as the men, and had so many rules that life was extremely difficult for them."[69]

The conversion ritual was called *siqqitirniq*. It was a blatant rejection of certain taboos, and an eager acceptance of opposite behaviours. Many taboos had centred around food, and siqqitirniq focused on this: "They cut the seal open and took out the intestines, the liver, the heart, the eyes, and the tongue and cut them into small pieces. . . . Everyone of us was given a piece of meat," recalled Elder Rachel Uyarasuk many decades later. "We did this because all those parts of the seal, the heart, and the intestine were all parts of the *pittailiniq*, the taboos. They were no longer to be observed. There wouldn't be any part of the seal that people would have to abstain from eating. This was not just the case for seal, but for all other animals as well."[70]

For some, conversion was controversial. Tagurnaaq remarked of Aua's daughter, who had recently given birth, that "Aapaq has become a Christian for her food."[71]

Siqqitirniq freed Inuit from one set of taboos while binding them to another, most notable of which was the prohibition of work, including hunting, on every seventh day. The siqqitirniq ritual was practised in the Pond Inlet area, at Iglulik, at Melville Peninsula, and as far south as Repulse Bay.

When Rasmussen spent his first lengthy period of time with the shaman Aua at his camp at Itijjariaq, the old man was recognized as an *angakkuq* ("shaman") and

68 Mathiassen, "Material Culture," 235.

69 Freuchen, *Arctic Adventure*, 340.

70 Tungilik and Uyarasuk, *The Transition*, 123-4.

71 Mathiassen, "Material Culture," 236.

adhered to the old beliefs. This meant there were many things he would not discuss with the ethnologist. But by the time Rasmussen visited him again for an extended period a year later, Aua had converted to Christianity and was much more forthcoming.

Umik had looked forward to the conversion of Aua as a particular challenge. At Iglulik he told Mathiassen that he would undoubtedly win over those living farther south, and he mentioned in particular Aua and his family at Itijjariaq. But it seems that when the old man finally decided to convert, in the fall of 1922, Umik played no direct part in it. Rasmussen wrote that Aua "met some families of the Aivilik tribe during his residence at Repulse Bay who held prayer meetings in an igloo."[72] Mathiassen wrote that Aua forsook his old beliefs and converted "after his eldest son [Nataq] had dreamt that it was the true faith."[73]

New beliefs required another new word to be added to the Inuit vocabulary. Those who had taken part in siqqitirniq and became Christians were now referred to as *majulajuit* (loosely glossed as "those who want to go to heaven;" the singular form is *majulajuq*). Rasmussen uses the word sparingly, in a plural Greenlandic spelling, as *majulasut*, and glosses it as "they who crawl upward, as indicating that they had already relinquished their foothold upon earth, and sought only to find release from the existence to which they were born."[74] Jacob Olsen, in his Greenlandic publication about the expedition, uses the word *majulassunik*[75] (the nominative plural form would be *majulasut*). These are variants of *majuaqtuq* (in some dialects, *majuraqtuq*), a word generally glossed as "climb." In fact, it signifies movement from a lower to a higher place. In that sense, it can be seen in opposition to *siqqitiqtuq* (the verbal form of *siqqitirniq*), which signified a transition from a higher to a lower surface, perhaps a humbling of oneself before God. Its opposite, *majulajuq*, signified the rising up towards heaven that followed.

Mathiassen thought Umik's new religion was a fad. He predicted that its popularity would be short-lived: "If no reinforcements in the form of missionaries arrive for this new 'religion,' if this collection of half digested or undigested maxims can be called a religion, it will presumably disappear just as quickly as it came when it no longer has the interest of novelty."[76]

Umik's version of Christianity survived. But it would be many more years before trained missionaries arrived in the district to transform his hodgepodge of beliefs into more conventional Christianity.

72 Rasmussen, translated and quoted by Laugrand and Oosten, *Inuit Shamansim and Christianity*, 52.

73 Mathiassen, "Material Culture," 236. There is no mention of a role for Umik in this conversion.

74 Rasmussen, *Across Arctic America*, 39-40.

75 Olsen, *Akilinermiulerssârut*, 54.

76 Mathiassen, "Material Culture," 236.

The Shaman Aua

Knud Rasmussen returned to Danish Island from his all-too-short trip to the inland Inuit south of Baker Lake in mid-September 1922. He had learned much about Inuit spirituality and shamanism on that trip. His documentation of their beliefs was groundbreaking, as were Birket-Smith's writings on their material culture. But those Inuit were, nonetheless, a minority group. Now, back on the coast, he needed to immerse himself once again in the beliefs of Inuit who dwelt on the shores of a marine environment, and whose actions and activities were guided by a need to be wary of and placate the forces that controlled the sea mammals.

Rasmussen knew that he needed to spend more time with the powerful shaman Aua, from whom he could learn much about the old ways of the coast dwellers. Rasmussen had first heard of Aua the previous December from his brother Ivaluarjuk at Repulse Bay.

Rasmussen had described a dramatic meeting with Aua on the land. It was late January and the sun had only just returned to the southern horizon of Foxe Basin. Perversely, this is the time of year when Arctic temperatures are at their most severe. Rasmussen and Qaavigarsuaq were hunting walrus at the floe edge near Cape Elizabeth. Rasmussen tells the tale: "It was bright starlight towards the close of the journey. . . . Suddenly out of the darkness ahead shot a long sledge with the wildest team I have ever seen. Fifteen white dogs racing down at full speed, with six men on the sledge. . . . A little man with a large beard, completely covered with ice, leapt out and came towards me, holding out his hand white man's fashion. Then halting, he pointed inland to some snow huts."[77] This was Aua, and he and Rasmussen were to become fast friends.

Rasmussen and Qaavigarsuaq accompanied Aua to his small village of snowhouses—five domed huts connected by passages, home to sixteen inhabitants. Rasmussen was fascinated to see the architecture of snowhouse construction carried to the extremes he observed in Aua's camp. Aua's wife, Urulu, introduced Rasmussen to the occupants of the little village, all of whom were related.

For the next two weeks the visitors accompanied Aua and the other Iglulingmiut—for that was their cultural affiliation—on hunting expeditions during the day. In the evenings, Rasmussen listened, and questioned sparingly, collecting material on the spiritual life of these particular Inuit.

Rasmussen took a practical approach to the collection of folklore: "One is altogether dependent upon the character and temper of one's sources; it is essential to have native authorities not only qualified in regard to knowledge of their subject but also gifted with the right appreciation of it themselves. They must be reliable, so that one can listen without criticizing all the time, and one should if possible be on

77 Rasmussen, *Across Arctic America*, 21.

friendly terms with them throughout."[78]

He elaborated: "All study of folk-lore is solely and entirely dependent on the sources from which the material is derived; it is necessary to find narrators not only gifted with knowledge and imagination, but thoroughly interested in the work as well. And they must be sufficiently reliable for the listener to take what they say without reserve, and without over-much criticism. Only thus is it possible to get the right colour and atmosphere: to give life to all the alien material in the mind of the reader."[79]

Aua and Urulu met Rasmussen's requirements perfectly, drawing on their symbiotic lifetimes of diverse experience through their storytelling. "What one did not know the other did,"[80] wrote Rasmussen in summation.

But Rasmussen believed he wasn't hearing everything. Aua was a shaman, after all, and "a faithful spirit conjuror," realized Rasmussen, "cannot disclose the secrets of his life without weakening his relationship to the supernatural."[81] And so the old man, while helpful and cooperative, displayed a certain reticence. Nonetheless, Rasmussen had learned a great deal from this first extended visit to him.

Rasmussen was fascinated by Aua's explanation of Inuit belief in spirits; he wrote that the Inuit believed "they are surrounded on all sides by spirits, the same spirits which the angakkut enlist in their service as helping spirits."[82] He distinguished between two types of spirits. The first, more tangible types, were earth-bound, somewhat analogous to what might appear in the folklore of other cultures as trolls or gnomes. The second type personified various things such as "fire, stone, a precipice, a feasting house or such like;"[83] the spirits of these entities were then described as the object's *inua* (its "owner or lord").

Examples of the first type were the *ijiqqait* ("beings living in the hills"). In fact, their dwellings were inside the hills, and shamans often saw them disappearing into crevices in the rocks. To ordinary folk they were invisible, but people could hear the ijiqqait whistling in the air. People feared them but were counselled not to show their fear, for the ijiqqait attacked only the timid and cowardly.

The ijiqqait had a distinctive appearance. Their eyes were set vertically rather than horizontally, as is the case with humans, so they blinked sideways. Their mouths were placed in a similar orientation. Otherwise, they were shaped like humans, lived in a similar way, and dressed the same too, save for a few peculiarities in the women's

78 Rasmussen, *Across Arctic America*, 120-121.

79 Rasmussen, "Iglulik Eskimos," 45.

80 Rasmussen, *Across Arctic America*, 121.

81 Rasmussen, translated and quoted by Laugrand and Oosten, *Inuit Shamanism and Christianity*, 53.

82 Rasmussen, "Iglulik Eskimos," 204.

83 Ibid.

clothing. They were known to be fast enough to chase down a caribou, and so strong that when one would catch a caribou, he would sling it over his shoulder and run home with it. On the occasions when they captured a human, they had a way of turning the human into a swift runner as well. But Inuit were well advised not to get caught, for the ijiqqait would never let them return to their own people again.

Shamans were able to see the ijiqqait and visited them on occasion. The ijiqqait were always well supplied with caribou meat, fat, and suet. They were known to have a strange implement—Aua described it as much like the mirrors that white men had. It glittered like mica, and served as both a mirror and a spyglass. The ijiqqait knew all about the lives of Inuit, for when one looked through this strange mirror, everything that was happening in the far-off dwellings of Inuit was reflected in it.

Aua told Rasmussen the following tale that had been told to him by his father, Qingailisaq, also known as Uqaaminiq ("the man with the sharp tongue"), who had encountered an *ijiraq* (singular form of *ijiqqait*) in the hills.

> My father was out once hunting caribou, and had killed four. He was just cutting them up when he saw four men coming towards him. They came over the crest of a hill, and he thought at first it was caribou. But they came closer, and he saw that they were ijiqqait, two men with their grown-up sons. One of the sons was quite a young man. All were big men, and they looked just like ordinary human beings, save that they had nostrils like those of the caribou. The oldest of the men seemed very excited, he at once grasped hold of Uqaaminiq, pressed his hands against his chest to throw him down, but Uqaaminiq remained calmly standing, and the angry ijiraq could not do anything with him.
>
> Then said the ijiraq: "Will you do any harm?"
>
> "I will do no harm; you need not be afraid of me," answered Uqaaminiq.
>
> Then the ijiraq at once loosed hold of him, and proposed that they should sit down on a stone and talk. And he told his son to cut up the caribou my father had been cutting up himself. The work was speedily done, though he had no knife; he flayed them in the same way as one does a lemming, simply tearing open the skin, but it was done more rapidly than by a man working with a knife.
>
> The ijiraq sat down on a stone and talked with my father. He said they lived in the country inland from Piling, near Nuvuk; they lived by hunting caribou. They had a small pocket in their tunics, in which they kept two small stones. They were mighty runners, and could outrun the caribou; when they came up quite close, they killed them with the stones in their pockets.
>
> The old ijiraq was out looking for a son that was lost—a son

> who had not come home from his hunting, and he now thought he must have been killed by human beings, and had at first believed that it was Uqaaminiq who had killed him. But Uqaaminiq said he had never seen an ijiraq before, and the other then grew calm, and they parted in friendship and mutual understanding.
>
> My father, who was a great shaman, went home and had a dress made like that of the ijiraq, but with a picture of the hands in front, on the chest, to show how the ijiraq had attacked him. It took several women to make that garment, and many caribou skins were used. There were a number of white patterns in the dress, and it became a famous dress which was bought by him who was called angakkuq [the well-known whaler and collector for the American Museum of Natural History, George Comer], and my father was paid a high price for the garment, which is the only ijiraq tunic ever made by human hands.[84]

When Qingailisaq returned to camp after his encounter with the ijiraq, he asked his wife, Ataguarjugusiq, to make him a coat like the old ijiraq had worn. He specified that he wanted the two hands of the ijiraq to be represented on the front of the parka, to show where the man had pushed him. His wife obliged, and so the famous coat was sewn. This is the "dress" to which Aua refers in his story, the memory of which lives on today in Inuit history. It differs from the normal *qulittaq* ("parka") in that it has no hood, and the sleeves are very short.

In 1902, American whaling captain George Comer purchased the coat from Qingailisaq. Comer had a deep interest in Inuit and their customs and collected both material and intellectual culture for the American Museum of Natural History at the behest of anthropologist Franz Boas. Although Aua claimed that his father was paid a "high price" for the parka, no one knows what value was ascribed to it by the museum, only that Comer sold a collection of a number of items to the museum at the end of that voyage for a total price of $550. The coat is a valued part of that collection.[85]

The museum published a picture of the coat and a short description in 1903. The account differs in a few details from that given by Aua two decades later: "The two hands signify that no supernatural being can touch the shaman, and the bears at the top of the back of the coat represent the guardian spirits of the owner, while the figure of an infant shown over the hands calls to mind a vision which the shaman had when he received his supernatural power."[86]

In 1907 Boas published an account of this parka in another museum publication, an account that differed slightly from the museum's earlier version. Both

84 Rasmussen, "Iglulik Eskimos," 205-206.

85 The coat is catalogued as item 1902-78, #60-4440: "Anticock [angakkuq] coat cap & gloved, Iglulic."

86 The American Museum of Natural History, "The Eskimo Collection," 8.

accounts are notable in not mentioning the assault by the ijiraq. In his account, Boas paraphrases information received from Comer about the initiation of an unnamed angakkuq, but who must have been Qingailisaq:

> One day when he was caribou-hunting near the peninsula Amittuq, he killed three caribou. On the following day he saw four large bucks, one of which was very fat. He struck it with an arrow, and the caribou began to run to and fro. Its antlers and its skin dropped off, its head became smaller, and soon it assumed the form of a woman with finely made clothes. Soon she fell down, giving birth to a boy, and then she died. The other caribou had turned into men, who told him to cover the woman and the child with moss, so that nobody should find them. They told him to straighten out her body; but he was only able to move one arm, because she was exceedingly heavy. After he had covered up the bodies, the men told him to return to his people and to tell them what had happened, and to have his clothing made in the same way as that of the woman.
>
> The garment . . . is the coat worn by this angakkuq, who claims that it is identical with that worn by the caribou woman, with the exception of the representation of her child, which he added to it. The hands, represented in white skin, are intended to ward off evil spirits. The animal figures represented on the shoulders were explained to represent "children of the earth."
>
> While the angakkuq was telling this story to Captain Comer, the women who were near covered their heads with their hoods, for fear of the angakkuq's protecting spirit. The cap and mittens which belong to the suit are also said to be of the same pattern as those worn by the caribou woman.
>
> In taking down this story, Captain Comer had his paper resting on a woman's shoulders. The angakkuq objected to this, because, as he said, his protecting spirit would not like to have the paper on which so important a story was recorded touch a woman. Captain Comer also remarks that the other Eskimo were somewhat skeptical in regard to this story, but that they did not dare express their doubts.[87]

In the 1980s Andy Awa, a grandson of Aua, told a different story of the garment's acquisition by Comer. He said that "Captain Comer's persistent efforts to obtain the clothing met with resistance from his [great-]grandfather, for to give away any spiritual object meant to relinquish its inherent power. Since Qingailisaq did not like to refuse the captain, he asked his wife to make a duplicate of the costume, which

87 Boas, "Second Report," 509-510.

consisted of coat, hat, and mitts. Awa believes that this duplicate is now in the possession of the American Museum of Natural History and that, in keeping with Inuit tradition, the original clothing was probably buried with his [great-]grandfather."[88]

Stories change over time. By 2015, another descendant of Aua explained the hands and the human image on the parka in another way. In this version, the parka was Aua's, not Qingailisaq's, and Aua had imagined the design in the early 1920s: "Aua says he thought someone was going to drown him. The pattern of the hands on his chest and little man in the middle of the parka were safeguards. It's a protection parka. Only he thought of it and wanted to design it, so he can save his life."[89]

The Wisdom of a Shaman

After his return from the inland Inuit, Rasmussen knew that he needed to spend more time with Aua. He planned to do this in early 1923, before departing on his grand sled trip to Alaska. But in the fall of 1922, something had happened that Rasmussen worried might throw a wrench into his plans. That fall Aua had converted to Christianity, as had most of his countrymen that same year.

Many of the Aivilingmiut had heard a little of Christianity from the Catholic priests to the south at Chesterfield Inlet, but apparently few of them had been converted by the priests. Most of the Iglulingmiut, farther to the north, were converted by Umik, the Inuit prophet who had arrived from Pond Inlet bringing his own version of Christianity. Rasmussen wrote that Aua's conversion had happened in the fall of 1922 at Repulse Bay.

When Rasmussen heard of the old man's conversion, he worried that this might cause Aua to be hesitant—perhaps to the point of refusal—to discuss the old beliefs.

And so it was with some trepidation that Rasmussen visited Aua's camp in January 1923. His reception was unlike the tumultuous greeting he had received a year earlier. He wrote:

> It was known that I was on the way, and above each hut waved a little white flag—a sign that the inmates had relinquished their old heathen faith and become Christians. As I drove up, men, women and children trooped out and formed up in line outside Aua's hut, and as soon as I had reigned in my team, the whole party began singing a hymn. The tune was so unlike what they were accustomed to in their own pagan chants that they bungled it a little, but there was no mistaking the

88 Driscoll, "The Inuit Parka," 212.

89 Awa, *As It Happens.*

> earnestness and pious feeling which inspired it. There was something very touching in such a greeting; these poor folk had plainly found in the new faith a refuge that meant a great deal in their lives.[90]

Dispensing with formalities, he cut to the chase in expressing his hope that the shaman's conversion to a new belief system would not hamper their working relationship. "To my great joy he answered that this would not be the case," wrote Rasmussen. "He explained that he indeed had sent away his helping spirits, as he had no more use for them, but that this was exactly the reason why he could now tell all the secrets, which had been too sacred for him to communicate in the past." He had been reticent before, he explained, precisely because to disclose the secrets of his life then would have weakened his rapport with the spirit world. Now the opposite was true. "All his knowledge was available to me. . . . I could write down extensive material on the spiritual culture of the Eskimos," Rasmussen wrote, and that material "later on also lay the foundation for my work among other tribes." [91]

Aua's conversion to Christianity, therefore, actually facilitated the transmission of his knowledge of shamanism to Rasmussen. When a shaman converted to Christianity, it turned out—at least in Aua's reasoning—he was then able to freely talk about his knowledge and previous practices without fearing the loss of his power. As the scholars Frédéric Laugrand and Jarich Oosten point out, the adoption of Christianity did not mean that Inuit had forsaken their belief in shamanism, but merely that they no longer practised it, and in Aua's case, that he had sent his *tuurngait* ("spirit helpers") away. In fact, Aua told Rasmussen that he had sent his helping spirits to his sister on Baffin Island.

Between January 2 and March 2, Rasmussen visited Aua at Sturges Island in Lyon Inlet, not far from Danish Island, on three occasions. On the first two, he was alone; on the third he was accompanied by Jacob Olsen.[92] Rasmussen's conversations with Aua and Urulu were extremely productive.

In addition to making two extended visits to Aua's camp, Rasmussen occasionally hosted the old man and his wife at expedition headquarters at Danish Island. On these occasions, too, the aging shaman shared his wisdom with the enquiring ethnologist.

Inuit life had been governed by a complex system of taboos that regulated behaviour. Inuit, guided by their leaders, of course knew what had to be done in any given

90 Rasmussen, *Across Arctic America*, 118.

91 Rasmussen, quoted by Laugrand and Oosten, *Inuit Shamanism and Christianity*, 52-53.

92 January 2-13 (alone); February 9-17 (alone); February 26-March 2 (with Jacob Olsen). Mathiassen, "Report on the Expedition," 63.

situation. But Rasmussen wanted to know more than what actions were required; he wanted to know *why*. The Inuit, frustrated, could often give no answer. And Rasmussen, perhaps equally frustrated, wrote, "They regarded it as unreasonable that I should require not only an account, but also a justification, of their religious principles."[93]

One evening, tired of the repeated question of "why," Aua suddenly invited Rasmussen to follow him outside, where a storm was raging. Aua calmly remarked, "In order to hunt well and live happily, man must have calm weather. Why this constant succession of blizzards and all this needless hardship for men seeking food for themselves and those they care for? Why? Why?"

At just that time hunters were returning unsuccessfully from a day's hunt for seal. Aua turned the tables again, and asked his companion, "Why?" Rasmussen had no answer.

The shaman led him to Kublu's iglu, where the *qulliq* ("seal oil lamp") gave little light and his children shivered under a skin blanket.

"Why should it be cold and comfortless in here?" the shaman asked. "Kublu has been out hunting all day, and if he had got a seal, as he deserved, his wife would now be sitting laughing beside her lamp, letting it burn full, without fear of having no blubber left for tomorrow. The place would be warm and bright and cheerful, the children would come out from under their rugs and enjoy life. Why should it not be so? Why?"

At the dwelling of his sister Natsiq, Aua asked, "Why must people be ill and suffer pain? We are all afraid of illness. Here is this old sister of mine; as far as anyone can see, she has done no evil; she has lived through a long life and given birth to healthy children, and now she must suffer before her days end. Why? Why?"

They returned silently to Aua's iglu. Aua explained:

> You see . . . you are equally unable to give any reason when we ask you why life is as it is. And so it must be. All our customs come from life and turn towards life. We explain nothing; we believe nothing. But in what I have just shown you lies our answer to all you ask.
>
> We fear the weather spirit of earth, that we must fight against to wrest our food from land and sea. We fear *Sila* ["the spirit of weather"].
>
> We fear dearth and hunger in the cold snow huts.
>
> We fear *Takannakapsaaluk*, the great woman down at the bottom of the sea, that rules over all the beasts of the sea.
>
> We fear the sickness that we meet with daily all around us; not death, but the suffering.
>
> We fear the evil spirits of life, those of the air, of the sea and the earth, that can help wicked shamans to harm their fellow men.
>
> We fear the souls of dead human beings and of the animals we have killed.

93 Rasmussen, "Iglulik Eskimos," 54.

> Therefore it is that our fathers have inherited from their fathers all the old rules of life which are based on the experience and wisdom of generations. We do not know how, we cannot say why, but we keep those rules in order that we may live untroubled. And so ignorant are we in spite of all our shamans, that we fear everything unfamiliar. We fear what we see about us, and we fear all the invisible things that are likewise about us, all that we have heard of in our forefathers' stories and myths. Therefore we have our customs, which are not the same as those of the white men, the white men who live in another land and have need of other ways.[94]

Aua had explained clearly and succinctly to Rasmussen why his question of "why" must remain unanswered. On another occasion, Aua explained some facts about death to Rasmussen:

> We ignorant Eskimos living up here do not believe, as you have told us many white men do, in one great solitary spirit that from a place far up in the sky maintains humanity and all the life of nature. Among us, as I have already explained to you, all is bound up with the earth we live on and our life here; and it would be even more incomprehensible, even more unreasonable, if, after a life short or long, of happy days or of suffering and misery, we were then to cease altogether from existence. What we have heard about the soul shows us that the life of men and beasts does not end with death. When at the end of life we draw our last breath, that is not the end. We awake to consciousness again, we come to life again, and all this is effected through the medium of the soul. Therefore it is that we regard the soul as the greatest and most incomprehensible of all.[95]

It was unusual, though, to think of such things. Aua explained: "In our ordinary everyday life we do not think much about all these things, and it is only now you ask that so many thoughts arise in my head of long-known things; old thoughts, but as it were becoming altogether new when one has to put them into words."[96]

Rasmussen had learned that a long period of training was required for a good shaman. Indeed, some parents, knowing that their as-yet unborn child was destined to

94 Ibid., 55-56.

95 Ibid., 60-61.

96 Ibid., 61.

be a shaman, "set all things in order for him beforehand by laying upon themselves a specially strict and onerous taboo."[97] Such a child, foreordained to be a shaman, was Aua. He told his story to Rasmussen:

> I was yet but a tiny unborn infant in my mother's womb when anxious folk began to enquire sympathetically about me; all the children my mother had had before had lain crosswise and been stillborn. As soon as my mother now perceived that she was with child, the child that one day was to be me, she spoke thus to her house-fellows:
>
> "Now I have again that within me which will turn out no real human being."
>
> All were very sorry for her, and a woman named Aarjuaq, who was a shaman herself, called up her spirits that same evening to help my mother. And the very next morning it could be felt that I had grown, but it did me no good at the time, for Aarjuaq had forgotten that she must do no work the day after a spirit-calling, and had mended a hole in a mitten. This breach of taboo at once had its effect on me. My mother felt the birth-pangs coming on before the time, and I kicked and struggled as if trying to work my way out through her side. A new spirit-calling then took place, and as all precepts were duly observed this time, it helped both my mother and myself.
>
> But then one day it happened that my father, who was going out on a journey to hunt, was angry and impatient, and in order to calm him, my mother went to help him harness the dogs to the sledge. She forgot that in her condition, all work was taboo. And so, hardly had she picked up the traces and lifted one dog's paw before I began again kicking and struggling and trying to get out through her navel; and again we had to have a shaman to help us.
>
> Old people now assured my mother that my great sensitiveness to any breach of taboo was a sign that I should live to become a great shaman; but at the same time, many dangers and misfortunes would pursue me before I was born.
>
> My father had got a walrus with its unborn young one, and when he began cutting it out, without reflecting that my mother was with child, I again fell to struggling within the womb, and this time in earnest. But the moment I was born, all life left me, and I lay there dead as a stone. The cord was twisted round my neck and had strangled me. Aarjuaq, who lived in another village, was at once sent for, and a special hut was built for my mother. When Aarjuaq came and saw me with my eyes sticking right out of my head, she wiped my mother's

97 Rasmussen, "Iglulik Eskimos," 116.

blood from my body with the skin of a raven, and made a little jacket for me of the same skin.

"He is born to die, but he shall live," she said.

And so Aarjuaq stayed with my mother, until I showed signs of life. Mother was put on a very strict diet, and had to observe difficult rules of taboo. If she had eaten part of a walrus, for instance, then that walrus was taboo to all others; the same with seal and caribou. She had to have special pots, from which no one else was allowed to eat. No woman was allowed to visit her, but men might do so. My clothes were made after a particular fashion; the hair of the skins must never lie pointing upwards or down, but fall athwart the body. Thus I lived in the birth-hut, unconscious of all the care that was being taken with me.[98]

Aua continued his story, telling of the many taboos that he and his family members had to follow in order that he might reach his full potential:

For a whole year my mother and I had to live entirely alone, only visited now and again by my father. He was a great hunter, and always out after game, but in spite of this he was never allowed to sharpen his own knives. As soon as he did so, his hand began to swell and I fell ill. A year after my birth, we were allowed to have another person in the house with us. It was a woman, and she had to be very careful herself. Whenever she went out she must throw her hood over her head, wear boots without stockings, and hold the tail of her fur coat lifted high in one hand.

I was already a big boy when my mother was first allowed to go visiting; all were anxious to be kind, and she was invited to all the other families. But she stayed out too long; the spirits do not like women with little children to stay too long away from their house, and they took vengeance in this wise: the skin of her head peeled off, and I, who had no understanding of anything at that time, beat her about the body with my little fists as she went home, and made water down her back.

No one who is to become a skillful hunter or a good shaman must remain out too long when visiting strange houses; and the same holds good for a woman with a child in her *amaut* [a woman's parka with a pouch for carrying a child].

At last I was big enough to go out with the grown-up men to the blowholes after seal. The day I harpooned my first seal, my father had to lie down on the ice with the upper part of his body naked, and the seal I had caught was dragged across his back while it was still

98 Ibid., 116-117.

alive. Only men were allowed to eat of my first catch, and nothing must be left. The skin and the head were set out on the ice, in order that I might be able later on to catch the same seal again. For three days and nights, none of the men who had eaten of it might go out hunting or do any kind of work.

The next animal I killed was a caribou. I was strictly forbidden to use a gun, and had to kill it with bow and arrows. This animal also only men were allowed to eat; no woman might touch it.

Some time passed, and I grew up and was strong enough to go out hunting walrus. The day I harpooned my first walrus my father shouted at the top of his voice the names of all the villages he knew, and cried: "Now there is food for all!"

The walrus was towed in to land while it was still alive, and not until we reached the shore was it finally killed. My mother, who was to cut it up, had the harpoon line made fast to her body before the harpoon head was withdrawn. After having killed this walrus, I was allowed to eat all those delicacies which had formerly been forbidden, yes, even entrails, and women were now allowed to eat of my catch, as long as they were not with child or recently delivered. Only my own mother had still to observe great caution, and whenever she had any sewing to do, a special hut had to be built for her.

I had been named after a little spirit, Aua, and it was said that it was in order to avoid offending this spirit that my mother had to be so particular about everything she did. It was my guardian spirit, and took great care that I should not do anything that was forbidden. I was never allowed, for instance, to remain in a snow hut where young women were undressing for the night. Nor might any woman comb her hair while I was present.

Even after I had been married a long time, my catch was still subject to strict taboo. If there but lived women with infants near us, my own wife was only allowed to eat meat of my killing, and no other woman was allowed to satisfy her hunger with the meat of any animal of which my wife had eaten. Any walrus I killed was further subject to the rule that no woman might eat of its entrails, which are reckoned a great delicacy, and this prohibition was maintained until I had four children of my own. And it is really only since I have grown old that the obligations laid on me by Aarjuaq in order that I might live have ceased to be needful.[99]

A man did not reach and maintain the status of great shaman solely through his own powers or through the tutelage of others. He was necessarily assisted by one

99 Rasmussen, "Iglulik Eskimos," 117-118.

or more helping spirits, invisible helpers that he could summon when needed. Aua continued his story with a discussion of the spirits that helped him achieve his power:

> Everything was thus made ready for me beforehand, even from the time when I was yet unborn. Nevertheless, I endeavoured to become a shaman by the help of others, but in this I did not succeed. I visited many famous shamans, and gave them great gifts, which they at once gave away to others, for if they had kept the things for themselves, they or their children would have died. This they believed because my own life had been so threatened from birth.
>
> Then I sought solitude, and here I soon became very melancholy. I would sometimes fall to weeping, and feel unhappy without knowing why. Then, for no reason, all would suddenly be changed, and I felt a great, inexplicable joy, a joy so powerful that I could not restrain it, but I had to break into song, a mighty song, with only room for the one word: joy, joy! And I had to use the full strength of my voice.
>
> And then in the midst of such a fit of mysterious and overwhelming delight I became a shaman, not knowing myself how it came about. But I was a shaman. I could see and hear in a totally different way. I had gained my *qaumaniq*, my enlightenment, the shaman-light of brain and body, and this in such a manner that it was not only I who could see through the darkness of life, but the same light also shone out from me, imperceptible to human beings, but visible to all the spirits of earth and sky and sea, and these now came to me and became my helping spirits.
>
> My first helping spirit was my namesake, a little *aua*. When it came to me, it was as if the passage and roof of the house were lifted up, and I felt such a power of vision, that I could see right through the house, in through the earth and up into the sky. It was the little aua that brought me all this inward light, hovering over me as long as I was singing. Then it placed itself in a corner of the passage, invisible to others, but always ready if I should call it.
>
> An aua is a little spirit, a woman that lives down by the sea shore. There are many of these shore spirits, who run about with a pointed skin hood on their heads; their breeches are queerly short, and made of bearskin; they wear long boots with a black pattern, and coats of sealskin. Their feet are twisted upward, and they seem to walk only on their heels. They hold their hands in such a fashion that the thumb is always bent in over the palm. Their arms are held raised up on high with the hands together, and incessantly stroking the head. They are bright and cheerful when one calls them, and resemble most of all sweet little live dolls. They are no taller than the length of a man's arm.

My second helping spirit was a shark. One day when I was out in my kayak, it came swimming up to me, lay alongside quite silently and whispered my name. I was greatly astonished, for I had never seen a shark before; they are very rare in these waters. Afterwards it helped me with my hunting, and was always near me when I had need of it.

These two, the shore spirit and the shark, were my principal helpers, and they could aid me in everything I wished. The song I generally sang when calling them was of few words, as follows:

Joy, joy,
Joy, joy!
I see a little shore spirit,
A little aua,
I myself am also aua,
The shore spirit's namesake,
Joy, joy!

These words I would keep on repeating, until I burst into tears, overwhelmed by a great dread. Then I would tremble all over, crying only: "Ah-a-a-a-a, joy, joy! Now I will go home, joy, joy!"

Once I lost a son, and felt that I could never again leave the spot where I had laid his body. I was like a mountain spirit, afraid of human kind. We stayed for a long time up inland, and my helping spirits forsook me, for they do not like live human beings to dwell upon any sorrow. But one day the song about joy came to me all of itself and quite unexpectedly. I felt once more a longing for my fellow-men, my helping spirits returned to me, and I was myself once more.[100]

On the first morning of his visit to Aua in 1923, Rasmussen recorded a sermon preached by the newly converted Christian in his iglu. It is the only Christian message recorded by a member of the expedition. It bore little resemblance to the incantations of the shamans that Rasmussen had become familiar with. As with many of the homilies preached by ministers to this day, it was built around one word. In Aua's case on that day, the word was *qujannamiik* ("thank you").

The gist of his message was that one must give thanks for everything that a person encounters in life, both good and bad:

100 Rasmussen, "Iglulik Eskimos," 118-120.

> Tolerance, mercy and helpfulness must be paramount in the conduct of one's life. People should freely confess their faith without worrying that others do not share their beliefs. Life's destiny must be faced calmly, and no annoyances should lead us to rage.
>
> Even if meat depots are plundered by foxes, wolves or bears, our speech should still show thankfulness, for all animals fear hunger in the same way as we do, only they do not have the wisdom of man that enables them to invent special weapons which assist them in the struggle for food. Therefore we must not be angry that they seek to satisfy their hunger, even if it is to our detriment. And what applies to animals applies even more to humans.
>
> As soon as you are told that people in a camp are in need, you must help them to the best of your ability. If you follow these commandments, you will in turn receive help throughout life—yes, protection against dangers and success in the hunt, and no power in the world can threaten misfortune.[101]
>
> Thus Aua spoke. His words made a deep impression on his audience.

"To Think I Had Been So Happy": Urulu's Story

Rasmussen revelled in collecting life stories of Inuit he met. These stories, he felt, were more than just the events of a life, but embodied the beliefs of the subject and the cultural context of that person's life.

In addition to his interviews with Aua, Rasmussen also interviewed his wife, Urulu, and recorded the events of her life as she recalled them. It is a story of hardship and happiness, of quiet struggle and triumph. It is one woman's story of life in a time now past.

Rasmussen described Urulu as being always busy, never idle for a moment. He was astonished at the amount of work she managed to get through each day. She was an expert seamstress and cheerfully performed all the other household duties one might expect of the wife of an expert hunter. She sang while she worked. Rasmussen asked her often to tell him about her life. She always maintained that there was nothing worth telling until one day, seated beside the lamp, sewing a pair of boots, she spontaneously began to tell her story:

---

101 Rasmussen, *Fra Grønland*, 323. (Translation by Kenn Harper. This story does not appear in any of Rasmussen's writings in English.)

I am called Urulu ("the difficult one"), but my name is really Aqiggiarjuk ("the little ptarmigan"). I was born at the mouth of Admiralty Inlet. While I was still a little child carried on my mother's back, my parents left Baffin Land and settled at Iglulik.

The first thing I can remember is that my mother lived quite alone in a little snow hut. I could not understand why my father should live in another house, but then I was told that it was because my mother had just had a child and was therefore unclean and must not be near the animals killed for some time to come. But I was allowed to visit her when I liked; only I could never find the entrance to that hut. I was so little that I could not see over the block of snow the others stepped across as they went in, so I had to stand there, calling out "Mother, Mother, I want to come in!" until someone came and lifted me over into the passage. And then when I was inside, the snow bench where she sat looked so high, so high, I could not get up there myself but had to be lifted. I was no bigger than that when I first began to remember things.

The next thing I remember is from Piling, a big hunting ground in Baffin Land. I remembered gnawing meat from the leg of a bird, a huge big thighbone, and I was told it was a goose. Up till then I knew nothing bigger than ptarmigan, and thought it must be a terrible big bird.

Then all my memories disappear, until one day as it were, I wake up again, and then we were living at a place called The Mountain. My father was ill. All the others in the place had gone off hunting inland, and I was left alone. Father had pains in his chest and lungs, and grew worse and worse. We were quite alone, my mother, my two little brothers and I, and mother was very unhappy.

One day I came running into the tent and called out: "Here are white men coming!" I had seen what I thought must be white men; but when my father heard it, he gave a deep sigh, and said, "Alas, I thought I might yet live and breathe a little while; but now I know that I shall never go out hunting anymore."

The men I had seen were ijiqqait, or mountain spirits. No white men ever came to our country in those days, and my father took it as a warning that his death was near.

Quite without thinking, I made no secret of what I had seen. But my little brother Siqussuk kept it secret, and died of it shortly after. One must never keep the matter secret when one has seen spirits.

My father grew worse and worse, and when we realized that he had not long to live, we set off and carried him on a sledge to a neighboring settlement, where there lived a man named Qupanuaq, with his wife Qikiqtaunak. Father died there. I remember he was tied up in a skin and dragged away from the village, and left lying out in the open with his face turned towards the west. My mother told me that was because he was an old man, and such must always be set to face the quarter whence the dark of night comes, children to face the morning, and young people towards the spot where the sun is seen at noon. That was the first time I learned that people were afraid of the dead, and had special customs on that account. But I was not afraid of father, who had always been kind to me. And I thought it was hard that he should lie all uncovered out in the open like that. But mother explained that I must thence-forward never think of my father in the body. His soul was already in the land of the dead, and he would feel no more pain there.

After my father's death we went to live with an old man who took mother to be one of his wives. A little after that my brother Siqussuk fell ill; his liver swelled up and he died. I was told it was because he had seen ijiqqait just before my father's death, the same ones I had seen. But he had kept the vision secret and if you do that you die.

In the autumn, when the first snow had fallen, Qupanuaq decided to go up country with his wife Qikiqtaunak and their son Tuurngaq ("the helping spirit"); my brother Qajakujjuk ("the little kayak") was to go with them. I remember my mother was very distressed about it, for she did not think the old man, armed as he was only with bow and arrows, would ever get any game. But she was not able herself to keep us, and had to agree to my brother's going with them.

Then a little while after, a strange thing happened. Mother had cooked some ribs of walrus, and was sitting eating, when the bone she held suddenly began to make a noise. She was so frightened, she stopped eating at once, and threw down the bone. I remember her face went quite white, and she burst out: "Something has happened to my son!" And so indeed it was. Soon after, Qupanuaq returned late one night, and before entering the house, he went around outside to the window and called out "Dear Little Thing. It is my fault that you no longer have a son!" "Little Thing" was a pet name Qupanuaq used for mother. And then he came in and told us how it had come about.

They had killed nothing, and had for several days been obliged to live on caribou dung. They were sadly worn out when at last they came to a place where he had stored away the carcass of a caribou he had killed some time before; but now they could not find the cache.

They divided into two parties, his wife going one way, and Qupanuaq with the two boys another. They searched and searched all about, but could not find the spot. The first snow had fallen, it was autumn, with the cold wind and driving snow, and they were poorly clad; so they laid down behind the shelter of stones to rest. All were much exhausted. The day was short, and the night very long, and they had to wait for daylight before they could begin searching again.

Meantime, Qikiqtaunaq had found the cache, but she did not know where to look for the rest of the party, and being anxious about them, she ate but little herself, and gave the child she was carrying a small piece of meat to suck. She had made a stone shelter like the others, and lay half dozing when suddenly she awoke, having dreamed of my brother. She dreamed that he stood there quite plainly before her, pale and shivering with cold, and spoke to her and said: "You will never see me again. It is because the earth-lice are angry at our having eaten their sinews and their dung before a year had passed since my father's death."

I remember this quite distinctly because it was the first time I realized that there were certain things one must not do after anyone had died. The caribou are called "earth-lice" in shaman language.

So lifelike was the dream that Qikiqtaunaq could not sleep any more that night. My brother Qajakujjuk was her favorite, and she used to say charms over him to make him strong.

Next morning, when it was light, and Qupanuaq was ready to start, my brother was so weak that he could not stand, and the others were too exhausted to carry him. So they covered him with a thin worn skin and left him. Later on they found the meat, but they did not go back to Qajakujjuk. He was frozen to death.

Next spring, we left there and went to Admiralty Inlet. We reached there just at the time when folk were laying up their sledges and belongings before going up country to hunt caribou. There was a man named Kipumi; his wife Kunualuk had given birth to a stillborn child a little while before, and was not allowed to go with the hunting party. So my mother went instead, and I went with her. We stayed inland all that summer. The men were successful in their hunting, and we helped them to drag the meat and store it in depots or cut off thin slices and laid them on stones to dry. It was a pleasant time. We lived in abundance, with all manner of dainties besides, and the day passed as in play.

Then one day, I remember, we were startled to hear a woman from one of the tents calling out: "Here, come and look, quick, come and see." We all ran to the spot, and there we saw a spider letting itself down to the ground. We could not make out where it came from; it looked as if it were letting itself down from the sky. We all saw

> it, and there was silence among the tents. For when a spider comes down from the sky, it means someone is going to die. And true it was; when people came up from the coast, we learned that four men had perished in their kayaks. And among them was my stepfather. And thus we were left alone and homeless once again.
>
> But it was not long before my mother was married again, this time with a young man, much younger than she was. They lived together until he took another wife, a young one about his own age. Then my mother was cast off, and we were alone again. Then my mother was married to a man named Augpilaaq ("the red one") and we had someone to look after us once more. This Augpilaaq wanted to go down to Ponds Inlet to look for white men. He had heard that whalers often came there in the summer. So he went off with my mother, and I was left alone in the care of Amarualik and his wife Tutuk. But I did not stay with them long, for Amarualik thought he had too many mouths to feed, so I went to live with Kanajuq.
>
> I was there when Uitaara, ("my new husband")—that is my pet name for Aua—came and fetched me, and that is the end of all my adventures. For one who lives happily has no adventures, and in truth, I have lived happily and had seven children.

Rasmussen asked Urulu, "What is the bitterest memory of all you can remember?"

Without hesitation, she answered:

> The bitterest I have ever known was a time of famine shortly after my eldest son was born. And to make matters worse, all our stores of meat from the previous hunting had been destroyed by wolverines. During the two coldest months of the winter, Uitaara hardly slept indoors a single night, but was out all the time hunting seal, and made do with a snatch of sleep now and then in the little snow shelters he built by the blow holes. We nearly starved to death, for in all that time he got only two seals. To see him go out, cold and hungry day after day to his hunting, in all manner of cruel weather, to see him grow thinner and weaker all the time—oh, it was terrible. But then at last he got a walrus, and we were saved.

Rasmussen then asked the obvious question, "And the happiest thing you can remember?"

The old woman broke into a broad smile and put down her sewing, as she recalled a time long ago. "It was the first time I came back to Baffin Land after I was married," she began. "I had always been a poor fatherless creature, passed from hand to hand; but now I was welcomed with great festivity by all in the village. My husband had come to challenge one of the others to a song contest, and there were many feasts on that occasion, feasts such I had only heard about, but never taken part in myself."

When she had finished her reverie, Urulu suddenly burst into tears. But they were tears of joy. She explained to Rasmussen, "I have today been a child once more. While I was telling you all about my life, I lived it over again, and saw and felt everything in the same way as when it really happened. There are so many things we do not think of until the memories are upon us. And now you have learned the life of an old woman from the very beginning to this day. And I could not help crying for joy to think I had been so happy."[102]

Mathiassen's Brush with Death

In mid-June 1922, Therkel Mathiassen left Danish Island again for another visit to Repulse Bay. He was accompanied by Peter Freuchen, Aaqqiuq, and Puursimaat. This would be a longer visit; its goal was the archaeological work Mathiassen had trained for at university and that interested him far more than the largely cartographic work of his earlier Baffin trip. Freuchen and the two Inughuit left him at Repulse Bay, where he put up in the Hudson's Bay Company house with manager George Cleveland, while they continued on to the Wager Bay area for another visit with trader Jean Berthie, also in the employ of the HBC.

Spring hunting occupied most of the Inuit at Repulse Bay, and Mathiassen was unable to hire help, so he worked alone. On June 24 he sent a letter to Freuchen, who was already back at Danish Island, asking him to send Jacob Olsen to help him. Olsen arrived on July 8. But he had cut his finger before he left the expedition's headquarters, and it was badly infected. This rendered him of little use in helping with the archaeology; he was, however, able to hunt and cook.

On July 20 the two moved into a tent, and the following day Cleveland left with his winter's haul of fox pelts for Chesterfield Inlet to await the HBC supply ship.

At Naujaat, Mathiassen excavated twelve house ruins, sixty square metres of a large midden, and fifty graves. He collected three thousand artifacts, which were taken back to Denmark. Two more house ruins were excavated at nearby Aivilik.

In mid-August, Mathiassen and Olsen took passage with a respected guide, Aullanaaq, to Duke of York Bay on Southampton Island, where Aullanaaq left them with his mother, Niviatsarnaq, and her husband, Angutimmarik.

102 Rasmussen, "Iglulik Eskimos," 48-52.

Niviatsarnaq's proper name was Siusarnaaq, but she was known to Inuit more commonly by her *aqausiq,* or pet name, Niviatsarnaq. She was then probably in her late sixties. She had led an interesting life at the junction of two cultures.

The American whaling captain George Comer had spent considerable time in northwestern Hudson Bay two decades before the arrival of the Fifth Thule Expedition. He lived for a time with an Inuit woman, Ukkuq, by whom he had one child, Pamiulik. Ukkuq died giving birth to Comer's second child; the baby did not survive. After Ukkuq's death, her sister Niviatsarnaq lived aboard ship as Comer's northern "wife" whenever the captain was in the country, although Comer had a Qallunaaq wife back home in East Haddam, Connecticut. Niviatsarnaq was one of two wives of an Inuk man, Auqqajaq, who worked with Comer and had saved his life in 1894 when Comer had fallen through thin ice. Aullanaaq was Niviatsarnaq and Auqqajaq's only child.

Joe Curley, the son of another Inuk who worked for whalers, said in the 1980s that he didn't know how many years Comer and Niviatsarnaq were together, but "whenever he [Comer] came up here, she would travel with the captain. They were looked upon as man and wife."[103]

Most whalers were incapable of pronouncing Inuit names correctly. Instead, they gave them nicknames. That's why they called Auqqajaq by the name Ben. His son Aullanaaq was known as John L., after a famous boxer, John L. Sullivan. He is the progenitor of today's many Ell families in the eastern Arctic. Of course, Niviatsarnaq was also given a nickname. She was called Shoofly, after a popular American song, "Shoo Fly, Don't Bother Me."

Auqqajaq's death in 1905 occurred the same year that Comer departed for the south after a two-year wintering. The following year, he wrecked his well-known ship, the *Era*, off Newfoundland on his way north. He would return the following year with another ship, the *A. T. Gifford*. By then, Niviatsarnaq had taken a new husband. He was Angutimmarik, a powerful shaman who had worked for many years for Scottish whalers in the bay. He was known to them as Scotch Tom.

Mathiassen thought Angutimmarik was a "highly respected shaman,"[104] but noted that he had a high estimation of his own worth. Angutimmarik told Mathiassen, "As to myself, I believe I am a better shaman than others among my countrymen. I will venture to say that I hardly ever make a mistake in the things I investigate and in what I predict. And I therefore consider myself a more perfect, a more fully-trained shaman than those of my countrymen who often make mistakes."[105]

Inuit interviewed by Dorothy Eber in the 1980s remembered that

---

103 Eber, *When the Whalers*, 114.

104 Mathiassen, quoted in Rasmussen, "Iglulik Eskimos," 132.

105 Rasmussen, "Iglulik Eskimos," 132.

Angutimmarik had a sophisticated understanding of illness. One Inuk woman remarked, "I think everyone remembers that man. Nobody was ever to use his things. . . . In our camp a couple of people were really sick, and Angutimmarik began doing his magical things to discover who was causing the illness. After using his magic, he knew I had used his cup, and he told me I was not to do this because in this way he would pass all his germs to me."[106]

Angutimmarik and Niviatsarnaq were "militantly anti-Christian."[107] Angutimmarik told Mathiassen that, although some in Repulse Bay had become Christians, he himself knew nothing of Jesus and as long as he knew nothing of him, he would stick with his old ways. He said that the Scottish whaler John Murray had made fun of him and said that shamans did not speak the truth. But, he told the Dane, Murray had once said to Itiruusiq, a shaman, "Take out your two big front teeth without touching them to show that you are a shaman." One of the man's teeth fell out. Murray then took hold of the other one but couldn't budge it, but shortly after it fell out too.[108]

The visit to Southampton Island was meant to be short. Mathiassen and Olsen excavated eleven house ruins in Duke of York Bay from August 20 until September 6. Aullanaaq returned on September 2, intending to take them directly to Danish Island, but the ice had already formed in Frozen Strait. And so the plan changed—he would take them back to Repulse Bay. But that plan was thwarted by a gale that caused them to return to their camp on September 13, when they reluctantly made the decision to winter.

It promised to be an unpleasant winter. They were low on supplies: two kilograms each of sugar, flour, and oatmeal, three kilograms of canned pemmican, two packets of tea, one kilogram of coffee, half a packet of mustard, and a little salt. They had just over one litre of petroleum and thirty boxes of matches. Fortunately, they had a good supply of tobacco—140 slabs of the popular Cavendish brand. Olsen had his gun but only thirty rifle cartridges and the same number of shot cartridges. Mathiassen had left his gun at Repulse Bay because he had no ammunition at all. Not expecting to winter, they had not brought their winter clothing with them; instead, they had woollen clothes, and each man had a pair of sealskin pants. It wasn't much, but, wrote Mathiassen, "the Eskimos promised to help with food and winter clothing as much as they could."[109]

But the Inuit were also short of ammunition.

106 Mary Ningeogan of Coral Harbour, quoted in Eber, *When the Whalers*, 82.

107 Carpenter, "Aivilik Relations," 2.

108 Rasmussen, "Iglulik and Caribou Eskimo Texts," 112.

109 Mathiassen, "Report on the Expedition," 55.

On October 4, with all their meat gone, the entire camp moved inland to a large lake, which Olsen named Hansine Lake after his wife back in Greenland. They lived there in skin tents and later snowhouses. At the end of the month they moved farther inland to a region with caribou, to a camp they named Darkness Lake. There were only six families on the island, and they were all at this winter camp. Olsen hunted with the Inuit as long as his ammunition lasted. Mathiassen, with neither a gun nor ammunition, spent most of his time in camp.

Years later, Joe Curley, adopted son of Angutimmarik, recalled, "They were poor. They were poor like little orphan boys."[110]

For both men, this sojourn at Darkness Lake was "dreary and insecure."[111] Food was scarce, but even worse, relations with the Inuit had gradually become less friendly. Their tea and tobacco, both good forms of payment in the days of barter, were gone. They could only "pay with nothing but promises"[112] of what they would provide once safely back at Danish Island.

That wasn't enough, because unfortunately they had also broken some taboos. In fact, Mathiassen recorded their transgressions in his own words: "They [We] had excavated ancient ruins, hammered stone samples out of the rocks, smashed caribou skulls with a hammer in order to eat the brain, etc., and when some of the Eskimos became sick, the shamans worked it out that the two strangers were the cause of it."[113]

Niviatsarnaq was, in Mathiassen's words, an "evil genius."[114] One night while the camp members were travelling, she suffered from a headache and convinced herself that her pains would not subside unless Angutimmarik killed the two strangers. Jacob Olsen overheard her imploring her husband to commit the deed and was able to prevent it.

Later, around New Year's, they moved in with Makkik, "who was more kindly disposed towards them."[115] Then an epidemic of sore throat broke out, and Mathiassen himself became seriously ill. Makkik began to doubt the wisdom of housing the two.

On February 5 a gun went off unexpectedly in the iglu, and the bullet made six holes in the folds of Mathiassen's inner coat, but he was unscathed. It was an accident, but it was nonetheless a close call. That same day Aullanaaq arrived, sent by Rasmussen to rescue his men. But before he could begin the homeward journey, he needed to hunt for dog food. Mathiassen, Olsen, and their rescuer finally reached Blæsebælgen on February 21, when Rasmussen hosted a huge feast to celebrate their arrival.

Mathiassen afterwards claimed that he had appreciated the experience, although it had been difficult because "he had lived on terms of intimacy with the Eskimos that otherwise would have been impossible."[116] He had learned much.

---

110 Joe Curley quoted in Eber, *When the Whalers*, 83.

111 Mathiassen, "Report on the Expedition," 57.

112 Ibid.

113 Ibid.

114 Ibid.

115 Ibid.

116 Ibid., 58.

A few years after the Fifth Thule Expedition, in 1926, both Catholics and Anglicans established mission stations on Southampton Island. The following year, Father Eugene Fafard commented on the extraordinary influence that Niviatsarnaq exerted on all the Inuit of the island. He referred to her by her nickname, Shoofly, and called her the queen of the island. She was an excellent seamstress, and he reported that she had created a sewing school where she taught several girls. Her waterproof sealskin boots were said to be the best. She was the first woman in her community to have a sewing machine. Joe Curley said of his stepmother, "She was a wise person. . . . People looked to her for advice. . . . She was regarded as one of the leaders among our people."[117]

Even men came to ask Niviatsarnaq's advice on various matters. In fact, she was so influential that Angutimmarik became jealous of her prestige. Another priest, reporting what he had heard from Father Fafard, wrote, "When he [Angutimmarik] had puppies, he kept a young female and called her 'Shoofly.' When she was six months old, he harnessed her and delighted in whipping her repeatedly, shouting each time 'Shooflyruluk!' ('wretched Shoofly')."[118]

George Comer eventually retired in Connecticut, but kept in touch with his northern family. John Ell—Aullanaaq—wrote to him in 1933, thanking him for a box of items sent the previous summer and giving him the sad news that his mother was in failing health. He wrote that he was employed by the Hudson's Bay Company and had purchased a large boat, and he asked for three barrels of gasoline and some Winchester rifles. "If you send me this, I will be very glad," he closed.[119]

Niviatsarnaq—the famous Shoofly—passed away in the 1930s, Angutimmarik in the 1940s.

Jacob Olsen: "No Taboo Performances Are Necessary"

The importance of Jacob Olsen on the Fifth Thule Expedition is often overlooked. He was the expedition's interpreter and secretary, as well as a dog-driver and hunter. Unlike the six Inughuit on the expedition who did not speak English or Danish,

117 Joe Curley quoted in Eber, *When the Whalers*, 114.

118 Letter from Father Guy Mary-Rousselière to Smithsonian Institution, November 16, 1982. Kenn Harper personal collection.

119 Letter of John Ell to George Comer, July 30, 1933, Southampton Island, courtesy of Melinda Tatty.

Olsen, a Kalaaleq from central west Greenland, spoke Kalaallisut (West Greenlandic) and Danish. The Inughuit spoke Inuktun, a dialect of the Inuit language that is related to Kalaallisut and all Canadian Inuktitut dialects. Knud Rasmussen spoke Inuktun and Kalaallisut, as well as Danish and English. Peter Freuchen spoke Danish, English, and Inuktun. The three other Danes did not speak Inuktun or Kalaallisut. All the Danes also spoke English to varying degrees.

The Aivilingmiut and Iglulingmiut who interacted with the expedition at Danish Island referred to the Inughuit as *Akukittut* ("the people with short flaps on their parkas"). They had heard of such people on trading trips north to Pond Inlet. That word today is used, generally with a "-miut" suffix—*Akukitturmiut*—for all Greenlanders. But Jacob Olsen was different from the Inughuit. He was a Kalaaleq, and the people of Melville Peninsula had no knowledge of West Greenlanders.

Olsen's father, Samuel Olsen, was the chief catechist in Sisimiut (then called Holsteinsborg). Jacob's older brother, Gustav, was a close friend of Rasmussen and had been the first missionary in the Thule district. Another brother, Julius, worked as a catechist among the Inuit of East Greenland. Jacob was born on November 22, 1890. After graduating from the seminarium in Nuuk, he took up duties at Qeqertarsuaq (then called Godhavn). He was, moreover, a skilled dog-driver and proficient in the use of the kayak. He was a natural for the expedition, and in the summer of 1921, Rasmussen recruited him. Olsen, who was labouring at the village of Ujarasussuk, had just three hours to think about Rasmussen's offer. He accepted, and left his family in Qeqertarsuaq, where they would remain during his absence.

In the early days of the expedition, Olsen made a number of trips from Danish Island to Repulse Bay. In the spring of 1922 he travelled to Chesterfield Inlet with ethnographer Kaj Birket-Smith. Olsen remained there while Birket-Smith continued on to Baker Lake, where he would wait for Rasmussen before visiting the inland Inuit. At Chesterfield, Olsen availed himself of the hospitality and knowledge of Inuktitut-speaking trader Solomon Ford. He also spent considerable time at the Roman Catholic mission, and got to know its founder, Father Arsène Turquetil, and the young priest Lionel Ducharme.

In addition to his work as an assistant to the Danish scientists, Olsen preached the gospel to Inuit he met, both at the expedition's headquarters and on his various trips. This was a time of religious upheaval in the Naujaat area. Inuit there were influenced by the Catholic mission at Chesterfield Inlet to the south at about the same time as the Inuk prophet Umik arrived from the Pond Inlet area with his version of Christianity. Into the mix came Jacob Olsen, a man with six years of theological training under his belt, speaking a dialect of the Inuktitut language, and with an interest in proselytizing.

In an interview in 1990, the well-known Inuk Anglican minister Noah Nashook said, "My first introduction to Christianity as a young boy took place near Naujaat from preachers from Greenland who had arrived by ship. I was so young

I don't remember my reaction."[120] Although not mentioned by name, Olsen is the only member of the expedition who might have been described as a preacher.

Of the six Inughuit, only the young woman Aqattaq had been baptized in Thule; the rest were baptized in Nuuk the day before leaving for Canada, all having attended baptismal preparations for the three years previous. But there is no indication that they proselytized.

Olsen kept a detailed diary in Greenlandic in which he recorded the songs and customs of the Inuit, as well as notes on his work in archaeology and the collection of artifacts. One man whom he met at Chesterfield Inlet was Pilakapsik. Olsen talked to him quite forcefully about Christianity, and eventually Pilakapsik said he wanted to hear more. As Olsen was leaving shortly, he referred him to Father Turquetil.

Another of the Danes, Helge Bangsted, wrote in his diary, "They [the Catholic fathers] very much want Jacob to go over to Catholicism and become a catechist here. 'But I will not do so,' said Jacob."[121] In his own writings, Olsen noted that the Catholic priests had made overtures to him on three separate occasions.

Peter Freuchen wrote about Olsen that he was too busy casting his seed among the Inuit to bother with any preaching. But this accusation is suspect. Freuchen had made similar aspersions, in almost the same words, against a West Greenlandic missionary in Thule. While there may well be truth to the accusations, it could just be Freuchen taking an opportunity to show his well-known dislike of missionaries.

In Greenland, Olsen was known as Jaakunnguaq, and the Canadian Inuit called him Jaaku. He admired the Inuit, got on well with them, and praised them for their kindness, friendliness, helpfulness, and hardiness. He particularly admired the Aivilingmiut for their skills and their speed in iglu construction. He marvelled at a multi-domed iglu complex he saw at Mattuq (Bury Cove), which housed four families. He even took notes on the calls used to direct the dogs in a team, and compared them to the calls used in Greenland.

Greenlandic scholar Robert Petersen summed up Olsen: "He was physically strong and skilled in all kinds of sports, and he was also endowed with a good sense of humour. He could in many areas prove himself among the Aivilingmiut and be accepted."[122]

The Aivilingmiut had given up the art of kayaking, but Jaaku had brought his kayak with him and demonstrated its use to them. They remembered it three decades later when they told Petersen how impressed they were at seeing Jaaku roll his kayak. (By contrast, the inland Inuit had retained the use of their kayaks for use on lakes. Knud Rasmussen wanted to show them how Greenlanders roll a kayak, but failed to realize that the Caribou Inuit kayak is not meant for such feats. He found himself in

120 Evaluardjuk, "Noah Nashook," 39-41; translated and quoted by Laugrand and Oosten, *Inuit, Oblate Missionaries*, 89. (Laugrand and Oosten identify Jacob Olsen incorrectly as "Poorsima" [Puursimaat].)

121 Bangsted, *Diary*, entry from April 25, 1922. This diary was offered as part of Bangsted material at a Bruun Rasmussen auction in Copenhagen in 2006; from notes I made on viewing the lot on November 30, 2006; its present whereabouts is unknown. Translation by Kenn Harper.

122 Petersen, "J. P. Jacob Olsen," 301.

a dangerous predicament—upside down in an unfamiliar kayak.)

Olsen was critical of the syllabic writing system that Inuit in the eastern Canadian Arctic had recently adopted. He wrote sarcastically, "They [the characters] are very well suited to what they are supposed to do! They are not able to show the words as they are. Thus there are many possibilities for misunderstandings. How, in fact, should one show the pronunciations of the syllables?" Robert Petersen, writing about Olsen and editorializing on the subject, summed it up this way: "It is practical to learn, but impractical to use."[123]

In 1922, when Olsen and Mathiassen travelled to Southampton Island, intending to spend a relatively short time there before returning to Danish Island, they were unfortunately forced to winter in trying circumstances with few supplies. In January, a woman named Nanuraq became ill and was treated by an angakkuq, her husband, Makkik. A few days later, the healing attempts were taken over by Angutimmarik himself. Olsen was present with Mathiassen at a healing ritual. He wrote down in detail what he saw; Rasmussen subsequently reviewed the report for accuracy with both Olsen and the shaman, and published it in English.[124] It transpired that the sick woman had broken a number of rules—discovered in part through audience participation and suggestion—and confessed her transgressions.

Olsen recorded another seance, in which everyone in the village was frightened to the point where no one dared to go out. Finally the shamans were requested to drive away the evil spirits. Angutimmarik began with a song to invoke the spirits:

> What can it be that moves
> which moves me
> somewhere out over the earth, away from here,
> which moves and will thus become visible,
> something without entrails,
> something that seeks to do evil,
> something moving straight towards us.
> Helping spirit Tipjarsi, Tipjarsi,[125]
> come, come to me,
> I consult you and I interrogate you
> And you must answer.[126]

Olsen wrote that at times the shamans were not content with merely singing: "They go out themselves to do battle with the evil spirits, and when they return, their hands and arms are bloody from the fight and their clothing in rags."[127]

---

123 Ibid., 300.

124 Rasmussen, "Iglulik Eskimos," 132-141.

125 *Tipjarsi* means "something along the shore that was washed up by the waves."

126 Rasmussen, "Iglulik Eskimos," 145.

127 Ibid., 147.

But he had his doubts about the power of the shaman. He stopped short of calling the Southampton Island shaman Saraq an outright fraud:

> I was witness to such a case, where a shaman named Saraq went out to fight against evil spirits, but I discovered that he had taken some caribou blood with him beforehand, and rubbed himself with this, without being discovered by anyone else. When he came in, he stated that the shaman who had been out with him had been unable to hold the evil spirit, but he, Saraq, had grasped it and stabbed it, inflicting a deep wound. . . . All believed his report, all believed that he had driven away the evil spirit which had been troubling the village, and no one was afraid any longer.[128]

Jaaku was also not above arguing with Inuit over their belief in taboos. He compiled a list of ninety taboos, before noting that the list even then was incomplete. He was frustrated by many of them. When sickness in the camp was blamed on his and Mathiassen's presence, he said, "I talked to them in such a way that they could understand it [my message], and pointed out that people were also getting sick and dying even before we came."[129]

When he killed a polar bear and got it to the snowhouses, he was told there were a number of precautions that the group must follow. They were to throw away all their clothes before going into the snowhouses. And they were not to use the fat of the bear for five days. But Jaaku ignored them. "No taboo performances are necessary for the animals that I kill," he said.[130] This pleasantly surprised the Inuit.

Throughout the dreadful winter of privation on Southampton Island, Jaaku maintained his faith. On Christmas Eve, 1922, he wrote in his diary, "I told them who we were celebrating and why He had come into the world. . . . I wish He would come into the hearts of those poor people."[131]

On March 23, 1923, with their work on Danish Island at an end, Olsen and Birket-Smith left Blæsebælgen with Aullanaaq as guide to begin their homeward journey. On April 17 they stopped at Cape Fullerton, where the HBC schooner was wintering, affording them an opportunity to say goodbye to trader Jean Berthie. A month later they reached Arviat (then called Eskimo Point), where the post manager, George Mitchell, was seriously ill with frostbite. They spent part of their

---

128 Rasmussen, "Iglulik Eskimos," 147.

129 Petersen, "J. P. Jacob Olsen," 297. Translation by Kenn Harper and Aviaq Harper.

130 Ibid. Translation by Kenn Harper and Aviaq Harper.

131 Ibid., 296. Translation by Kenn Harper and Aviaq Harper.

time there at an Inuit camp on Sentry Island. They had hoped to travel inland to further investigate the Paallirmiut, but the lateness of the season and the inability to get dog food spelled the end of that idea. They continued on to Churchill, then made their way via The Pas and Winnipeg to New York, where they caught a ship to Copenhagen.

Olsen published a book on his experiences called *Akilinermiulerssârut* (which might be translated as "Report on the Canadian Inuit") in 1927.[132] It has never been translated into either Danish or English.

Robert Petersen thought that Olsen's purpose in writing his book was simply to portray Canadian Inuit as they were. Some of his early remarks may have seemed a trifle condescending, as when he noted of the first shaman he met, "He seemed pretty ridiculous."[133] But overall, Olsen presented an even-handed description of his experiences and of the culture of Inuit, particularly the Aivilingmiut.

Olsen became very fluent in the Aivilingmiut dialect during his time in Arctic Canada. He kept his expedition diaries in Greenlandic, but as he recognized more and more the differences between Kalaallisut and *Aivilingmiutut* (the Inuktitut dialect spoken by the Aivilingmiut), he modified his script. When his book was published, another Greenlandic author and pastor, Otto Rosing, criticized the work for having so many expressions in Aivilingmiutut that in several places it was "unintelligible."[134] This was an overly harsh criticism, as the book was popular among Greenlandic readers anxious to know about their relatives across the sea.

After his reunion with his wife, Hansine, and children in Greenland, Olsen returned to Denmark for a year, on contract to assist Knud Rasmussen in interpreting and writing up some of the Inuit folklore collected. Other trips to Denmark for the same purpose followed.

Jacob Olsen died of scarlet fever in Nuuk on July 10, 1936. He was only forty-five years old. He was the first to be buried in the new cemetery there.

Canadian Inuit remembered him as unique among expedition members. There were Qallunaat, there were Akukittut, and there was Jaaku, a Kalaaleq.

The Misadventures of Peter Freuchen

Peter Freuchen was a giant of a man. Standing almost two metres tall, he towered over the other members of the Fifth Thule Expedition and the Inuit of Melville Peninsula. Inuit called him Piitarjuaq ("big Peter," or Piitarsuaq in Greenlandic).

132 Olsen, *Akilinermiulerssârut*. Translation by Kenn Harper and Aviaq Harper.

133 Petersen, "J. P. Jacob Olsen," 298. Translation by Kenn Harper and Aviaq Harper.

134 Rosing quoted in Petersen, "J. P. Jacob Olsen," 295. Translation by Kenn Harper and Aviaq Harper.

He was born in Denmark on February 20, 1886. As a young man he dropped out of university to participate in an expedition to northern Greenland in 1906. Once back in Denmark, he was working as a reporter when he met Knud Rasmussen. The two became fast friends.

In 1910 they established the North Star trading post in the heartland of the Inughuit of northern Greenland. Freuchen became chief trader there. But he was much more than a merchant. He travelled and explored, adding to the geographical knowledge of northern Greenland. He also collected zoological, botanical, and meteorological specimens for museums. But, most importantly, he learned the language of the local Inughuit and immersed himself in their customs.

A year after his arrival in the district, and intending to make his life there, Freuchen married a girl named Navarana. In Denmark, this marriage would have at least turned heads if not earned the ire of the local authorities, for Navarana was only thirteen years old, while Freuchen was twenty-six. But in Thule, it was seen as normal. Hunters needed wives, and most women married young. The local missionaries took a dim view of this Inuit custom marriage, but it suited Freuchen just fine. He wrote to a friend, "I am hated by the mission and loved by the Eskimos. What more can I ask for?"[135]

When Navarana, who was to have accompanied the expedition as a seamstress and general assistant, died before the expedition left Greenland, Peter decided to continue without her.

According to Freuchen, the original plan had been that he and Qaavigarsuaq would leave the expedition's ship, the *Søkongen,* at or near Kinngait (then called Cape Dorset) on Baffin Island, where they would overwinter. They would then sled north the following spring, cross to Melville Peninsula in the Iglulik area, and then sled south to join the main party, which had initially hoped to establish its base at Winter Island, mapped a century earlier by William Edward Parry.[136] It is just as well that this plan was abandoned, probably because of the lateness of the season, for the area of the Baffin coast they would have traversed is notoriously sparse in game resources.

In later years, Freuchen became well-known worldwide as a writer and storyteller. Many have cast doubt on the veracity of his stories. But, for almost all of them, there was a basis of fact, although Freuchen was certainly not averse to embellishing his tales. Many of his best-known stories were the results of his experiences on the Fifth Thule Expedition.

One of those was of a map-making trip he made with Helge Bangsted and guides Aaqqiuq and Palluq. At one point Freuchen became separated from the group and then lost when a storm arose. That posed no problem, he thought. He would simply build an iglu and wait out the storm. Unfortunately, the snow conditions were not right for building an iglu. Here, in his own words, is what he did:

---

135 Peter Freuchen in a letter to Johan Skjoldborg, October 29, 1914, quoted in Christensen, "Jeg er hadet," 74. Translation by Kenn Harper.

136 Freuchen, *Arctic Adventure*, 329.

> I began digging in the solid snow and soon I had a depression long enough for me to lie down in. I put my sled on top of this strange bed. . . .
>
> On my sled I had the skin of a bear's head I had killed some days before, and I took this along for a pillow. Finally as I crawled into my snug little shelter, I pulled my small sleeping bag in place with my foot, so that it covered the opening like a door.
>
> I was well protected against the sub-zero temperature, dressed like an Eskimo in two layers of fur. . . . I had heavy boots and good gloves. . . . Warm and comfortable at last, I soon fell asleep.
>
> When I finally woke up I was very cold. I knew I had to get out and move about at once. What worried me the most was the fact that my feet did not hurt any more—a sure sign of danger.

Freuchen was trapped in his little cave. He had intended to simply push the sled away when he awoke, but snow had drifted over it and he was unable to move it. He rolled over and pushed up on it with his back, but the sled wouldn't budge. Hoping to dig his way out, he discovered that the condensation from his breath had turned the walls of the tiny cavity into ice. He tried scratching with his hands, but that proved futile. Freuchen was buried alive!

Desperate, he managed to pull the skin of the bear's head down from the end of the cave. He chewed on the edge of it until it was saturated with spit, then let it freeze. He was able to dig a little with the frozen skin, but it softened quickly. Nonetheless, he managed to create a small hole. Then things got worse:

> I pushed with all my strength but the hole was much too small. I got out far enough to expose my face to the drifting snow. My long beard was moist from my breathing and from the spit which had drooled from my bearskin. The moment my face got through the hole my beard came in contact with the runners of the sled and instantly froze to them. I was trapped. The hole was too small to let me get through, my beard would not let me retire into my grave again. I could see no way out. But what a way to die—my body twisted in an unnatural position, my beard frozen to the sled above, and the storm beating my face without mercy. . . .
>
> With all my strength I pulled my head back. At first the beard would not come free, but I went on pulling and my whiskers and some of my skin were torn off, and finally I got loose. I withdrew into my hole and stretched out once more.

After resting for a time, Freuchen had a new idea. He explained:

> I had often seen dog's dung in the sled track and had noticed that it would freeze as solid as a rock. Would not the cold have the same effect on human discharge? Repulsive as the thought was, I decided to try the experiment. I moved my bowels and from the excrement I managed to fashion a chisel-like instrument which I left to freeze.
>
> This time I was patient. I did not want to risk breaking my new tool by using it too soon. While I waited, the hole I had made filled up with fresh snow.... At last I decided to try my chisel, and it worked! Very gently and very slowly I worked at the hole. As I dug I could feel the blood trickling down my face from the scars where the beard had been torn away.[137]

Freuchen managed to work his body into the hole, and to move the sled that had blocked his passage.

Peter Freuchen had saved his life by fashioning a chisel from his own feces to free himself from an ice cave that had threatened to become his early grave. He ended his description of that adventure with the ominous statement, "Fortunately I then did not know the ordeal was to cost me my foot."[138]

And thus begins another tale.

The map-making expedition on which Freuchen, Bangsted, Aaqqiuq, and Palluq had embarked was quickly brought to an end. The party had to return to base camp as fast as possible if Freuchen's foot was to be saved.

Back at Danish Island, gangrene set in and the flesh began to peel from his foot. Palluq's wife, Tagurnaaq, (Freuchen calls her Apa in his telling, but he is in error) used an Inuit treatment. "She captured lemmings," wrote Freuchen, "skinned them, and put the warm skin on my rotting foot with the bloody side down. Every time she changed this peculiar kind of dressing, some of my decayed flesh peeled off with it, but she insisted on this treatment until there was no more flesh left.... At night when I could not sleep I stared with horrible fascination at the bare bones of my toes."[139]

She also told stories about her experiences treating frozen limbs: "She knew a number of people who had lost both legs, others their arms or hands, but many had been killed because they were far too much trouble to take care of."[140]

Gangrene, Freuchen noted, is smelly: "As long as I kept my foot inside the warm house, the odor was unbearable, so we arranged to keep the foot outside. We

137 Freuchen, *Vagrant Viking*, 176-180.

138 Ibid., 180.

139 Ibid., 182.

140 Ibid., 181-2.

made a hole in the wall by the end of my bunk, and I put my foot out into the freezing temperatures whenever the odor became too overpowering."[141]

From the relative comfort of his bed at Danish Island, he wrote a letter to the fur trader Henry Toke Munn on March 21, 1923, in which he made light of his situation: "Just now I am at bed, having some frozen toes to take care of. Hope they will drop of [*sic*] pretty soon."[142]

Tagurnaaq offered Freuchen something else to take his mind off his troubles: "One day [Tagurnaaq] told me that I needed a woman to take my mind off my pains. She brought along a young girl, Siksik, whose husband, Qingaq, had kindly put her at my disposal while he went off on a trip with Captain Berthie. I felt like King David, who was given young girls to keep him warm at night, but I told Siksik that I was in no condition to take advantage of the kind offer."[143]

Perhaps. But Freuchen loved female companionship, and if he did not make Siksik his bedmate, he certainly did with another woman, Qakuqtingniq, a young Nattilik woman. Little is known of the circumstances, except that about nine months later, Qakuqtingniq bore Freuchen's child.[144]

Freuchen was candid about his relationships with Inuit women. He described an encounter he had with a hunter he met while returning once to Danish Island. The hunter was accompanied by his two wives. "He asked us to spend the night in his igloo," wrote Freuchen, "and generously offered me one of his women. This gesture of friendship could not be turned down, but it caused trouble between the two women. During the night the old man woke me up to say his other wife was insulted because she had not been put at my disposal, with the result that I had to spend another night there."[145]

Freuchen continued his description of his recovery: "The gangrene did not spread beyond the toes. Once the decay had bared all five toes to the roots, it did not go farther, and the flesh stopped peeling. I could not stand the sight, however, and one day I decided to do something about it." He had decided to amputate his own toes!

"I got hold of a pair of pincers," he wrote, "fitted the jaws around one of my toes, and hit the handle with a heavy hammer. The excruciating pain cut into every nerve of my body, an agony I cannot describe."[146]

Freuchen later remarked flippantly, "Perhaps one could get used to cutting off toes, but there were not enough of them to get sufficient practice."[147]

He admitted that he cried with self-pity when he had finished cutting off his

141 Ibid., 182.

142 Letter from Peter Freuchen to Henry Toke Munn, March 21, 1923, quoted in Lloyd, "Station Diary," 74-75.

143 Freuchen, *Vagrant Viking*, 182.

144 Ole Itinnuar was born in late December or early January 1924. His exact birthdate is unknown but he was baptized on January 15, 1924. Source: Peter Itinnuar correspondence, May 24, 2022.

145 Freuchen, *Vagrant Viking*, 173.

146 Ibid., 182.

147 Ibid., 182-3.

toes, but it was a great relief to have the toe-stumps off since they had kept him from walking and putting on his sealskin boots. "Now I could at least get on my boots and hobble around," he wrote.[148] By March 27 he was able to be up for three hours, and two days later for two additional hours. By April 19 he was able to make short sledge journeys near the station. In fact, he learned quickly to walk quite well; toes are important, certainly, but the balls of one's feet provide the most balance, as other explorers who have lost toes in the Arctic also learned.

On June 6 Freuchen and Helge Bangsted travelled to Beach Point, just south of Repulse Bay, where they met Aullanaaq, who took Freuchen in his sailing boat to Chesterfield Inlet, which they reached on July 9. Freuchen's purpose was to see the doctor on the HBC supply vessel the *Nascopie*. He whiled away his time doing archaeological digs while awaiting the ship.

Dr. Hart told Freuchen that he needed an operation immediately if the foot was to be saved. Some reports say this operation took place in the company's staff house, others say it was aboard the ship. In fact, it took place in the ship's mess hall on a dining table.

Freuchen was a non-drinker. But the doctor apparently had no anaesthetic. Freuchen reportedly downed half a bottle of rum before the operation. Dr. Hart, assisted by William Douglas, now an HBC clerk, then performed the operation.[149]

Despite the fact that this is an often-told story, it's unclear just what came off during the procedure. Freuchen claims he himself had amputated five toes from the frozen foot, but the expedition's official report says that on the ship "Freuchen had his frost-bitten great toe amputated."[150] What is likely is that Freuchen had made a bit of a mess of amputating the big toe—its bone mass would have been larger than that of the other toes. Dr. Hart needed to clean up Freuchen's job on the big toe, and probably remove dead flesh from various parts of the foot, including the heel, which had also been frostbitten.

The doctor advised Freuchen to go out on the *Nascopie* to get further treatment in the south. But he was unwilling to do so. He still had work to do, and returned to Danish Island. Back in Denmark in 1926, he ended up having his left foot amputated and was fitted with a prosthetic foot—all this the result of a night's carelessness in seeking temporary shelter while lost on the land.

148 Freuchen, *Vagrant Viking*, 183.

149 Ibid., 185. Freuchen calls him Sergeant Douglas, but Douglas had left the RCMP and joined the HBC as clerk at Repulse Bay on July 1, 1923.

150 Mathiassen, "Report on the Expedition," 74. In Rasmussen's letter of March 5, 1923, to George Cleveland, he says that Freuchen has suffered "the loss of three toes . . . the toes have just begun to fall off." See Lloyd, "Station Diary," 68.

Mathiassen and the Thule Culture

By March 1923, the work of the Fifth Thule Expedition that could be undertaken from its base at Blæsebælgen on Danish Island had largely been finished. It was time for most scientific members of the expedition to complete their work plans and leave for Denmark, albeit by varying routes. Their work, though, would continue en route.

On the morning of March 11, the last Expedition Council was held. Despite its grandiose name, this was simply a meeting of the personnel to ensure that everyone was aware of what expectations remained for them. European food supplies were almost exhausted, and coal was running low.

Early the same afternoon, Knud Rasmussen left with Qaavigarsuaq and Arnarulunnguaq on the great sled journey that would take them across the top of North America to Alaska and Siberia.

On March 23, Kaj Birket-Smith and Jacob Olsen began their homeward journey by heading south, initially with the help of the trusted guide Aullanaaq.

A day before their departure, Therkel Mathiassen had left for Iglulik and Pond Inlet, where he would conduct further archaeological work in the summer.

Mathiassen had done important archaeological work at Naujaat, a few kilometres east of the trading station at Repulse Bay, at Aivilik just west of that station, and at Southampton Island. He had found solid evidence of what had been supposed before—the existence of a culture ancestral to that of modern Inuit. He was anxious to continue the cartographical and geographical work he had begun the previous year and make an ethnographic study of the Tununirmiut, the people of the Pond Inlet area. He would, of course, do archaeological work at Pond Inlet, which was about midway between Repulse Bay and Thule, the site where earlier examples of the technology of the new culture had been excavated.

Immediately upon leaving Danish Island, Mathiassen spent a few days at Aua's camp at Sturges Island. He had spent time at the shaman's various camps on many occasions since the start of the expedition. But the attraction there was more than just the information he was able to glean from the old shaman. Mathiassen had taken a young woman of the camp as his lover.

She was Arnaujaq, the young wife of a man named Quviq.[151] She later took the Christian name of Leah. She was the daughter of Kassungiaq, a woman born about 1875, who was married to Qipanniq at the time of Arnaujaq's birth in 1901.[152] Arnaujaq's biological father, however, was not Qipanniq but a Scottish whaling captain, Alexander Murray Junior.[153]

Mathiassen may have had more than one lover in the camp. In the movie *The*

151 Trébaol, "Genealogical compilation," 16-117. Trébaol spells the man's name as Koverk. Mathiassen spells it as Queq in his census (Mathiassen, "Material Culture," 17).

152 Ibid., 118. Trébaol spells Qipanniq's name as K'epanerk, and Arnaujaq as Arnauyark.

153 Ibid. Trébaol reports that Kassungiak lived with Captain Comer, but this is probably a mistake, her whaler "husband" being Murray.

Journals of Knud Rasmussen, a fictionalized version of some events on the expedition, Mathiassen is infatuated with Aua's daughter Aapaq. A character outline for Mathiassen prepared by Isuma TV has Mathiassen saying, "I became friendly with Apak [Aapaq], the daughter of Aua. She was so beautiful, but unhappy in her marriage to Tapaqti and defiant of her father. She shared her worries with me, for she felt she had endangered her daughter and family by the taboos she had broken. I wanted to take her away, maybe even home to Denmark, but couldn't, although for a box of bullets, Tapaqti would have allowed it. Even if I could have chosen her, we all knew she would never go."[154]

On Mathiassen's final stay at the camp, Aua joked with Mathiassen about the young Dane's wives, telling him that he must remember to tell Asta (Mathiassen's wife in Denmark) "who was your wife here."[155]

Regardless of whether or not he had more than one lover, we know that only Arnaujaq bore his child, a girl named Amaktlak. Unfortunately, there is no accurate record of her birth date, it being recorded only as "around 1924."[156] Whether Mathiassen knew that he had left a child behind is unknown. In the book he wrote about the expedition, there is no mention of Arnaujaq. Aapaq is mentioned only in a fleeting reference in which he notes Tagurnaaq's sarcastic comment that Aapaq had become a Christian for her food, a reference to the fact that those who adopted Christianity no longer were bound to follow food taboos.[157]

During his two years in the Canadian Arctic, Mathiassen was known to the Inuit as Tikili. Some have hypothesized that this nickname was really Tikilik ("the one with the thimble"), because archaeologists often use thimbles on their fingers while digging. That may be a convenient coincidence, but his name Tikili was simply an Inuit attempt to pronounce his first name.

Mathiassen reached Iglulik on April 17, but found that all the "men of any importance"[158] had already left to trade at Pond Inlet, where a new trading post had been established by the HBC two years earlier. He continued on through Steensby Inlet, which he had earlier named after the Danish geographer whose theories had initially fanned Rasmussen's interest in the question of Inuit origins. On the island Maniqtuq, he learned that the hunters there had also left for Pond Inlet. This dashed his hopes of mapping the unknown Baffin coast between Iglulik and Piling.

At Iglulik, his guide, Puursimaat, and his wife, Aqattaq, turned back to Danish Island, and Mathiassen continued on with Palluq and his wife, Tagurnaaq. He described them as "most helpful and pleasant travelling companions."[159] They traversed Baffin Island heading north and reached the head of Milne Inlet on May 13. There they got

154 Isuma, "Therkel Mathiassen," accessed January 2, 2022.

155 Email from Dorte Mathiassen (Mathiassen's granddaughter), January 2, 2022.

156 Trébaol, "Genealogical compilation," 117.

157 Mathiassen, "Material Culture," 236.

158 Mathiassen, "Report on the Expedition," 70.

159 Mathiassen, "Material Culture," 71-2.

four caribou. After that, soft snow made progress slow. Travelling along the south coast of Eclipse Sound, they visited numerous Inuit camps before finally reaching Pond Inlet on the 21st. Mathiassen stayed with HBC trader Gaston Herodier and used his post as a base for his summer scientific work. He excavated near the station, at Button Point on Bylot Island, and at the rich site Qilalukan near the trading station.

A few days after Mathiassen's arrival, Umik, "the prophet from Iglulik,"[160] arrived. Many in Pond Inlet had already converted to his religion before his departure for Iglulik the previous year. Now they "assembled on the shore, and his sled stood a few steps from them, and they sang a hymn; only then did they rush forward and shake him by the hand; even the dogs were taken by the paws!"[161]

That summer the Canadian government ship the *Arctic* brought the apparatus of Canadian judicial procedure to Pond Inlet, and Mathiassen observed the trial of three Inuit accused of the murder of a trader, Robert Janes. He wrote that the trial was "an enormously tedious process of which the Eskimos understood very little."[162]

He left Pond Inlet with his collections on September 18 aboard the *Nascopie* after "exactly two years on Canadian soil."[163] Travelling via Montreal, Ottawa, and New York, he reached Copenhagen on October 30.

In addition to his popular Danish book *Med Knud Rasmussen Blandt Amerikas Eskimoer* (With Knud Rasmussen among America's Eskimos) (1926), Mathiassen authored major works in the reports of the Fifth Thule Expedition: *Archaeology of the Central Eskimos* (1927), *Material Culture of the Iglulik Eskimos* (1928), *Contributions to the Physiography of Southampton Island* (1931), *Contributions to the Geography of Baffin Land and Melville Peninsula* (1933), and *Report on the Expedition* (1945).

George Comer was a man with insatiable curiosity about the culture of the Inuit among whom he worked for so many years. He whaled in the general area where the Fifth Thule Expedition was based, although two decades earlier. In 1915, effectively retired from Hudson Bay whaling, Comer went for the first time to northwestern Greenland as ice master of the *George B. Cluett*, a rickety ship on charter to Donald MacMillan's Crocker Land Expedition. In 1916, always interested in archaeology and long a collector of artifacts for scientists, he excavated a large midden in Greenland that became known as Comer's Midden. Coincidentally, he was assisted in those excavations by Peter Freuchen, then the trading station manager at Thule. Comer sent artifacts from those diggings to the American Museum of Natural History, where they were analyzed by archaeologist Clark Wissler and described as symptomatic of

160 Mathiassen, *Med Knud Rasmussen*, 115. Translation by Kenn Harper.

161 Ibid., 115. Translation by Kenn Harper.

162 Ibid., 122. Translation by Kenn Harper.

163 Mathiassen, "Report on the Expedition," 72.

a previously unidentified Inuit culture. Therkel Mathiassen actually visited the site in August of 1921 during preparations for the Fifth Thule Expedition, but had no time then for any excavation.

Five years later, Mathiassen's excavations at Naujaat showed definitively that the culture whose artifacts he was unearthing was the immediate precursor of that of modern Inuit and differed from a previous culture, eventually known as the Dorset culture, which was not ancestral to the Inuit.

Mathiassen naturally was interested in what the newly identified or newly confirmed culture would be called. He decided early in his investigations that it should be called the "Naujan Culture," after the place where he had "found" it.

This caused some controversy among Danish members of the expedition. Peter Freuchen decided to write to Thomas Thomsen, leader of the Ethnographic Department of the National Museum in Denmark, on the subject. Thomsen was also a member of the expedition's steering committee. Freuchen wrote his letter on May 16, 1923, when he was alone at Blæsebælgen, almost two months after Mathiassen had left for Pond Inlet. By that time, only Helge Bangsted, Freuchen, and four Inughuit remained at Danish Island, but Bangsted was away at thc timc.

Freuchen's letter read:

> While today packing some boxes of collections, my thoughts turn quite natural to you and my fears are many. . . . This brings me to the main topic of this letter: You will have heard of Mathiassen's excavations at Repulse Bay; he is certainly making a grand thing of it—I cannot judge if it is not perhaps too much. It is always tempting for a young man, the first time he is out, to believe that he has created a world epoch. Now he has a new "culture." As this is the same as we found at Thule on the Second Thule Expedition, I suggested to him that we call it the Thule culture. It would thereby be forever linked to Knud's name and to Denmark, but he is indeed unyielding with his "Naujan culture." I would therefore ask you, as a committee member and as Knud's friend, to propose to Mathiassen that he calls his discovery the Thule culture.[164]

Freuchen alluded to a dispute between Rasmussen and another Danish scientist, Lauge Koch, a close friend of Mathiassen, which he claimed led to periodic dissension between Rasmussen and Mathiassen: "It has often been clear to all of us on this expedition that, behind the many kind words from both sides, there has been a disagreement of disposition between the two. This is a shame for Knud and will not benefit Mathiassen in the least. But Mathiassen knows, and he knows that we know, that it would delight Knud to have the name of Thule linked to these ruin findings."[165]

---

164 Freuchen quoted in Gulløv, "The Concepts," 150.

165 Ibid.

He pointed out that items of the Thule Culture were first found at Thule and described by Clark Wissler of the American Museum of Natural History: "Moreover, it should also be said that the items were first found in Thule and described (albeit badly) by Wissler; no honour will be taken from Mathiassen, and I would ask you to explain this to him. I beg you, however, to talk to Birket about it at first; he is a reasonable man."[166]

Freuchen's letter was discussed by the expedition committee, whose chairman, Marius Ib Nyeboe, wrote to Thomsen: "In particular, I am pleased that the name 'Thule Culture' strikes you as natural, and I hope you will support the proposal in that name, if Mr. Mathiassen should express a wish for the other name, as I said the other day."[167]

Mathiassen conceded, and in his preliminary report on the expedition he wrote: "This wealthy old Eskimo culture . . . I will call the Thule culture; the reason for this name is that the first discovery of this culture is the one which was done by members of the Second Thule Expedition near the station at Thule in the Cape York District in North Greenland. . . . Then that the distribution of this culture across the American continent and the Arctic Archipelago has been demonstrated on the Fifth Thule Expedition."[168]

Mathiassen's description of the Thule Culture bears repeating: "The Thule culture, as we know it from these old finds, shows us a highly developed and remarkable Eskimo culture. It presents to us a people, living in permanent winter houses by the coast, in conical tents in summer, hunting the whale, the walrus, the seal, the bear and the caribou, trapping foxes, catching birds and salmon, all by means of a highly developed implement technique. They had all the typical Eskimo forms of weapons and implements: the dog sledge, the kayak, the women's boat, the harpoon with moveable foreshaft, loose head and bladder; the ice-hunting harpoon . . ."

He went on to include a long list of technological items uniquely diagnostic of the Thule Culture, and concluded: "They mastered a highly developed proficiency in ornamentation and carving and were also familiar with the snow house. It is an Eskimo culture which, in many respects, is richer and more developed then that met with among the present day Central Eskimos. The Thule culture is by no means a primitive culture."[169]

This is the culture, defined by Mathiassen, that is ancestral to modern Inuit.

166 Ibid.

167 Ibid.

168 Mathiassen, "Foreløbig," 206, quoted in Gullov, "The Concepts," 150.

169 Mathiassen, "Archaeology," 6.

The Departure of Freuchen and the Inughuit

In late December 1923 or early the following month, Peter Freuchen became a father for the third time. His lover from the previous spring, Qakuqtingniq, bore a son whom she named Ole. The exact date he was born at Wager Inlet is not known, but he was baptized on January 15 in the Roman Catholic Church at Chesterfield Inlet. Whether Peter knew of the birth is not known, but family lore says that he certainly knew of the pregnancy and had considered taking the young woman back to Denmark with him, but her family intervened to keep her with them.

Shortly after the baptism, Freuchen left expedition headquarters on Danish Island for the last time, beginning the long trek to Greenland, accompanied by Puursimaat and his wife, Aqattaq; Aaqqiuq and his wife, Arnannguaq, and their baby daughter, Navarana.[170]

One of the expedition's long-time local guides and assistants, Anarqaaq, accompanied the party for a time before turning back. Curiously, he would later wed Qakuqtingniq and raise Freuchen's son as his own.

The building at Blæsebælgen and the gear not taken along were divided among four faithful Inuit who had been employed by the expedition: Inuujaq, Tapaqti, Palluq, and Aqaut.

The trip was long and dangerous. It is one of the great unsung episodes of stamina and determination in the history of Arctic travel.

Two days north of Lyon Inlet they met Akuanu and his wife, Qinuruna, who decided to accompany them to Greenland. From there they travelled to Iglulik, and then on to Baffin Island, described as "the very seat of all the traditions of the Eskimos. It was, in a sense, sacred ground for a student of these people."[171] When they reached Milne Inlet, they encountered deep soft snow that made for hard sledding. After two days they reached better ice and continued on to Pond Inlet.

Shortly thereafter they left for Lancaster Sound, but a gale in Eclipse Sound left them stormbound for several days. They met Inuit there who were starving, and Freuchen sent Akuanu and Qinuruna back to Pond Inlet with a note informing the police of the condition of the unfortunate people. They never saw the couple again.

Freuchen's plan was to duplicate the Lancaster Sound crossing of a legendary Inuit shaman named Qillarsuaq, who had led a party across the sound, around the east coast of Devon Island, and up the east coast of Ellesmere Island in the 1860s to Greenland, where some intermarried with Inughuit. Freuchen had heard of that epic trip from old Miqqusaaq, the grandfather of his first wife, Navarana.

At one point on Freuchen's journey, they were caught on an ice pan. The

---

170 Mathiassen in his "Report on the Expedition" says the departure was January 19, 1924. Rasmussen in *Across Arctic America* says December 28, 1923.

171 Freuchen, *Peter Freuchen's Adventures*, 285.

men made a shelter for Arnannguaq, who was nursing her baby. Then, recounts Freuchen,

> "The ice . . . parted between the women; Aqattaq had grabbed up the child and had run with her. The mother's arms were inside her coat, and she could not get them out in time. Thus the two mothers were parted by open water, and I ran after Aqattaq and Navarana. I took the child—who had been lying on her mother's lap with no kamiks [*kamiik*, "a pair of skin boots"] on her feet—and stuffed her inside my coat with her feet down inside my pants. She thought this was very funny, and laughed hilariously, but her position prevented my jumping back to my friends, and after a few seconds the water was too broad to leap over."[172]

Finally they found a place where the two floes were relatively close. Freuchen took off his coat, wrapped Navarana up in it, and threw it across the water "like a sack"[173] to her father, who caught it. Navarana was safe with her mother again. Freuchen and Aqattaq finally found a spot narrow enough to jump across, and the parties were reunited.

They had left Pond Inlet with thirty-four dogs, but by the time they reached what Freuchen reckoned to be the middle of Lancaster Sound, that number was reduced to sixteen. Many of their supplies had been lost in crossing from ice pan to ice pan; they had no kerosene and no Primus stove. Freuchen was lucky to have saved his notebooks and wrote, "It was only by good luck that I had not lost my sled and load." He figured they could reach either side of the sound in about one sleep. If they went north, though, they would be in "unfamiliar, uninhabited country."[174] If they went south, they might find a settlement of Inuit and replenish at least some of their supplies. He knew too that the expedition vessel the *Søkongen*, under Captain Pedersen, would leave Thule soon for Pond Inlet to pick him and his party up, if they were there. Reluctantly, they turned south.

It took them two nerve-wracking days of crossing ice pans to finally reach land, but they were far to the west of the point from which they had left.

They took refuge in a cave and waited there until their clothes dried and they had regained some strength and caught up on sleep. Once their death-defying crossing was behind them, Freuchen noted in his unique style, "We discussed our adventures on the ice as if they had been arranged for our pleasure," adding, "Eskimos are great people."[175]

Heading east, they reached the mouth of Admiralty Inlet, where they

---

172 Ibid., 287.

173 Ibid., 288.

174 Ibid., 289.

175 Ibid., 290.

encountered open water. Travelling into the inlet, they reached a point that Aaqqiuq had reached from the south on an earlier trip with Mathiassen. He advised travelling farther east in the inlet to where he thought some rivers might lead eastward to Milne Inlet.

Finally they encountered a group of starving Inuit, thirteen in all. Freuchen wrote, "They looked strange to us, unlike any people we had ever seen before. Their faces were hollow and their eyes sunk deep in their skulls. They had no real clothes but were covered with scabrous-looking rags and filth. They were starving. . . . We thought they were ghosts at first, but I talked to them."[176]

Instead of replenishing their own supplies, Freuchen's party gave seal meat to the starving people. This new group accompanied Freuchen's party, and slowly they all moved northward along the east coast of Admiralty Inlet. Eventually, they reached a point called Uluksan, near present-day Arctic Bay, where they remained for some time.

At Uluksan, Peter Freuchen and his Inughuit companions rested and regained their strength in the company of the starving Inuit they had encountered on their harrowing trip. Freuchen noted that the Inuit were in fact rich in goods that could eventually be traded at the Hudson's Bay Company post in Pond Inlet. In particular, they possessed two sled loads of narwhal tusks. "They were not badly off," he wrote, "but the things they possessed could not be eaten."[177]

At Uluksan, Puursimaat became ill, and Freuchen decided that the entire party of Inughuit should remain in Admiralty Inlet while he, in company with a young man, would walk to Pond Inlet. Freuchen had taken a liking to the young man, Mala, whom he described as being always cheerful and optimistic.

Their route took them across a plateau that Freuchen named the Magda Plateau. He had plenty of time to think on this arduous trip, to ponder what the future might hold for him. In his later life as a popular writer, he wrote much about his earlier relationship with his deceased wife, Navarana. But on this journey to Pond Inlet, his thoughts were not on Navarana, nor on Qakuqtingniq, the mother of the child he had left behind in the Kivalliq region. He wrote instead about his love for a woman back in Denmark, Magdalene, a woman to whom he had written from Danish Island asking her to marry him on his return.

Much of the Magda Plateau was soft clay, into which they sank while walking. "I must have slept as I walked, because suddenly I toppled over and fell face down in the disgusting stuff," he wrote. "I could not get my breath, yet I did not have the initiative to raise my head out of it, and only came to when Mala

176 Freuchen, *Peter Freuchen's Adventures*, 291.

177 Ibid., 292.

stood over me, shouting and yanking at my hair." He continued, "I was going through this purgatory to get home to Magdalene. . . . If it had not been for the thought of her, I could never have gone on." He named the "stretch of clay and hell" after her, noting, "If it was named after her I could cross it somehow—there must be something good about it."[178]

Eventually they finished the crossing of the plateau and reached the seacoast. Taking turns with their one gun, they shot and missed or lost a number of seals basking on the ice before Freuchen finally bagged one. "It was our big day that gave us back our lives," he wrote.[179] They had only four bullets left.

They reached Milne Inlet and travelled three days to an Inuit camp. From there they accompanied a family to Button Point. Mala became enamoured of the daughter in the family and remained at Button Point with them, hunting narwhal. It was already August, and Freuchen needed to get to Pond Inlet, where he hoped that the *Søkongen* would arrive by prearrangement to pick him up.

Freuchen never saw Mala again, but wrote that "it is to him that I owe my life."[180] Once back in Denmark, when Freuchen took up his new life as a writer, he immortalized Mala as the main character in his novel *Eskimo*. That book would eventually be made into a movie by MGM Studios. Set in the Canadian Arctic, but filmed in Alaska, the role of Mala was played by a part-Inuk local actor named Ray Wise. He became so captivated by the role that he changed his name to Ray Mala. And so the name Mala, now rare in the eastern Arctic, lives on in the surname of an Alaskan Inuit family.

The *Søkongen* made it through the ice to Pond Inlet under the able command of Captain Pedersen. With Freuchen on board, the stalwart vessel headed for Admiralty Inlet, where it took aboard the Inughuit and set course for northern Greenland. Ice conditions made it impossible to reach Cape York, and the Inughuit disembarked farther south at Cape Seddon, from where they made their way home.

Peter Freuchen travelled down the coast and reached Denmark aboard the steamer the *Hans Egede*. Magdalene met him on the dock, and another chapter in his adventurous life began.

---

178 Ibid., 293.

179 Ibid., 296.

180 Ibid., 297.

Part 3:
ACROSS ARCTIC AMERICA

Part 3: Across Arctic America

Urpingalik: Poet of the Nattilingmiut

On March 11, 1923, Knud Rasmussen began the trip he had dreamed of for so long. He left Danish Island to head over the top of North America to Alaska, to visit as many Inuit groups as he could, including many with little experience of the Qallunaat culture that would so rapidly encroach on their ways of living. He would be accompanied on the journey by only two Inughuit, the young man Qaavigarsuaq and his female cousin Arnarulunnguaq.

They used two long sleds of the type used by the Aivilingmiut, fitted with peat and ice shoeing, and each drawn by twelve dogs. Each sled carried about five hundred kilograms of supplies, two thirds of which was dog food; the rest was tea, coffee, flour, tobacco, goods to trade with Inuit, clothing, guns, and ammunition.

A day earlier, Anarqaaq and Aaqqiuq had left for Repulse Bay with a letter from Rasmussen for the Hudson's Bay Company manager, George Cleveland, to try to sort out some difficulties between the two. Rasmussen headed first for Repulse Bay, where he made peace with Cleveland, then left with his party on March 18, heading northwest across Rae Isthmus.

Helge Bangsted and Anarqaaq, along with Tapaqti, Aua's son-in-law, would accompany Rasmussen's party as far as Pelly Bay, transporting additional supplies. Both Anarqaaq and Tapaqti were immigrant Nattilingmiut who had relocated to Repulse Bay and could be expected to know the Nattilingmiut Rasmussen hoped to meet.

While crossing Rae Isthmus, Tapaqti told a story to explain the presence of fossilized sea animals on the land:

> Here once lived the giant Inugpasugjuk who used to catch salmon down in a precipitous ravine at the head of Pelly Bay. The ravine is called Kitingujait.

> Sometimes Inugpasugjuk would go hunting seal by wading out into the sea and killing them with a stick. Once he waded out in Pelly Bay to catch seals, but before this he moved all the people living by the low shores up on to the highest islands in the world. Inugpasugjuk was very eager when hunting, and once he fell; as he slipped he shovelled the water aside with one hand so violently that a wave rose and washed in over the land. This big wave washed shoals of small fish on to the shore; there were sea scorpions, cod, flounders, sand-skippers, sticklebacks, in fact all the small animals of the sea, and when the wave dropped back again, all these fish remained on the land and in time turned to stone. These are the fossils lying about everywhere, and we call them *taqqutit*, because they are used as wick trimmers for our blubber lamps.[1]

They reached Committee Bay on March 28. There, in a snowstorm, they encountered Inuit.

Anarqaaq, who was outside repairing their iglu, removed the snow block from the doorway and shouted in that he had seen men. Rasmussen rushed outside and saw two "stoutly built men"[2] approaching the camp. Meeting strangers was a serious matter in this land. The men carried snow knives and harpoons. Rasmussen, unarmed, approached them and greeted them in their own language: "You can put your weapons away! We are peaceful people who have come to visit your country."[3]

The Inuit were astonished to be greeted by a stranger in their own language, and the greeting broke the ice. "We are just ordinary people, and you need expect no harm from us," they replied.[4]

The two men were father and son, Urpingalik and Kanajuq, members of the *Arviligjuarmiut* (people from Arviligjuaq, "the place with bowhead whales") group of Nattilik Inuit. They were on their way to Repulse Bay to trade their fox pelts for guns and ammunition. They were curious to know all about the trio of strangers who had appeared unexpectedly in their land and shared their language. Rasmussen and his party soon decamped and moved, at Urpingalik's invitation, to the latter's camp, two interconnected snowhouses accommodating eight people.

Rasmussen stayed with Urpingalik's extended family for eight days, "as he proved to be pleasant and interesting."[5] He wrote of the occasion, "We met as if we had known one another for years, and an encounter between old friends could not have been more cordial."[6]

---

1 Rasmussen, "Netsilik Eskimos," 9-10.

2 Ibid., 10.

3 Ibid., 11.

4 Ibid.

5 Mathiassen, "Report on the Expedition," 85.

6 Rasmussen, "Netsilik Eskimos," 13.

British explorers had previously encountered the Nattilingmiut in the 1800s, but their interests had been largely confined to collecting geographical information and learning what the Inuit knew about the fate of the missing Franklin expedition. Rasmussen's goal was quite different. He wanted to record the social life and the religious beliefs of the Inuit before both were irrevocably altered by an expected influx of white traders.

Urpingalik was a shaman who was held in high esteem, well versed in the old traditions of his people, intelligent and witty. He was an expert archer and the quickest kayaker of all his people in pursuing caribou at the river crossings. Rasmussen collected many folk tales from his host.

Urpingalik was more than a shaman; he was also a poet. Rasmussen, clearly impressed with the man, described him thus: "His imagination was a luxuriant one, and he had a very sensitive mind; he was always singing when he had nothing else to do, and he called his songs 'comrades in solitude,' or he would say that his songs were his breath, so necessary were they to him."[7]

Urpingalik also offered him the words to a number of magic songs. Rasmussen had to pay for these, and he did so by trading magic songs he had earlier learned from the Iglulingmiut.

Rasmussen asked Urpingalik how many songs he had composed, and the hunter-poet responded, "How many songs I have I cannot tell you. I keep no count of such things. There are so many occasions in one's life when a joy or a sorrow is felt in such a way that the desire comes to sing; and so I only know that I have many songs. All my being is song, and I sing as I draw breath."

Rasmussen entitled one of Urpingalik's songs, in translation, "A poor man's prayer to the spirits." It was used when hunting seal in winter:

> You, fatherless and motherless,
> You, dear little orphan,
> Give me
> Kamiks of caribou.
> Bring me a gift,
> An animal, one of those
> That provide nice blood-soup,
> An animal from the sea depths
> And not from the plains of earth.
> You, little orphan,
> Bring me a gift.[8]

---

7 Ibid., 15.

8 Ibid., 14-15.

In all his meetings with Inuit on his journey over the top of North America, Rasmussen busied himself with documenting their beliefs, legends, songs, taboos, and magic words. He was particularly interested in true stories from their lives. This was also the case when he had the good fortune to meet Urpingalik.

A year before Rasmussen met him, Urpingalik had suffered a tragedy and lost one of his sons, Inugjaq.

On a journey in the interior, Urpingalik and his youngest son had been ferrying their belongings on an ice pan over a wide and swift-running river. The current was strong, and suddenly it caught the pan and forced one side down so deep into the river that it turned over. Both father and son were immediately at the mercy of the river as it carried them downstream.

Urpingalik was knocked unconscious against a rock. When he came to, he was lying half in the water and half on the riverbank, his head being knocked against a stone by the regular wash of the waves. The pain quickly brought him to his senses, and a glance at the sun told him that he had been unconscious for some time. Suddenly, he realized his circumstances and began to look frantically for his son. He found Inugjaq further down the river.

Rasmussen continues the story:

> He carried him up to the bank and tried to call him to life with a magic song. It was not long before a caterpillar crawled up on the face of the corpse and began to go round its mouth, round and round. Not long afterwards the son began to breathe very faintly, and then other small creatures of the earth crawled on to his face, and this was a sign that he would come to life again.
>
> But in his joy Urpingalik went home to his tent and brought his wife to help him, taking with him a sleeping skin to lay their son on while working to revive him. But hardly had the skin touched the son when he ceased breathing, and it was impossible to put life into him again. Later on it turned out that the reason why the magic words had lost their power was that in the sleeping skin there was a patch that had once been touched by a menstruating woman, and her uncleanness had made the magic words powerless and killed the son.[9]

Another powerful Nattilingmiutaq shaman, Qakuqtingniq, later offered Rasmussen some insight into Urpingalik's tragedy: "People say that the ice floe on which Urpingalik was crossing the river was so large that it ought not to have capsized in the current. But they say that it was as if the floe suddenly met with some resistance that forced it down under the waters of the river. Therefore it is believed

9 Rasmussen, "Netsilik Eskimos," 11-12.

that the cause of the disaster was magic words, bad magic words that rebounded upon their own master: *irinaliut utiqtuq inungminut.*"[10]

Qakuqtingniq offered Rasmussen an explanation of what he assumed to be the cause of the ill fortune that had befallen Urpingalik and cost the life of his son. Uncharacteristically, it involved a white man, but this is perhaps indicative of the rapid culture change that was beginning to occur in that isolated part of the Arctic.

From their limited encounters with Qallunaat, the Nattilingmiut had formed a conclusion: "It is generally believed that white men have quite the same minds as small children. Therefore one should always give way to them. They are easily angered, and when they cannot get their will they are moody and, like children, have the strangest ideas and fancies."[11]

But the white man of whom Qakuqtingniq spoke was clearly a cut above the average. During the previous year, Captain Jean Berthie, the trader with the Hudson's Bay Company whom Peter Freuchen had met at Bury Cove near Wager Inlet in 1921, had made a trip to Pelly Bay to trade. Urpingalik's son Inugjaq had been blamed for tampering with one of the trader's observation instruments that lay on his sled, and the trader scolded the young man.

Urpingalik felt offended by this but said nothing to the trader. Instead he composed some evil magic words that were intended to kill Berthie before the end of the year. But the words had not been powerful enough to do the job.

Qakuqtingniq explained that "a formula of wicked words like that must kill if there is any power in it; and if it does not kill the one it is made for, it turns against its creator, and if it cannot kill him either, one of his nearest must pay with his life."[12]

The Inuit believed, quite simply, that Captain Berthie was a greater shaman than Urpingalik, and that the magic words had no choice but to turn against their source. But Urpingalik was also a shaman of some repute—when the evil words were unable to kill him either, they turned and killed his son.

Captain Berthie spoke Inuktitut well and was apparently a popular man among the Inuit. But he was unaware of any of this, or of the shamanic power that had been ascribed him by the Inuit. He had scolded the young man and that, as far as he knew, was the end of it.

Rasmussen, always analytical, found this whole episode to be illustrative of two characteristics of Inuit; the habit of concealing anger while contemplating revenge, and the exaggerated family feeling of *sirnaarniq*, which ensures that an Inuk will always side with his family. Rasmussen observed simply, "They do not tolerate having their children corrected by others."[13]

---

10 Ibid., 201.

11 Ibid., 128.

12 Ibid., 201.

13 Ibid.

Of the beliefs of the Nattilingmiut, Rasmussen wrote, "The religion of these people is based upon a constant fight against evil invisible spirits who interfere in their daily life in a variety of ways, but especially by means of sickness and bad hunting. To protect themselves against all these perils they have only their amulets in combination with their taboos and magic formulas."[14] To personalize it, Rasmussen recorded what he had learned from Ugpik, an "intelligent and interesting man," during a long night of conversation: "His philosophy of life was to the effect that we human beings know so very little of life and its controlling forces that we have an imperative duty, not only to ourselves but also to those we hold dear, to live as carefully as possible; that is why we are furnished with all the amulets that can assist us through the difficulties of life, and that is why we must bear in mind all the demands made upon us by the taboo rules."[15]

Rasmussen asked the shaman Qakuqtingniq what he desired most of life. He answered,

> I would like at all times to have the food I require, that is to say animals enough, and then the clothes that can shield me from wind and weather and cold. I would like to live without sadness and without pain, I mean without suffering of any kind, without sickness. And as a man I wish to be so close to all kinds of animals that in the hunt and at all kinds of sports I can excel over my countrymen. All that I desire for myself I desire also for those who through relationship are near to me in this life.[16]

When Rasmussen asked him what he would do to attain all he desired, he replied:

> I must never offend Nuliajuk or Naarsuk [Sila].
>
> I must never offend the souls of animals or a *tuurngaq* so that it will strike me with sickness.
>
> When hunting and wandering inland I must as often as I can make offerings to animals that I hunt, or to dead who can help me, or to lifeless things, especially stones or rocks, that are to have offerings for some reason or other.
>
> I must make my own soul as strong as I can, and for the rest seek strength and support in all the power that lies in the name.
>
> I must observe my forefathers' rules of life in hunting customs and taboo, which are nearly all directed against the souls of dead people or dead animals.
>
> I must gain special abilities or qualities through amulets.

14 Rasmussen, "Netsilik Eskimos," 40.

15 Ibid., 46.

16 Ibid., 224-5.

> I must try to get hold of magic words or magic songs that either give hunting luck or are protective.
>
> If I cannot manage in spite of all these precautions, and suffer want or sickness, I must seek help from the shamans whose mission it is to be the protectors of mankind against all the hidden forces and dangers of life.[17]

On April 5, when Rasmussen's time at Urpingalik's camp was at an end, everyone broke camp. Urpingalik and his family would continue on to Repulse Bay to trade. Rasmussen and his companions would sled westward in the hope of meeting Urpingalik's son Igsivalitaq. When the two parties were a little distance apart, Urpingalik's group stopped and waved their hands. The shaman's son Kanajuq called out, "May we all travel without evil spirits following us!"[18]

Igsivalitaq the Outlaw

Before Knud Rasmussen and his travelling companions parted from Urpingalik, Rasmussen had purchased a cache of meat from the man. But in order to find it, he had first to find Urpingalik's son, Igsivalitaq.

This was no easy task, for a few years earlier Igsivalitaq had murdered another man in a fit of temper. Then, knowing that the RCMP had established a detachment at Chesterfield Inlet and fearing that they might come in search of him, he had fled with his wife and son into the mountains near Pelly Bay.

Many Inuit feared Igsivalitaq. Rasmussen's guide Anarqaaq told him, "That meat you bought is going to cost you dear."[19] The other guide, Tapaqti, was also apprehensive about encountering the fugitive, for Tapaqti had married the widow of Igsivalitaq's victim. Both men feared that Igsivalitaq, an expert marksman, might think that they had been sent by the police, and shoot them on sight.

But Rasmussen was undaunted by the prospect of the meeting. Before he left Urpingalik's camp, Urpingalik's wife, Uvlunnuaq, the mother of the outlaw, sang for him a song that she had composed in sadness over her son's fate:

---

17 Ibid.

18 Ibid., 18.

19 Ibid.

Eyaya - eya.
I recognize
A bit of a song
And take it to me like a fellow being,
Eyaya - eya.

Should I be ashamed
At the child I once carried
With me in my back-pouch,
Because I heard of his flight
From the haunts of man?
Eyaya - eya.

Truly I am ashamed:
But only because he had not
A mother who was blameless as the blue sky,
Wise and without foolishness.
Now people's talk will educate him
And gossip complete the education.
I should perhaps be ashamed,
I, who bore a child
Who was not to be my refuge;
Instead, I envy those
Who have a crowd of friends behind them,
Waving on the ice,
When after festive leave-taking they journey out.

Oh, I remember a winter,
We left the island "the squinting eye";
The weather was mild,
And the feet sank, gently creaking, into the thawing snow.
I was then as a tame animal among men;
But when the message came
Of the killing and the flight,
Then I staggered,
Like one unable to get a foothold.[20]

Three days after leaving Urpingalik's camp, Rasmussen and his party finally met the object of their quest. Igsivalitaq had heard their dogs first and so was expecting visitors, but had no way of knowing if they were friend or foe. Rasmussen took the initiative of announcing himself in much the same way that the fugitive's father

20 Rasmussen, "Netsilik Eskimos," 16-17.

had introduced himself some days earlier: "We are only ordinary people who think of no evil."[21] Igsivalitaq, at first ill at ease and suspicious, finally relaxed.

Igsivalitaq told Rasmussen his own version of the circumstances that had caused him and his family to live apart from others:

> Others have told you why I live by myself; now I would rather tell you the whole story myself.
>
> About two years ago I was living not far from Repulse Bay . . . in order to be near to the places where I could buy guns and ammunition from white men.
>
> In this new country I had a hunting companion, and we often had contests. We were equally fast, equally skilful at hunting, but he was the stronger. We were always alone when we practised our sports, and my companion, who could not run so far as I can, made use of every opportunity to let me know that he was not afraid of me. And so it happened one day that to prove his superiority he rubbed his muck on me, and that was an insult I could not forget. When a man does that in our country it is an insult that means that he had an inclination to kill one. The treatment I had received tormented me so much that I could not tell anyone about it. Hatred grew up in me, and every time I met my old companion out caribou hunting it was as if I loathed myself; thoughts that I could not control came up in me, and so one day when we were alone together up in the mountains I shot him.
>
> Now if there had been no white men in our country the dead man's relatives would take vengeance upon me, and I would not be afraid of that; but now I was told that white men would come up from Chesterfield and take me away to punish me in the white man's way. White men were masters in our country and they would take me home to their own land, where everything would be wild and strange to me. So I grew afraid and came back to my old country and now live in the mountain regions where no white man has ever been before.
>
> When you came . . . I thought you belonged to the white men whom the Aivilingmiut call Police. I thought you were coming for me, and if I was to be taken away against my will I would rather die; so I had sharpened all my weapons to be ready. . . . You came as friends instead, and you must know that as long as you are with us everything I have is yours too.[22]

Rasmussen sympathized with the man and thought that he should not be punished according to laws with which he was unfamiliar. And he tried to explain

21 Ibid., 20.

22 Ibid., 20-21.

to him the sixth commandment—thou shalt not kill—by telling him that "people should be tolerant and sociable and do no harm to each other."[23] But Igsivalitaq was not naïve enough to believe that white men actually lived according to this precept. "The effect of my words was weakened," wrote Rasmussen, "because via Repulse Bay he had heard a trader's account of the Great War."[24]

Farther along on his trip westward, Rasmussen would encounter another incidence of Inuit clashing with the Canadian justice system—one with tragic consequences.

Summer at Maliruālik

After their encounter with Igsivalitaq, Rasmussen and his party spent some time near Pelly Bay. Tapaqti and Helge Bangsted left them on April 23 to return to Danish Island. Anarqaaq remained, having taken a local woman as his wife.

With two Nattilingmiut guides, Rasmussen left the camp the following day and travelled north to where he came upon a large village of thirty-two snowhouses near the North Magnetic Pole. There he traded for ethnographic specimens, among them a large collection of amulets. For some, he paid with locks of his own hair that, he noted, the "Eskimos considered possessed unusually great powers of protection."[25] On May 20, after an absence of almost a month, he returned to the camp, where Qaavigarsuaq and Arnarulunnguaq awaited him.

Arnarulunnguaq had busied herself in his absence with the preparation of spring and summer clothing. Qaavigarsuaq had hunted seal for dog food in preparation for a trip west to Kent Peninsula with a local man, Usugliq. They left on May 23, their purpose to take the artifact collections to the Hudson's Bay Company post there, from where the company would ship them to Copenhagen. He would also purchase ammunition, food, and tobacco, which were all running low.

In the meantime, Rasmussen and Arnarulunnguaq travelled with a hunter named Inuuttuk and his family to Back River, also known as Great Fish River, to visit the isolated *Utkuhikhalingmiut* (people from Utkuhikhalik, "the place where there is soapstone"). They reached their settlement of nine tents on Lake Franklin on the last day of May. This group had been briefly visited by the British explorer George Back in 1833, by Franklin searcher James Anderson in 1855, and by another Franklin searcher, Frederick Schwatka, in 1879, but little was known of them. Joseph Bernard, a trader who had briefly visited them a few years earlier, had written, "Utkuhikhalingmiut

23 Rasmussen, "Netsilik Eskimos," 21.

24 Ibid.

25 Mathiassen, "Report on the Expedition," 89.

are probably the most miserable people in the winter time I have ever seen or heard of."[26] Rasmussen's opinion was the complete opposite, perhaps because he visited at a milder time of year; he wrote, "Utkuhikhalingmiut will always remain in my memory as the most elegant, the most handsome and the most hospitable people I met on my long journey, in fact, the healthiest and the happiest I have ever associated with."[27]

By June 13, Rasmussen and Arnarulunnguaq had relocated to Malirualik on King William Island, where they were to meet Qaavigarsuaq. He, however, was overdue. This was cause for concern because Rasmussen was "quite devoid of the accustomed things that add zest to life: no tea, coffee, sugar or tobacco. . . . unable to conclude a long day's march without a pipe."[28] Eventually even their matches began to run out. Inuit there told him that the *Killinirmiut*,[29] their neighbours to the west, were very dangerous people and had probably killed Qaavigarsuaq. A respected female shaman held a seance and reported to Rasmussen that Qaavigarsuaq was still on his way home and not far off. "He had killed two bears on the way," she said, "and had had many other difficulties to fight against."[30] Despite her report, the common belief was still that Qaavigarsuaq and his companion had been murdered by the Killinirmiut.

Finally Qaavigarsuaq returned on September 3. The collection had been delivered to the HBC at Kent Peninsula. But fox trapping had been so good for the Inuit there that all the store's trade goods were sold out. Qaavigarsuaq was able to get only enough ammunition to use on his way back. On his arrival he shouted out to Rasmussen, "Very little ammunition, no tobacco, no tea, coffee, sugar or flour! But we are alive and kicking, and that hasn't always been as natural as you might think."[31]

Despite the lack of supplies, Rasmussen and Arnarulunnguaq had spent a pleasant enough summer at Malirualik. The Nattilingmiut assembled there in the summer, coming from numerous winter settlements. There the caribou crossed Simpson Strait from Adelaide Peninsula, and the rivers abounded with salmon. Rasmussen wrote of "the summer joys of the Nattilingmiut. . . . Never in my life have I ever seen such frolicsome and happy people, so gaily starving, so cheerfully freezing in miserable, ragged clothing."[32]

With its large summer population, Malirualik was also an ideal place from which to make excursions out to other summer communities, and to investigate the intellectual culture of the people. He divided the Nattilingmiut into five groups: Arviligjuarmiut; Killirmiut; Nattilingmiut proper; *Qikiqtarmiut*, the island dwellers on King William Island, including Malirualik; and the *Ilivilirmiut* of Adelaide Peninsula.[33]

---

26 Ibid.

27 Ibid.

28 Rasmussen, "Netsilik Eskimos," 59.

29 Rasmussen refers to this group both as the Killirmiut and the Killinirmiut.

30 Rasmussen, "Netsilik Eskimos," 73.

31 Ibid., 75.

32 Ibid., 62.

33 Ibid., 91-92.

Rasmussen was concerned that the Nattilingmiut wanted payment for most of their interactions with him. He was very low on trade goods and wrote, "At first I felt put out at the arbitrary 'something for something': but I became more patient when I realized that after all these people were certainly in the right." But Rasmussen noticed something peculiar—that for information on traditions, religious beliefs, old stories, and songs, they only requested payment when he wrote it down. "For them it was not an exchange of thoughts, such as they were accustomed to between the strangers they usually met with among their own kinsmen. My writing them down made these things 'something I would take home with me' . . . and the art of writing—an art so inconceivable to them, one that could make flourishes and strokes to speak—made their simple words everlasting, or eternally talking, and this in their opinion must give them a new value."[34]

Rasmussen and Arnarulunnguaq also conducted archaeological excavations that summer. At the end of August, they decided to build a stone house of the type that the Inughuit built in northern Greenland, a warm place in which to write. Rasmussen carried stones to the site while Arnarulunnguaq did the building. Among the Inughuit in Greenland, the women generally built the winter houses while the men hunted.

On September 21 a surprising event occurred: a ship arrived under full sail. The young Inuit there had never seen a ship before. They wondered, "Wherever could they have got all that wood from? And it swam over the water like a big bird, the sail spreading out from the hull like great white wings!"[35] The vessel was the *El Sueno*, "an old worn-out yacht"[36] from San Francisco, owned by the Hudson's Bay Company. It was manned by a Swede, Peter Norberg, and a Dane, Henry Bjørn, who were there to establish a trading post on King William Island. Rasmussen was impressed—Norberg had forced his way through Queen Maud Gulf, the most difficult part of the Northwest Passage, without charts or navigational aids.

The arrival of the *El Sueno* spelled salvation for Rasmussen; he was able to acquire all the ammunition he needed. And so he was able to spend his last month on King William Island "free of cares,"[37] occupied only with preparations for the upcoming winter's long sled journey.

Winter began in mid-October; the lakes froze over and the ground was covered with snow.

34 Rasmussen, "Netsilik Eskimos," 52.

35 Ibid., 80.

36 Ibid.

37 Ibid.

The Deep Footprints of Tired Men

In October 1923, before the ice formed, Knud Rasmussen travelled with Peter Norberg, the Swede who had arrived to establish a trading post on King William Island, and the shaman Qakuqtingniq to Qallunaarsiurvik ("the place where one looks for white people") on the east coast of Adelaide Peninsula. There they found exactly what Qakuqtingniq had told them to expect: the sun-bleached bones of members of the long-lost Franklin Expedition, as well as some pieces of cloth and leather. Rasmussen claimed that he was the first outsider to visit the spot. He gathered the bones, built a cairn over them, and raised two flags at half mast—the British and the Danish—giving the lost explorers their last honours. Respectfully, he wrote, "The deep footprints of tired men had once ended in the soft snow here by the low, sandy spit, far from home, from countrymen."[38]

The Nattilingmiut were certainly the most isolated Inuit Rasmussen encountered. They had had very limited interactions with white explorers, starting with a visit by the British explorer John Ross, who eventually abandoned his ship, the *Victory*, on their shores in 1832. The wreck had long provided timber and iron for hunters resourceful enough to salvage them. And the experience of the Franklin expedition that cost the lives of over one hundred men a decade and a half later was still fresh in the memories of some.

Rasmussen collected two accounts of the meetings that had happened seven decades earlier between Nattilingmiut and the men of the Franklin expedition, some struggling to survive, some already dead.

From Iggiaraarjuk, he heard this brief story:

> My father Mangaq was with Titqatsaq and Qablut on a seal hunt on the west side of King William's Land when they heard shouts, and discovered three white men who stood on shore waving to them. This was in spring; there was already open water along the land, and it was not possible to get in to them before low tide. The white men were very thin, hollow-cheeked, and looked ill. They were dressed in white man's clothes, had no dogs and were travelling with sledges which they drew themselves. They bought seal meat and blubber, and paid with a knife. There was great joy on both sides at this bargain, and the white men cooked the meat at once with the aid of the blubber, and ate it.
>
> Later on the strangers went along to my father's tent camp and stayed there the night before returning to their own little tent, which was not of animal skins but of something that was white like snow. At that time there were already caribou on King William's Land, but the

38 Ibid., 131.

strangers only seemed to hunt wildfowl; in particular there were many eider ducks and ptarmigan then. The earth was not yet alive and the swans had not come to the country.

Father and his people would willingly have helped the white men, but could not understand them. They tried to explain themselves by signs, and in fact learned to know a lot by this means. They had once been many, they said; now they were only few, and they had left their ship out in the pack-ice. They pointed to the south, and it was understood that they wanted to go home overland. They were not met again, and no one knows where they went to.[39]

And from Qakuqtingniq, Rasmussen collected this story:

Two brothers were once out sealing northwest of Qikiqtaq (King William's Island). It was in spring, at the time when the snow melts away round the breathing holes of the seals. Far out on the ice they saw something black, a large black mass that could be no animal. They looked more closely and found that it was a great ship. They ran home at once and told their fellow-villagers of it, and the next day they all went out to it. They saw nobody, the ship was deserted, and so they made up their minds to plunder it of everything they could get hold of. But none of them had ever met white men, and they had no idea what all the things they saw could be used for.

One man, who saw a boat hanging up over the gunwale, shouted: "A trough. A gigantic trough! I am going to have that!" He had never seen a boat and so he thought it was a meat trough. He cut through the lines that held the boat, and it crashed down on to the ice bottom upward and was smashed.

They found guns in the ship too, and as they had no suspicion of what they were, they knocked the steel barrels off and hammered them out for harpoons. In fact, so ignorant were they about guns that they said a quantity of percussion caps they found were "little thimbles," and they really thought that among the white men there lived a dwarf people who could use them.

At first they dared not go down into the ship itself, but soon they became bolder and even ventured into the houses that were under the deck. There they found many dead men lying in their beds. At last they also risked going down into the enormous room in the middle of the ship. It was dark there. But soon they found tools and would make a hole in order to let light in. And the foolish people, not understanding white man's things, hewed a hole just on

39 Rasmussen, "Netsilik Eskimos," 129.

the water-line so that the water poured in and the ship sank. And it went to the bottom with all the valuable things, of which they barely rescued any.

The same year, well into spring, three men were on their way from King William's Land to Adelaide Peninsula to hunt for caribou calves. There they found a boat with the bodies of six men. In the boat were guns, knives, and some provisions, showing that they had perished of sickness.

There are several other places in our country where we still see bones of these white men. . . .

That is all I know about the *pelrartut* as we call the white men who once visited our country and who were lost without our forefathers being able to help them.[40]

Among the Inuinnait

On October 31, 1923, Peter Norberg, the Hudson's Bay Company manager, hosted a farewell party for Knud Rasmussen and his two Inughuit travelling companions in the house he had erected at Malirualik. All the Inuit at the post were invited. Rasmussen had spent just over seven months among the Nattilingmiut and it had been a productive time for him, both in terms of ethnographic information gathered—stories, songs, and legends—and material objects purchased or excavated.

The following day, Rasmussen, Qaavigarsusaq, and Arnarulunnguaq, accompanied by local guides, set out on their long journey westward. They crossed the treacherous ice of Queen Maud Gulf and on November 13 met the first of the allegedly hostile Killinirmiut Inuit group, the first of the so-called Copper Eskimos, now known as Inuinnait. These people, Rasmussen wrote, "seemed to live on a constant war footing with all strangers."[41] They were the people that the Nattilingmiut had warned him to be wary of.

Rasmussen immediately noticed a marked difference in the way of life of these new people compared with those he had left behind in the east. For one thing, they lived closer to a trading post. In the home of the first man he visited, Rasmussen noted that "enamel dishes had replaced the fine, blubber-shiny wooden trays that are made of driftwood; aluminum pans took the place of stone pots, and even the handsome Eskimo lamp of soapstone had had to surrender to a shiny basin of tin."[42]

40 Ibid., 130-131.

41 Rasmussen, "Copper Eskimos," 10.

42 Ibid., 19.

The following day, he and his party reached the Hudson's Bay Company post at Kent Peninsula, established only in 1920, where they enjoyed the hospitality of Hugh Clarke, "an intelligent and likeable young man,"[43] and his assistant, a Dane named Rudolf Jensen. There Rasmussen met another Dane who would join his expedition, Leo Hansen. Hansen was a photographer and filmmaker who had been sent out by the expedition's committee to join Rasmussen in the central Canadian Arctic. Hansen would accompany Rasmussen as far as Point Barrow, Alaska, and later rejoin him in Nome.

Rasmussen stayed a week at Kent Peninsula, to read the mail that had accumulated for him there, and to feed and rest his dogs. Indeed, Rasmussen offered a special note of thanks to Hugh Clarke for the splendid way Clarke treated his dogs: "On Arctic journeys one is apt to give second place to the kindness shown to oneself; the man who feeds one's dogs wins one's heart."[44]

On November 22 they continued on to the Inuit camp at Malirisiurvik, a camp of the *Umingmaktuurmiut* ("muskox people").

Again Rasmussen commented on the marked difference between these people and the Inuit further east: "One thing that could not fail to be observed at once was the infectiously bright spirits they were always in: they were not only full of fun, they were almost defiantly self-assured and so free in their manners that it was often necessary to keep some of them down a little."[45]

This joie de vivre was a mixed blessing for the ethnographer. He knew that his time among the Inuinnait would be limited, but, he wrote, as a consequence of their enthusiasm, "what I had least of in this joyous snow-hut camp was peace and quiet in which to work. Our hut was always full of visitors, and as they were all fond of talking together it was not easy to concentrate on writing."[46]

As a result, after a visit to a large settlement of thirty snowhouses at Bathurst Inlet, Rasmussen moved back to Kent Peninsula, where Clarke gave him the use of a company hut where he could work in relative quiet. Rasmussen convinced a few of the Umingmaktuurmiut—"those members of the tribe whom I had found would suit me best to work with"[47] —to accompany him back to Kent. These were an aging shaman, Hiiq, who was "an expert of outstanding merit in mystic matters,"[48] his wife, Hikhik, his son Tatilgaq, and a young man, Natsit, only about twenty but recognized as the best storyteller of the group, having been raised by a respected shaman.

Rasmussen found the Umingmaktuurmiut to be "as poets perhaps the most gifted and inspired Eskimos I have ever fallen in with."[49]

---

43 Rasmussen, "Copper Eskimos," 11.

44 Ostermann, "Mackenzie Eskimos," 5.

45 Rasmussen, "Copper Eskimos," 14.

46 Ibid., 15.

47 Ibid.

48 Ibid., 16.

49 Ibid.

He was not impressed, though, with the shamanic performances he witnessed: "All the seances I attended with the Umingmaktuurmiut were extremely naïve in tendency and performance. . . . the audience is credited with almost fabulous faith in the trustworthiness of the shaman and the actual presence of the spirits. . . . their conjuring tricks were so childish."[50]

In his report on the expedition, Therkel Mathiassen summed up Rasmussen's brief time among the Copper Inuit thus: "With the study of the Umingmaktuurmiut in the region of Kent Peninsula, one of Knud Rasmussen's principal objects on the Expedition, an investigation of the intellectual culture of the Central Eskimos, was on the whole completed. The thing now was quickly to get forward to the Western Eskimos, whose most eastern group lived in the Mackenzie Delta . . . 2,200 miles from Kent."[51] Rasmussen himself wrote, "The distance had to be traversed as rapidly as possible, but there would have to be halts here and there for the purpose of studying the people with whom we fell in."[52]

They left Kent Peninsula on January 16 with the temperature hovering at minus forty-two degrees Celsius. They travelled on two sleds, Rasmussen and Arnarulunnguaq on one drawn by six dogs, Qaavigarsuaq and Hansen on the other with a heavier load that included the photographer's equipment, drawn by ten dogs.

They visited Inuit briefly at Agiaq before reaching Tree River on January 22. Both the HBC and RCMP had posts there. Six days later they left in bitter cold and drifting snow to traverse Coronation Gulf to Cape Krusenstern, where they spent only a day among the *Nuvungmiut* ("people from the point"), whom Rasmussen described as "presumptuous and restless people."[53] They continued on to Bernard Harbour, where the HBC post manager was another Dane, Peder Pedersen. Rasmussen had no qualms about spending only a little time there, as it had been the headquarters of the earlier Canadian Arctic Expedition, which had done detailed ethnographic work in the region.

In early February he spent ten days at a large hunting camp in Dolphin and Union Strait, and with that his time among the Inuinnait was at an end. It had been brief—only three months. He left on February 15 on the nine-hundred-kilometre sled journey west to the next HBC post at Baillie Island.

As Rasmussen travelled farther west through Inuinnait territory and into the Mackenzie Delta, he came upon more and more small trading stations built to trade for

50 Ibid., 31.

51 Mathiassen, "Report on the Expedition," 94.

52 Rasmussen, "Copper Eskimos," 52.

53 Ibid., 96.

furs with the local Inuit. Some of these were the property of the giant Hudson's Bay Company, but others belonged to independent traders trying to eke out a living in a harsh land.

One of the traders who had built such posts was a Dane, Christian Klengenberg.

Klengenberg was twenty-four years old when he jumped ship in Point Barrow, Alaska, in 1893 and began his life among the Inuit. Soon he married an *Inupiaq* (Indigenous person of northern coastal Alaska) woman, whose name he recorded as Gremnia. He supported himself through whaling and trading.

The following year he took a boatload of supplies to the whaling fleet at Herschel Island, a wild and lawless outpost of American whaling just east of the Alaskan border in Canadian waters. From there he travelled northeast to an island that the whalers assumed to be uninhabited. But while there he claimed to have seen human footprints. Time did not permit him to investigate, but he determined that someday he would return and find these unknown people. But the pressures of supporting a growing family kept Klengenberg at home in Alaska for the next decade.

In 1905 Captain James McKenna, impressed by the young Dane's knowledge of sea ice, hired him to accompany him and his two ships, the *Charles Hanson* and the *Olga*, to travel once again to Herschel Island. There McKenna put Klengenberg in charge of the *Olga,* and the two ships headed east into largely uncharted waters. Klengenberg had been ordered to keep in sight of the other ship, but the two separated in heavy fog. The *Charles Hanson* returned to Herschel Island, where it wintered, its captain assuming that the *Olga* was lost and that her crew had perished.

The following summer, though, the *Olga* returned with Klengenberg and his family and five of its nine crewmen. Klengenberg reported that ice had prevented him from returning the previous year and that he had wintered on what he thought was Banks Island. In fact, it turned out to be Bell Island, off Victoria Island's southwestern shore.

That summer a young Icelandic-Canadian adventurer, Vilhjalmur Stefansson, then new to the Arctic, reached Herschel Island. There he met Klengenberg, just returned from his wintering on the *Olga*. Klengenberg told Stefansson about the Inuit he had met to the east and showed him a collection of artifacts he had acquired from them, including a number of knives made of copper. For that reason, the people, who were Inuinnait, came to be known as the Copper Eskimos or Copper Inuit.

But it was Klengenberg's description of the people themselves that intrigued Stefansson. He told Stefansson, or so the explorer later claimed, that these Inuit had never seen a white man before, and yet some looked very much like white men themselves, having blue eyes and fair hair.

Stefansson spent sixteen months in the Arctic on that expedition before returning south. Immediately he began planning another expedition, one that he hoped he would head. He secured the backing of the wealthy American Museum of Natural History in New York and the Canadian government, which appointed Rudolph M. Anderson as the expedition's co-leader. In April 1908 the expedition headed north, where the explorers and scientists would spend four years.

Two years into the expedition Stefansson and his Inuit guides finally reached a camp on Victoria Island, where he encountered the people who had been on his mind since his meeting with Klengenberg, the Copper Inuit. He wrote in *My Life with the Eskimo*, "I knew I was standing face to face with an important scientific discovery. . . . When I saw before me these men who looked like Europeans in spite of their garb of furs, I knew that I had come upon either the last chapter and solution of one of the historical tragedies of the past, or else that I had added a new mystery for the future to solve: the mystery of why these men are like Europeans if they be not of European descent."[54]

Stefansson spent a year among the Inuinnait, then returned to Herschel Island and Alaska. In 1912 he returned south, first to Seattle, then to New York. His claim to have discovered Inuit who resembled Europeans—whom he called the "Blond Eskimos"—was picked up by the press and spread around the world. The *Seattle Daily Times* carried a headline: "American Explorer Discovers Lost White Tribe, Descendants of Leif Ericsson."

Lost tribe stories were always great fodder for newspapers. Stefansson, as an Icelander, was familiar with the saga accounts of the Icelanders who had colonized Greenland under Eric the Red almost a thousand years earlier, and whose descendants had disappeared a few centuries later. Craving fame, he would love to have been the man who unravelled the mystery of their fate. What a romantic notion that they could have crossed into Canada and moved west, intermarried with the Inuit, and survived as a mixed race in the last part of the Canadian Arctic to be explored! What a twist of fate that an Icelander should be the man to "discover" them and bring them—and himself—to the attention of an incredulous world!

But the reports also made Stefanssson suspect in the eyes of some of his scientific peers. Had the man lost his objectivity? Had he simply convinced himself that he had found what he wanted to find? The Norwegian explorer Roald Amundsen called Stefansson's claim one of the most ridiculous ever to have come out of the Arctic.

Rasmussen was well aware of Stefansson's theory of the "blond Eskimos" but found no evidence to support it in his time among the Inuinnait. He debunked the theory, stating that "all the anthropological measurements taken do not indicate any new infiltration in the tribe."[55]

Stefansson, perhaps in an attempt to salvage his reputation, later complained that the media had embellished his reports and that only about ten of the thousand Inuit he had met were blue-eyed. But his protestations were disingenuous. He himself had written letters to the museum about the blue-eyed Inuit, and he had gone so far as to suggest that their language resembled Icelandic, a Scandinavian language. There is absolutely no basis for such a suggestion, except for the stubborn desire of Stefansson to believe it.

---

54 Stefansson, *My Life with the Eskimo,* 192.

55 Rasmussen, "Copper Eskimos," 74.

Icelanders wanted to believe that Stefansson was correct. Even within the last few decades, Icelandic anthropologists carried out a study, with the cooperation of the Inuit of the Central Arctic, called the Inuit Genetic History Project. It proved that the Inuinnait are not descended from the lost Greenland colony, and should put to rest Stefansson's quaint and self-serving theory.

The man had deluded himself and seen what he desperately wanted to see, and what no other credible observer saw. In the process—not coincidentally—he had gained fame. It would not be the last time that Vilhjalmur Stefansson sought self-aggrandizement and hoodwinked the world.

The Hanging of Alikammiq and Tatamirana[56]

While travelling in the eastern reaches of Inuinnait territory, Knud Rasmussen heard a story about the enforcement of Canadian justice on two Inuit who had committed murders.

In 1921 word reached Constable W. A. Doak at the newly established Tree River RCMP detachment that five Inuit had been murdered on Kent Peninsula. Doak set out to investigate. He discovered that a number of the reported killings had occurred because of domestic disputes. One man, Tatamirana, had killed two other men, then together with his nephew Alikammiq, a young man said to be between sixteen and eighteen years of age, killed a third man, Pangnaana. Doak arrested both men and took them back to Tree River.

The officer took a personal interest in young Alikammiq and made him a kind of servant. Alikammiq cleaned the house, looked after Doak's clothing, and did other menial work. On April 1, Doak rose from bed and called for his young servant to bring him his sealskin boots. Alikammiq threw them to him, but Doak threw them back at him, telling him that the soles were not supple enough and needed to be chewed. This was women's work, as Alikammiq well knew. He also spilled the slop bucket, and was chastised and thrown out of the house. Alikammiq brooded throughout the day. That night he went to a storehouse and came out with a rifle and four bullets. He entered the house and, with no warning, shot Doak in the upper leg. He then sat down and calmly watched as the officer bled to death.

The trader Otto Binder, who lived nearby, was in the habit of making a morning call on Doak. The next morning, when Binder was halfway to the police post, Alikammiq broke out a windowpane and fired one shot through the trader's heart. He died instantly.

---

56 These men have previously been much written about in the historical record under the names used officially in their trials, Alikomiak and Tatamigana. I have also used these spellings in my writings about them in the past.

Alikammiq then went to Binder's house and told the trader's Inuit common-law wife what he had done, and announced that he was going to the camp nearby to kill all the other white men. One of the Inuit secretly sent his son ahead to warn the whites, and Sergeant Woolams arrested Alikammiq, who had just finished boasting that killing a white man was as easy as killing a ptarmigan.

That summer Alikammiq and Tatamirana were both taken to Herschel Island aboard a Hudson's Bay Company ship. They would be tried for murder. But the policy-makers in Ottawa had made a strategic decision. Sinnisiak and Uluksuk, two Inuit who had earlier been tried for the killing of two priests, had been treated leniently, to no avail; the leniency shown them had not deterred further murders. This time there would be no leniency. Tatamirana and Alikammiq would be found guilty and hanged.

The RCMP wrote to the Department of the Interior in 1922, recommending that a trial be held in the Arctic, where Inuit could see first-hand the workings of white man's justice. T. L. Cory, solicitor for the Northwest Territories Branch, concurred when he wrote, "The advantage in having the accused murderers tried in their own country among their own people, will be to bring home to the natives the result of their comrades' actions. . . . As kindness has failed in the past I strongly recommend that the law should take its course and those Eskimos found guilty of murder should be hanged in a place where natives will see and recognize the outcome of taking another life."[57] Amazingly, only a few months later, Cory was appointed to defend the very men he had thought should be hanged.

Judge Lucien Dubuc of Edmonton, a stipendiary magistrate of the Northwest Territories, was assigned to carry out the trial at Herschel Island. The jurors were all white.

Tatamirana was convicted of the murder of one man, Ikpakuhaq, but the six-man jury recommended mercy. Both Tatamirana and Alikammiq were next convicted of killing Pangnaana and sentenced to death. Finally, Alikammiq was tried for the murder of Constable Doak. The trial occurred on July 18, 1923, and took only one day. The verdict was guilty.

But the trial, regardless of the guilt of Alikammiq, was a sham. The lumber to build the gallows had accompanied the judge's party when it left Edmonton. A hangman travelled incognito with the court party. But most damning is the existence of a telegram from the Deputy Minister of Justice to Judge Dubuc *before* the judge's departure from Edmonton for Herschel Island. It reads, "Eskimo trials you should consult police authorities as to the date and place of execution, understand they favour Herschel Island."[58]

So the authorities had decided before the trial that a verdict of guilty would be the result, and that the inevitable sentence of death would result in a hanging.

Judge Dubuc waited some weeks before actually passing sentence. By the

57 Cory, written correspondence to O. S. Finnie.

58 Deputy Minister of Justice, Telegram to Judge Dubuc.

time he did, the gallows had already been constructed in the Herschel Island bone house, an old building for drying whale bone, left over from whaling days. After sentence was passed, Alikammiq, grinning and uncomprehending, left the prisoner's dock and handed the judge a cigarette as he passed the bench.

A storm of protest in southern Canada had resulted from the convictions of Tatamirana and Alikammiq. It was led by Bishop J. R. Lucas of the Church of England. It was he who first brought to the attention of the public that the court party had been accompanied by a hangman, had carried lumber for the construction of a gallows, and even that the graves for the reception of the bodies of Alikammiq and Tatamirana had been dug before sentence was passed. Lucas painted a pathetic scene of what took place in the Herschel Island courtroom—only a dozen spectators, mostly Inuit, had attended. The defendants appeared not to understand what was going on, Alikammiq laughing often and at inappropriate times. He was, some argued, probably only sixteen years of age.

Lucas portrayed the killings on Kent Peninsula as responses to cultural conflict, not as reflections of the criminal character of the Inuit. He blamed one of the victims, the trader Otto Binder, and northern white society generally, for destabilizing the traditional society of the Copper Inuit. As he well knew, the traditional society of the Inuit in the western Arctic had been ripped pitilessly from its moorings in an extremely short period of time by an insurgence of white traders in search of fur.

Lucas's efforts succeeded in having the hangings postponed. But in the end he failed to stop them.

The executions took place on February 1, 1924. At dawn on that date, Alikammiq and Tatamirana were led to the gallows. They appeared to be in high spirits and shook hands with everyone there. Alikammiq offered the executioner a cigarette and gave a small ivory carving to the wife of the police superintendent. But once he stood on the scaffold, his final words were a declaration that the police had long been the enemies of his people. Both men were buried in the graveyard at Herschel Island.

Alikammiq and Tatamirana were the only Inuit ever executed by the Canadian government.

In January 1924 Knud Rasmussen was at Tree River, a guest of the Hudson's Bay Company. There he learned the story of the sentences passed on Tatamirana and Alikammiq—who would be hanged in a little over a week. Later, he learned that the hangings had taken place. He knew of the rapid culture change that was taking place in the western Arctic, and he was sympathetic. He wrote about the hangings this way:

> Heavy and cumbersome machinery was required to get the two murderers sentenced. Judges, jury and witnesses had to be summoned from long distances. . . .
>
> All that great show of judges, jurymen and witnesses made no particular impression on them; they seemed to be at peace with their conscience. Both were sentenced to death, but first the sentence had to be confirmed by the highest Canadian authorities. Thus it happened that one evening late in winter, while following their customary occupation of making salmon nets, they were informed that they were to be hanged next morning at three o'clock. Young Alikammiq received the news with a smile. The other man, who was somewhat older, felt as if he were choking and asked for a glass of water. Having taken a drink he too was ready to meet his fate. Just before they were to be executed they gave the wife of the police sergeant some small souvenirs carved in walrus ivory, as a sign that they bore no malice toward the police. They ascended the scaffold with great calmness and met death without fear.[59]

Rasmussen then described the sad fate of the father of one of the men:

> One of the two men had an old father living on Kent Peninsula. When he got to know that at the command of the white man his son had to undertake the long journey to the eternal hunting grounds, he realized that he must not go up there unless someone was there to receive him. This could only be if he [the father] killed himself, but the old man was to learn that human life is a tenacious thing. First he tried to shoot himself in the chest with a rifle. When this failed he tried to stab a knife into his heart. As this did not cause death either, he cut his throat and then at last was able to fulfill his self-imposed obligation towards his son.[60]

In early February 1924 Rasmussen took the time to visit the grave of the deceased and wrote sensitively about the powerful emotions he felt there:

> It chanced that one winter's day I stood by the old man's grave, which was only protected against wild beasts by one or two simple skins and some blocks of snow. A cold north wind swept over the ground; the drifting snow enveloped me; yet I could not help feeling a stream of warmth through my body, and I had to bow in reverence to the destiny that rested in that lonely grave. Somewhere far away a boy had been

59 Rasmussen, "Copper Eskimos," 64.

60 Ibid., 64-65.

hanged by strange men; but on this spot an honourable old heathen had taken his part in expiating the crime by giving his life too.[61]

Among the Mackenzie Inuit

Rasmussen and his party began their journey out of Copper Inuit territory on February 15, 1924. This marked the end of his research into the customs of Inuit known as the "Central Eskimos." What followed was a westward journey of approximately nine hundred kilometres to Baillie Island, a route along which few Inuit lived but one that was populated by white trappers lured there by high prices for furs, particularly the pelt of the white fox.

On March 3 they met the first of many Alaskan Inuit immigrant trappers, also enticed by the promise of furs. They were hospitable and, to Rasmussen's surprise, spoke good English. Six days later they passed Cape Parry and reached Horton River on the 15th. The following day they passed the "smoking mountains" where fire had burned in a coal seam for many years.

Rasmussen recorded a legend about the smoking mountains that he heard from a man named Aunaraitsiaq:

> In the early infancy of man, people were never alone, whether they lived in a settlement or were travelling on long journeys.
>
> They were surrounded by a spirit people, ijiqqait, who lived as human beings and were in fact human beings—except that they were invisible.
>
> Their bodies were not for our eyes, or their voices for our ears. And when people travelled and pitched camp and began to build their snow huts, one might see round about the snow-drifts that the snow blocks began to move, being lifted out of the drifts in cubic form and piled together into a snow house which seemed to grow of itself. Occasionally one might see the glitter of a copper knife—that was all!
>
> They were clever people, the ijiqqait, and they did not mind people coming into their houses, which were arranged just like those of human beings.
>
> All their belongings were visible, and people could trade with them very profitably. If one wished to buy something, all that was necessary was to point to it and at the same time show what one was prepared to give for it.

61 Rasmussen, "Copper Eskimos," 65.

If the spirit agreed, the object required lifted itself up and moved towards the man who wanted it. But if they declined the bargain, the object remained where it was.

So people were never alone; they always had small silent and invisible spirits around them!

But one day it happened that during a halt a man seized his knife and cried:

"What do we want with these people who are always right on our heels?"

Saying this he flourished his knife in the air and thrust it in the direction of the snow huts that had made themselves. Not a sound was heard, but the knife was covered with blood!

From that moment the spirits went away. Never again did anyone see the wondrous sight of snowdrifts forming themselves into snow huts when one made camp, and for ever the people lost their silent, invisible guardian spirits.

It was said that they had gone to live inside the mountains in order to hide from man, who had mocked and wounded their feelings.

That is why to this day one can see the mountains smoking from the enormous cooking fires flaming inside them.[62]

The next day they reached the Hudson's Bay Company post at Baillie Island, where another Dane, Henrik Henriksen, was the manager. Here, Rasmussen noted, he "felt almost as if he were in Greenland, among Eskimos who spoke of whales and white whales, seals and bearded seals, kayaks and umiaks [*umiat*, "skin boats"], people with a way of living entirely different to that of the Central Eskimos. . . . Instead of snow-huts they had houses of wood or earth, and even their language was more like that at home. And yet they were very different from the Greenlanders, first and foremost because they were much more prosperous, thanks to the profitable fur hunting and the keen competition among the pelt buyers."[63]

Many were wealthy and owned their own motor schooners. They drove hard bargains but, wrote Mathiassen in his report on the expedition, "with Knud Rasmussen's unique powers of associating with Eskimos it was not long before they thawed and told him all he wanted to know without having to wave dollars under their noses."[64]

---

62 Ostermann, "Mackenzie Eskimos," 60-61.

63 Mathiassen, "Report on the Expedition," 97.

64 Ibid., 98.

On March 25 Rasmussen and his party continued westward. At Liverpool Bay they spent four days with an excellent storyteller, Apagkaq. In early April they were the guests of a chief named Mangilaaluk, who hosted them in his imposing log cabin. On April 8 they reached Kitigaaryuk, "the ancient main Eskimo settlement in the Mackenzie district."[65]

The Mackenzie Eskimos had once been numerous, numbering about two thousand in the middle of the nineteenth century. About half of those had lived at Kitigaaryuk. Since then, epidemics had reduced the population to about four hundred, but half of those were immigrant Alaskan Inuit lured by employment in whaling's heyday and later by furs. When Rasmussen arrived, Kitigaaryuk was an HBC post, but the company faced stiff competition from "cash buyers" who came down the Mackenzie River and paid better prices for furs. A white fox pelt sold for thirty dollars, and many Inuit became well-to-do. Many had bought schooners, some costing as much as three thousand dollars. The women used sewing machines. Many men had their own typewriters. Hair clippers, safety razors, and cameras were common.

Mathiassen's report noted, "Kayaks are never seen nowadays; one that Dr. Rasmussen bought at Single [Shingle] Point was thought to be the last in the whole of the Mackenzie region."[66]

At Shingle Point they encountered a community of Inuit suffering from influenza and all members of the expedition became ill, Arnarulunnguaq seriously so. They struggled on to Herschel Island, where HBC manager A. A. Carroll nursed them back to health. They remained there from April 17 until May 5. There Inspector Stuart Taylor Wood of the RCMP took an interest in Rasmussen's work. A report prepared from Rasmussen's notes states that Wood "seemed to share his [Rasmussen's] opinion that a legal system like the Canadian, based as it is on laws and principles quite unknown to the people who infringe them, is unsound and involves a feeling of fear and uncertainty, and that the ground should first be prepared by a work of education."[67]

While there, Rasmussen collected a great deal of folklore from the Mackenzie Inuit and the Alaskan immigrants.

On May 5, they left Herschel Island and shortly crossed the unmarked border into Alaska.

Rasmussen's time among the Mackenzie Inuit had been short, only a month and half. But, although short, it had been productive. Rasmussen wrote: "I have succeeded, in spite of the short time, in collecting a whole lot of material regarding the customs and habits of the natives, their religious traditions and a very comprehensive folk-lore; and finally, I have also been able to get a handsome collection, about 300 specimens, of implement items, flints, etc. from the time prior to the white man."[68]

---

65 Mathiassen, "Report on the Expedition," 98. (Kitigaaryuk is today's modern Inuvialuit spelling; Rasmussen spelled it Kitikârjuit.)

66 Ostermann, "Mackenzie Eskimos," 55.

67 Ibid.

68 Ibid., 163.

He devoted less time to the Alaskan immigrant Inuit he met there, with one exception being Apagkaq, the storyteller at Liverpool Bay. Rasmussen noted, "This is the first time I have encountered story-telling regarded as an art and cultivated as such since I left West Greenland, and the result I obtained was unique and good."[69]

Rasmussen noted also that he had "never any language difficulty," but the work was exhausting. "More work than I could manage," he wrote. He had to get rest on the sled while travelling, as he was "continuously moving in all kinds of weather."[70]

Knud Rasmussen died before he had an opportunity to prepare his notes on the Mackenzie Inuit for publication. They were edited by Hother Ostermann, his childhood friend, who had worked as a pastor and teacher, and later as a historian, writer, and translator. They were published as part of the *Report of the Fifth Thule Expedition 1921-24* under the title *The Mackenzie Eskimos, after Knud Rasmussen's Posthumous Notes* (1942). He also edited *The Alaskan Eskimos, as Described in the Posthumous Notes of Dr. Knud Rasmussen* (1952), which was completed after his own death by the ethnologist Erik Holtved.

Alaskan Interlude

Knud Rasmussen left Herschel Island on May 5, 1924, by dogsled, bound for Point Barrow, Alaska. His party consisted of three other travellers: Qaavigarsuaq, Arnarulunnguaq, and the Danish filmmaker and photographer Leo Hansen, who had joined the expedition in the central Canadian Arctic. There followed eight hundred kilometres of coastline sparsely populated with small Inuit camps and the cabins of white trappers.

They reached Barrow on May 23. It was the most northerly settlement in Alaska and the largest town that Rasmussen and the Inughuit had seen since leaving Nuuk almost three years earlier. It boasted a school and a hospital; about 250 Inuit and a few Qallunaat called it home.

One of those Qallunaat was Charles Brower, an influential trader who eventually wrote a best-selling book about his own life in the Arctic, with the captivating title *Fifty Years Below Zero*. Brower—known to outsiders as the "King of the Arctic"—

69 Ibid.

70 Ibid., 164.

proved of great assistance to Rasmussen, whose time was limited, by directing him to the best storytellers.

Rasmussen had initially thought there would be little to learn from Inuit living in such close proximity to non-Inuit culture, with its school and other amenities. He quickly realized that he was wrong. As his posthumous notes make clear, "New perspectives opened up, especially in folklore and mythology."[71]

The trading and mission buildings at Barrow were at Cape Smith, and the community is today known as Utqiaġvik ("the place where one hunts owls").

It was a busy time of year in Barrow—the bowhead whaling season. The point was on the annual migration route for this large Arctic whale, the prey of traditional hunting by Inuit even before it attracted Qallunaat whalers to the Arctic. Now, with whaling by Qallunaat a thing of the past, it remained a regular part of Inuit life. As Rasmussen pointed out, it had always allowed for "a period of cultural florescence in this region."[72]

After a much-too-short visit, Rasmussen and the two Inughuit left Barrow on June 3, leaving Leo Hansen behind to film the whalers' festivities. He would travel later by ship, with the expedition's collections of artifacts, and rejoin them in Nome.

Rasmussen's party passed Wainwright and reached Icy Cape on June 8. A whale had just been taken there, and for two days the visitors were present for a grand feast held to celebrate the occasion. The hunt was a more or less traditional hunt by Inuit, supplemented with useful technology they had garnered from the earlier presence of American commercial whalers. The Inuit feasted and held drum dances far into the night. Rasmussen was in his glory. He remained there as long as he could, collecting folklore.

But by June 30 he had to move on. This marked the end of his epic sled journey, in which he logged about six thousand kilometres of travel from Danish Island in fifteen months. Summer was advancing. They would have to continue their journey by boat. Rasmussen gave all but four of his dogs to Ugpirsaun (Ukpiksaut), an Inuk trader at Icy Point who took him and his companions on a three-day journey by skin boat to Point Lay, where he turned back. At the Inuit settlement there, Rasmussen hired another boat to take them two more days west. From there, the ice was close to the shore, so they walked westward along the coast, wading through many swift rivers along the way.

After six days they reached Pitmigiaq, where they met Inuit reindeer herders. They hired yet another boat there, this one small and unsound, to take them to Point Hope, which they reached on July 16. It was a large settlement, which Rasmussen called the "ancient centre of Alaska's whaling."[73] It had once been even larger, inhabited by the powerful and feared *Tikirarmiut* ("people of the small point of land"). There he found 122 Inuit house ruins—more than he had seen anywhere

71 Ostermann and Holtved, "Alaskan Eskimos," 11.

72 Ibid., 21.

73 Ibid., 102.

else—and a large number of graves. He acquired a large collection of artifacts that the Inuit were happy to dig up and sell to him.

And there he met an old man, Qalajauq, who provided him with more folklore. From him, Rasmussen recorded a myth about the origin of Point Hope:

> In the days long past there was no low land in front of the mountains, and the people lived on the top of the big Mount Irrisugssuk, southeast of Kotzebue Sound. This was the only land that rose out of the sea, and on the top there are still whale bones and whale skeletons from the first people's hunting. It was at the time when the people still went about on their hands with their heads downwards—it is that long ago.
>
> But one day wise Raven—the same who made the sky and the earth—was paddling out at sea in his kayak, far out at sea, and on the water he saw something dark moving and rippling. He paddled up and harpooned it, and blood flowed from the wound. Raven thought it was a whale, but then saw it was an enormous mass without beginning or end. Slowly the life ebbed out of it, and he made his towing-line fast and towed it in to the mountains to the south of Uivfaq [Uivvaq]. There he moored it, and next day when he examined it he found it rigid: it had become land. To this day there is a hole in the ground at the settlement, the place where Raven harpooned *Tikitaq*.[74]
>
> That is how Point Hope was made.[75]

While in Point Hope, Rasmussen gave a Sunday lecture in the local church on "Greenland and the Greenlanders," in which he focused on his theories on the origin of Inuit.

They left Point Hope on July 31 by a small boat with an outboard motor and sailed past Cape Thompson, where they visited more reindeer herders at Elektuna. An Inuk herder there was the first to own tame reindeer—when Rasmussen met him, he had a herd of almost eight hundred.

Finally, on August 7 they reached Kotzebue, a town of about one thousand people at the time, from where Rasmussen was able to send a telegram to his committee in Denmark announcing the success of his expedition.

He made a quick trip to the "model settlement" of Noorvik, built by the Department of Education. He was accompanied by an old man, Nasuk, who regaled him with local folklore, which made the trip worthwhile. Rasmussen took a profound dislike to the Quaker missionaries he met there and elsewhere. In Kotzebue,

74 Rasmussen spelled the Inupiat name for Point Hope as "Tikeraq." "Tikitaq" may be a misspelling of "Tikeraq" by his posthumous editors. Modern Alaskan orthography spells it "Tikiġaq." Rasmussen gave the meaning as "the point which runs out like a forefinger."

75 Ibid., 48.

he attended a Quaker service and sat near the back of the gloomy room where it was held; the minister came and asked him if he would not prefer to sit among the white people. In fact, he was so disgusted with the missionaries that he wrote in his notebook, "To hell with their christianity!"[76]

On August 22 they left Kotzebue by the mail boat the *Silver Wave* and reached Nome on the last day of the month after a stormy voyage. Leo Hansen left Barrow on the schooner the *Teddy Bear* and reached Nome four days after his compatriots did.

Siberia: The Promised Land

In the telegram that Rasmussen sent from Kotzebue announcing the success of his expedition, he included the noteworthy information, "Greenland tongue readily understood from Magnetic North Pole to Bering Strait."[77] In fact, it was an understatement, for his "Greenland tongue" had served him and his companions well long before they reached the Magnetic North Pole in the territory of the Nattilingmiut; he had had little or no difficulty among the Iglulingmiut, the Aivilingmiut, or the inland Inuit of the Kivalliq.

This felicitous linguistic situation would change once he reached Nome. Inuit and *Yupiit* were there from all parts of Alaska to exploit the tourist season and sell curios to tourists. This was an ideal situation in which to study Indigenous Alaskans who had gathered from the north and the south. But it also meant that Rasmussen would occasionally need the assistance of an interpreter. His posthumous editor Hother Ostermann wrote, "Here [in Nome] for the first time on all his travels round Arctic America, Dr. Rasmussen encountered linguistic difficulties. Wherever he had gone he had understood the dialects with very little trouble, and had also made himself understood to the natives. Now it appeared that south and west of the Yukon [River] the dialectal differences were so great that he was unable thoroughly to discuss problems and other matters without the aid of an interpreter."[78]

In his own words, Rasmussen wrote, "The Eskimos from the south and west of the Yukon [River] spoke a dialect differing so considerably from the others that I found it, contrary to all previous experience, impossible to discuss difficult questions such as matters of faith and ceremonial, without the aid of an interpreter."[79]

The language family known as Eskimo-Aleut split into the separate languages

---

76 Ostermann and Holtved, "Alaskan Eskimos," 53.

77 Mathiassen, "Report on the Expedition," 103-4.

78 Ostermann, "Alaskan Eskimo Words," 9.

79 Rasmussen, *Across Arctic America*, 349.

of Eskimo and Aleut thousands of years ago. Aleut, which has several dialects, is spoken only in the Aleutian Islands and the Pribilof Islands. The Eskimo languages in turn divided into two (or perhaps three) languages about one thousand years ago, in the estimate of linguists. One branch is the Inuit language, spoken in Greenland, Canada, and northern Alaska—a huge geographic extent. This is the area through which Rasmussen had the good fortune to travel all the way to Nome. This language has many dialects, but neighbouring dialects are quite similar and mutually intelligible. This is known as a "dialect chain." The differences accumulate over distance, so that speakers of widely separated dialects may find mutual comprehension difficult or impossible. An East Greenlander who flew from Ammassalik to Nome would find it difficult to comprehend the dialect spoken in Nome. But Rasmussen and the two Inughuit had the advantage of having travelled slowly from one dialect area to another, making maximum use of the dialect chain concept.

The other branch of the Eskimo language family is Yupik. These languages, some of which are mutually incomprehensible, are spoken in western and south-central Alaska and in Chukotka, a part of Russia. The line separating the Inuit languages from Yupik is the Yukon River, which empties into the Bering Sea south of Norton Sound. (A third purported branch of this language family was Sereniksi, spoken in and around one village in Chukotka; it became extinct in 1997.)

It is because Yupik speakers do not call themselves Inuit that the term "Eskimo" is often used in Alaska and in discussions of Alaska when an overarching term is needed for the speakers of both Inuit and Yupik languages.

It is unclear when Rasmussen first formulated a plan to visit the small Yupik-speaking population in Siberia. He wrote, "It is hard to say when I got the idea for it, for it has grown up together with me."[80] The idea had been with him since 1905, when he first talked of his grand plan for an expedition to North America. At times since then, as his plans and funding requirements changed, he downplayed the idea, sometimes eliminating it completely from the plans he made public or formulated with the committee responsible for overseeing the Thule Station. But an analysis of those various plans, as they had evolved over the years, indicates that the hope was always there.

Certainly he harboured the idea throughout the expedition, because he wrote to Marius Ib Nyeboe, chairman of the Thule Committee, on July 29, 1921, from Greenland (after the expedition members had left Denmark but a month before they sailed for Canada) that he would like to cross from Cape Prince of Wales in Alaska to Cape Dezhnev in Siberia. He wrote at that time about his "strong wish to reach as far as possible all the most important areas in Alaska, inhabited by Eskimos, and—of course—in addition, a trip across the Bering Strait to the Yuits [Siberian Yupik]."[81] But in his telegram from Kotzebue there is no mention of a side trip to Siberia, only that the expedition had been a success.

---

80 Rasmussen, *Fra Grønland*, 5; translated and quoted by Michelsen, "Plans for the Fifth Thule Expedition," 24.

81 Letter from Rasmussen to the Thule Committee, July 29, 1921, translated and quoted by Michelsen, ibid., 33.

Travelling from Kotzebue towards Nome on the *Silver Wave*, off Cape Prince of Wales, Rasmussen encountered Siberian Yupik visitors. He wrote, "It was a party of Siberian Eskimos from East Cape, on their way home from Teller, where they had been to trade. It was a hurried meeting, but thrilling in its way, and left me more than ever keen to visit these people on their own ground. In the extreme eastern corner of Siberia live the most westerly of all the Eskimos, and here surely was the most fitting point at which to end the Expedition."[82]

Perhaps it was at that moment that he firmly resolved to cross Bering Strait.

In old age, Qaavigarsuaq told the story of his life to the Greenlandic author Hans Larsen. He reminisced about sitting on the shore in Alaska with Arnarulunnguaq by his side. They could see the Siberian coast across the water, a feat quite possible under certain atmospheric conditions. "The sight of it was beautiful," he said. "We could not simply remain where we were. We must travel on again. We must cross that body of water that separates Alaska from Asia."[83]

He also told his son-in-law Arrutaq Kristiansen about the crossing: "We were once again travelling as three people just as before: Arnarulunnguaq, Kunuut [Rasmussen], and me Qaavigarsuaq."[84]

In a telegram from Kotzebue, Rasmussen had asked the Danish consul in Seattle to "cable Soviet Vladivostok information that expedition is purely scientific without trading interests requesting special privilege during stay East Cape."[85] He waited in vain for a reply.

Rasmussen considered various ways of getting across Bering Strait. (Ironically, the strait was named after another Dane, Vitus Bering, who had named it while in service to the Russians almost two centuries earlier.) He ruled out crossing in an *umiaq* ("Inuit skin boat") because it would be too time-consuming. He asked for the use of a United States government schooner but was declined because of political complications—the United States did not officially recognize the recently formed USSR, and would not do so until 1933. He hesitated to use a trading vessel because the new Soviet government in Siberia, although unstable, was trying to exert its authority in isolated Chukotka. The situation was tense because many small American companies had been trading into the region for years with no licenses and objected to being asked to pay for permission now.

In the end, he opted for a trading vessel run by a captain who was alleged to be popular on both sides of Bering Strait. That was Joseph Bernard, a Canadian from

82 Rasmussen, *Across Arctic America*, 357.

83 Larsen, *Qaavigarsuaq*, 17. Translation by Kenn Harper and Aviaq Harper.

84 Kristiansen, "K'avigarssuak," 190. Translation by Kenn Harper and Aviaq Harper.

85 Michelsen, *Knud Rasmussen: Ambassador*, 144.

Prince Edward Island who had traded throughout the western Canadian Arctic, Alaska, and Siberia for years. His vessel, the *Teddy Bear*, was small—only fifty-four feet long with a fourteen-foot beam—and sported an auxiliary gas engine.

From Nome, Rasmussen sent another telegram asking for an entry permit to the USSR. He waited three weeks with no response. He hoped to spend about a month at East Cape in the Yupiit community of Naukan. In the end, running out of time, he decided to go without papers.

Rasmussen and his party left Nome with Captain Bernard on the *Teddy Bear* on September 8, 1924. An American filmmaker, Earl Rossman, was also aboard with an assistant named Roy, who was either Inuit or Yupik. But a violent storm forced them to wait two days behind Sledge Island. On September 11 they returned to Nome. Only then did Rasmussen send another telegram to Copenhagen informing his committee that he was going without official permission.

The following day they departed again, but once again bad weather intervened, so they put in at Teller. While there Rasmussen went ashore and put his time to good use, compiling a list of about five hundred Inuit words from a man from Cape Prince of Wales. Rossman abandoned the trip at Teller. It is not known whether the mysterious Roy did as well; he is not mentioned again.

They finally departed on September 16 at about midday. In the evening they passed Cape Prince of Wales, America's most westerly point, and set course for the Diomede Islands in the middle of Bering Strait, both inhabited at that time. Little Diomede is an American island with a population of less than one hundred today. It is 3.5 kilometres away from Big Diomede, now uninhabited, which belongs to Russia. They are separated by more than politics—the International Date Line runs between them.

Qaavigarsuaq, in his memoir, mentions clearly that Arnarulunnguaq accompanied them on the trip. But in the details he presents of subsequent events, he does not mention her at all. She may not yet have completely recovered from the bout of influenza that affected her in northern Alaska. Probably she set off on the trip to Siberia, but changed her mind after the rough weather that beset the *Teddy Bear* on its first attempt, and remained in Nome.

Fog prevented a landing on Little Diomede. Rasmussen described the scene:

> I was tired out after the restless threshing about of those stormy days, and turned in early that night, but next morning at dawn, Captain Bernard came in and roused me; we were nearing Diomede Island. I turned out at once; it was still barely light and I could just make out a great dark mass rising sheer and inhospitable from the sea, with

> thousands of seabirds wheeling and screaming over the cliffs, while the water broke in a scurry of foam on the rocks below. . . . Yet the place was inhabited, though it looked like a bird cliff and nothing more. We made in towards the headland, intending to anchor, but just then a mass of fog came up, and the island vanished as suddenly as it had appeared. We gave up the idea of a visit for the time being, and made straight for East Cape.[86]

East Cape was beset by dense ice, so Bernard made land at a small trading post he called Emmatown, known to Russians as Dezhnev; it was several miles southwest of Naukan. Rasmussen was greeted there by a long-time English-speaking resident, the Australian trader Charley Carpendale; a Russian policeman named Alyaev;[87] and a Russian interpreter whose name was recorded only as Leo. Alyaev escorted Rasmussen and Bernard to the police station. The next day Rasmussen was taken by a Chukchi-speaking guide across the eastern end of Chukchi Peninsula to Uelen,[88] a trip of about fifteen kilometres through barren marshy tundra in heavy rain, to see the local governor and seek permission for his stay. He reached the community of about 250 by nightfall and was hospitably treated by the governor, Nikolaus Losseff,[89] but was denied permission to remain in Siberia.

A factor in Rasmussen being denied permission was probably his old nemesis, Vilhjalmur Stefansson. Rasmussen wrote:

> I learn that the reason for the concentration of officials is the strained relations with the surrounding world because no one will recognize the Soviet and Russia's right—and particularly the formal right to the Wrangel Islands, to which a warship had been despatched that very summer.
>
> Scientists do not seem to be popular after Vilhjalmur Stefansson planted the British flag on Wrangel Island, a territory which the Soviet regards as Russian. As the British did not back up the annexation, Stefansson himself started a trading company on the island, but later transferred his rights to a partnership at Nome, which transported Alaskan Eskimos to the disputed colony.[90]

The ubiquitous Stefansson had sent five settlers to Wrangel Island in 1921. They claimed the island for Canada, although only one of the party was Canadian. In 1923 Ada Blackjack, an Alaskan Inuk woman who was the sole survivor of the

86 Rasmussen, *Across Arctic America*, 359-360.

87 Rasmussen gives his name as Allayeff. See Shokarev, "Dezhnevo," 201.

88 Rasmussen gives its name as Wahlen.

89 His correct name was Nikolaevich Losev. See Shokarev, "Dezhnevo," 202.

90 Ostermann and Holtved, "Alaskan Eskimos," 90-91.

party, was rescued by a vessel that left new settlers on the island, an American and twelve Alaskan Inuit. They were removed by the Soviets in 1924, by the warship that Rasmussen mentioned in his notes.

The governor's knowledge of the drama unfolding around Wrangel Island did not augur well for Rasmussen. He was told that he could remain in Uelen overnight, but must return to Dezhnev the next day and leave immediately aboard the *Teddy Bear*. On September 18 he reached Dezhnev, where Bernard was waiting for him; the next day they sailed for Alaska.

On September 19, the ice lay close to shore and the *Teddy Bear* was forced to wait a while off East Cape, near the Yupik village of Naukan, which Rasmussen called by its Yupik name of Nuvuqaq.[91] The engine broke down and the captain went ashore. Rasmussen did not accompany him because he had no permit. "It was like looking into the promised land that one was not fated to enter," he wrote. "Young men and children came running down, out on the ice itself, and right up to the ship. A few came on board and stayed with us for an hour." He noted briefly, "How benevolent it was to understand him [a man from Naukan] and to be understood."[92]

Rasmussen had met a few elderly Yupiit at both Emmatown and Uelen "with whom I could talk."[93] The editor of his notes goes further in saying that they were "a few elderly Eskimos whose dialect he understood and with whom he could converse" and that "with their assistance he acquired some ethnographical details concerning the Eskimo tribe living in the neighbourhood."[94]

But Joseph Bernard's memoir provides more details on his meeting with at least two Yupiit at Emmatown after his return from Uelen. Bernard and Rasmussen were standing talking in front of Charley Carpendale's house when two men approached, coming down the hill from East Cape. Bernard recognized them as East Cape Yupiit. "When they came up to me, I introduced him [Rasmussen] to them and he started to speak to them in the Greenland Eskimo language.... After he got through talking one of the men turned to me and said, 'This man has been with the Eskimos a long time and he must have been here before because he speaks as we do.'"[95]

It may have been these Yupiit who provided Rasmussen with the short word list he compiled for Naukan or East Cape.[96] He makes no other mention of how he communicated with Inuit in Siberia. In a telegram he sent to his committee from

91 Rasmussen spells it Novoqaq.

92 Rasmussen, "Efterladte papirer"; quoted in Schwalbe, "Siberian Legacy," 179.

93 Ostermann and Holtved, "Alaskan Eskimos," 91.

94 Ostermann, "Alaskan Eskimo Words," 10.

95 Bernard, "In the Arctic," 13.

96 Ostermann, "Alaskan Eskimo Words," 10.

Nome on his return, he said, "Severe voyage East Cape where Eskimo understood Greenlandish perfectly."[97]

Did his linguistic skills and his Greenlandic mother tongue allow him to instinctively grasp some of the differences of the Yupik language so that he could communicate with the people he met? Did he use an interpreter? Was there a simplified *lingua franca*, a trade jargon, in use there? After all, the Yupik speakers from Chukotka Peninsula and the Inuit of Kotzebue Sound had been trading together for decades and must have developed a method of communication. Alternatively, did some of the few Yupiit he met speak English, as a result of their years of trading with Americans like Joseph Bernard or the Australian Carpendale? The record is silent.

On the return journey to Nome, the party spotted four walruses. Joseph Bernard and Qaavigarsuaq set out in a small boat and killed all four.

They were also storm-bound for a time off Little Diomede Island. They lay at anchor very near the Inuit houses. Rasmussen went ashore "to have a talk with the men,"[98] who would have spoken a dialect of Inupiaq, as the Alaskan Inuit dialect was called. But it was an old woman's story that he recorded in his notes. He visited her in company with a "companion," apparently a local person, who awakened the old lady, Majuaq, with the words, "Here's a man who is not a missionary or a trader either; all he wants is for you to tell him something about the people who lived in our land before the white men came with their customs." Majuaq asked, "How shall I talk with a man who does not understand our language?" "He says he is one of us," answered the guide.[99] Majuaq scrutinized her visitor and asked him some questions before stating, "You have the face of a white man, but our tongue."[100]

Rasmussen's visit to the old lady was maddeningly short, dictated by the changing weather and Bernard's desire to get back to Nome. From her he had time to record only one story, an account of the creation of song. It is very reminiscent of knowledge he learned in the eastern Canadian Arctic from Aua, Igjugaarjuk, and Urpingalik:

> In days gone by, every autumn, we held big feasts for the soul of the whale, feasts which should always be opened with new songs which the men composed. The spirits were to be summoned with fresh words; worn-out songs could never be used when the men and women danced and sang in homage to the big quarry. And it was the custom that during the time when the men were finding the words for these hymns, all lamps had to be extinguished. Darkness and stillness were to reign in the festival house. Nothing must disturb them, nothing divert them. In deep silence they sat in the

97 Telegram from Knud Rasmussen to Nyeboe, September 24, 1924, reproduced in Nielsen, "for mig en Oplevelse," 234.

98 Ostermann and Holtved, "Alaskan Eskimos," 100.

99 Ibid., 101.

100 Ibid.

dark, thinking; all the men, both old and young, in fact even the youngest of the boys if only they were old enough to speak. It was this stillness we called *qarrtsiluni* [*qaaqsiluni*], which means that one waits for something to burst.

For our forefathers believed that the songs were born in this stillness while all endeavoured to think of nothing but beautiful things. Then they take shape in the minds of men and rise up like bubbles from the depths of the sea, bubbles seeking the air in order to burst. That is how the sacred songs are made![101]

On September 22 the *Teddy Bear* reached Nome. While rowing ashore in a dinghy, Rasmussen saw a man "running backward and forward on the beach, waving something in his hand."[102] It proved to be a telegram addressed to Rasmussen. On August 16 Nyeboe had finally contacted the Danish Foreign Ministry, asking them to seek permission from Moscow for Rasmussen's visit. Fortunately, Denmark had formally recognized the USSR two months earlier, on June 18. Five days later, the ministry sent a request to the People's Commissariat for Foreign Affairs in Moscow. On September 12, Moscow granted permission. But it was too late. Rasmussen was already on his way across Bering Strait, and there was no way for Moscow to directly inform the officials in Chukotka. The telegram the man on the beach presented him was from the Danish Foreign Ministry, granting the belated permission for his visit.

Najagnir: "I Have Searched in the Darkness"

Rasmussen and the two Inughuit had a month to wait in Nome before taking passage south on the first leg of what would yet be a long journey home. Nome had been the centre of an Alaskan gold rush a quarter of a century earlier. In 1899 the population skyrocketed to 10,000 people, but by 1910 it had fallen to 2,600. In 1924 it was still an important commercial centre.

As he had at Kotzebue, Rasmussen observed racism in Nome. In Nome, he noted that the many Inuit and Yupiit there for the tourist season lived on the outskirts of town and were not admitted to the best restaurants. When he and the two Inughuit, dressed in Inuit clothing, entered one restaurant, "Mrs. Nichelingos' pretty

101 Ostermann and Holtved, "Alaskan Eskimos," 102.

102 Rasmussen, *Across Arctic America*, 379.

and lively waitresses were forbidden to serve us."[103] Rasmussen, Qaavigarsuaq, and Arnarulunnguaq often spent afternoons at the "Dream Theatre," where silent movies were shown, a novelty to the Inughuit. They also occasionally rode in a Ford car to the outskirts of the community where the Eskimos lived.

Rasmussen realized that in Nome he would be able to learn about various Inuit and Yupiit groups, some of whom had travelled great distances for the late summer trading and tourist season.

On his last day in Nome, he had the good fortune to meet an angakkuq from Nunivak Island, the last shaman of the many he met on his journey. The man's name was Najagnir.[104] He was a man wild in appearance, and had just been released from a spell in prison for having killed several people. But such was his power that no witnesses would testify against him, and the authorities had no choice but to set him free.

He was full of stories of his time in jail. He opposed the increasing dominance of white men over Inuit in his own homeland and lost no opportunity to rail against their influence. So he was not impressed by the foreign lifestyle he saw in Nome. He was impressed, however, by seeing on the street a white horse pulling a heavy cart. This was the inspiration for a story with which to impress the people in Nome. He told them that white men had killed him ten times during the past winter, but each time he had vanquished death by sacrificing one of his ten helping spirits, which were—of course—ten white horses. For this reason, Rasmussen called him the ten-horsepower wizard.[105]

Rasmussen had only a brief time to interview Najagnir on that last morning. He was surprised to discover that, at this far westerly end of Alaska, this angakkuq's words echoed much of the wisdom that he had learned from shamans all along his route from the east.

Here is what Najagnir told Rasmussen when he was asked what he thought of the way men live: "They live brokenly, mingling all things together; weakly, because they cannot do one thing at a time. A great hunter must not be a great lover of women. But no one can help it. Animals are as unfathomable in their nature; and it behooves us who live on them to act with care. But men bolster themselves up with amulets and become solitary in their lack of power. In any village there must be as many amulets as possible. Uniformity divides the forces; equality makes for worthlessness."[106]

Rasmussen asked him how he had learned these things. Najagnir replied, "I have searched in the darkness, being silent in the great lonely stillness of the dark. So I became an angakkuq, through visions and dreams and encounters with flying

---

103 Ostermann and Holtved, "Alaskan Eskimos," 59.

104 Rasmussen spells his name Najagneq. I have used the standard orthography in use on Nunivak Island, following Pratt, "Tracking Najagnir," 141.

105 Rasmussen, *Across Arctic America*, 384.

106 Ibid., 384-385.

spirits.... The ancients devoted their lives to maintaining the balance of the universe; to great things, immense, unfathomable things."[107]

He went on to explain that he believed in a power called Sila, "a strong spirit, the upholder of the universe, of the weather, in fact all life on earth—so mighty that his speech to man comes not through ordinary words, but through storms, snowfall, rain showers, the tempests of the sea, through all the forces that man fears, or through sunshine, calm seas or small, innocent, playing children who understand nothing.... No one has ever seen Sila. His place of sojourn is so mysterious that he is with us and infinitely far away at the same time!"[108]

> Children hear a soft and gentle voice, almost like that of a woman. It comes to them in a mysterious way, but so gentle that they are not afraid; they only hear that some danger threatens. And the children mention it as it were casually when they come home, and it is then the business of the angakkuq to take such measures as will guard against the peril. When all is well, Sila sends no message to mankind, but withdraws into his own endless nothingness, apart. So he remains as long as men do not abuse life, but act with reverence towards their daily food.[109]

For Rasmussen, Najagnir's words showed the unity of Inuit belief across the top of the world, from Greenland, through Arctic Canada, and northern Alaska. They reminded him of the words of Igjugaarjuk, the Caribou Inuit angakkuq: "All true wisdom is only to be found far from the dwellings of men, in the great solitudes; and it can only be attained through suffering."[110]

And with that the expedition was at an end.

At the end of October Knud Rasmussen and Leo Hansen, accompanied by Qaavigarsuaq and Arnarulunnguaq, travelled by tourist steamer from Nome to Seattle. From there they continued by train to Washington, D. C., where they met President Calvin Coolidge. In New York, Rasmussen was awarded the coveted Daly Medal by the American Geographical Society, only the second Scandinavian—after Roald Amundsen—to receive it.

Qaavigarsuaq and Arnarulunnguaq arrived in Copenhagen on the vessel the *Hellig Olav* on November 20. On December 2, Rasmussen and Hansen arrived on

---

107 Ibid., 385.

108 Ostermann and Holtved, "Alaskan Eskimos," 99.

109 Rasmussen, *Across Arctic America*, 386.

110 Ibid., 381.

the *Oscar II*. The expedition committee's publicity machine had been busy. Three aircraft escorted the ship into harbour, where crowds awaited Rasmussen's arrival. He had become Denmark's national hero. The Prime Minister hosted a gala dinner attended by members of government. King Christian X, who had been the expedition's protector, issued medals. And Rasmussen, who had attended university, was awarded an honorary doctorate by the University of Copenhagen.

The Inughuit: "We Do Not Even Have a Memorial of Them"

In 1927, Rasmussen wrote a popular account of the great sled journey over the top of North America. In it he said, "The Eskimo is the hero of this book. His history, his present culture, his daily hardships, and his spiritual life constitute the theme and the narrative."[111]

The Danish anthropologist Kirsten Hastrup has written about the relationship between Rasmussen and the two Inughuit who accompanied him on the great sled journey. She points out that not only were they friends, but they were also his surrogate family on the trip. She suggests that what resulted was a "collaborative ethnography" because "the Polar Eskimos were no longer being studied but studying with him, and clearly Rasmussen sees the American Inuit very much through Inughuit eyes."[112]

In New York, Rasmussen stood atop a skyscraper looking over the city with Qaavigarsuaq and Arnarulunnguaq by his side. Perhaps the two Inughuit thought of their fellow Inughuit who had been to this gigantic metropolis almost three decades earlier—Uisaakassak and Minik—and the stories they told back home of its size and mysteries.

Arnarulunnguaq sighed, contemplating her new surroundings:

> And we used to think Nature was the greatest and most wonderful of all! Yet here we are among mountains and great gulfs and precipices, all made by the work of human hands. Nature is great; Sila, as we call it at home; nature, the world, the universe, all that is Sila; which our wise men declared they could hold in poise. And I could never believe it; but I see it now. Nature is great; but are not men greater? Those tiny beings we can see down there far below, hurrying this way and that. They live among these stone walls, on a great plain of stones made with hands. Stone and stone and stone—there is no game to be seen

111 Rasmussen, *Across Arctic America*, vii.

112 Hastrup, "Knud Rasmussen," 132.

> anywhere, and yet they manage to live and find their daily food. . . .
>
> I see things more than my mind can grasp; and the only way to save oneself from madness is to suppose that we have all died suddenly before we knew, and that this is part of another life.[113]

Dressed in Qallunaat clothing, she called New York the coldest place she had ever been. She was fascinated by the elevators in the tall buildings and couldn't get enough of them.

Rasmussen mused on Arnarulunnguaq's words. The events of the expedition in Inuit territory, full of new experiences to a white man, had just been everyday life to the two Inughuit. Now it was their turn to wonder at the marvels of the white man's world. "Their expedition was beginning," wrote Rasmussen. And his thoughts returned to the Inuit, "to the people we had left, to the men and women who had spoken so simply and yet so powerfully of the greatest and the smallest things." And he gave his interpretation of Arnarulunnguaq's words, not that man had triumphed over nature, but that the indomitable spirit of the men and women of the Arctic had found ways to deal with "hunger and feasting, happiness and adversity, the daily round and the great moments of life," as part of nature. "Here," he wrote, "face to face with a chaos and confusion of marvels, Arnarulunnguaq found the very words for all it meant: Nature is great; but man is greater still."[114]

Arnarulunnguaq had been an integral part of the expedition; on the great sled journey she was responsible for cooking and clothing, but she also assisted in collecting botanical specimens and caring for the zoological items. She also helped Rasmussen in archaeological excavations at Malirualik on King William Island. In addition, she made drawings of Canadian Inuit women's tattoos as a contribution to the expedition's ethnography. Rasmussen wrote, in a magazine article in 1925, "She, the only woman who has ever traveled the Northwest Passage, must go down in Danish-Greenlandic history as one who must never be forgotten."[115]

On arrival in Denmark at the end of the expedition she was diagnosed with tuberculosis and hospitalized for some time. She returned to Uummannaq in 1925 and married Kaalipaluk Peary, son of Robert Peary, three years later. Unfortunately she suffered from illness for the rest of her life; she passed away in 1933 in the hospital in Uummannaq.

---

113 Rasmussen, *Across Arctic America*, 387.

114 Ibid., 387-388.

115 Rasmussen, quoted from a 1925 article in *Tidens Kvinder*, in makko.dk, "Hvem var Arnarulunnguaq?" English translation by Google Translate.

Kaalipaluk remembered her as "a very talented woman. She was perfect for all kinds of women's work. Preparation of catch and skins, sewing, preparation of food, everything perfect. She could even steer a dog sled quite impeccably."[116] But she never talked about the great sled journey.

Arnarulunnguaq was commemorated on a Greenlandic stamp in 1996, in a popular song by musician Ole Kristiansen in 1991, and in a poem by the Greenlandic politician and activist Aqqaluk Lynge in 1982. She has been the subject of book chapters and of modern artwork. In an article in 1925, Rasmussen quoted Arnarulunnguaq expressing her hesitancy at receiving the silver medal of merit from the king—an award given to all six Inughuit who participated in the expedition: "I have only been on this expedition as a woman and have only followed in the footsteps of men. It is those who broke the road, and not those who just followed along, who should be honored. That is why I think it is difficult for me to accept such an award."[117]

The comment is often made that she and Knud Rasmussen were bedmates during the expedition. The supposition is, perhaps, a natural one, given that they lived together under the same roof. In 1923, during Qaavigarsuaq's long absence from Nattilik country, they were the only two people under that roof. But there is no evidence to support the statement, and in fact, Qaavigarsuaq explicitly told his biographer that such statements were not true.

Rasmussen wrote of Arnarulunnguaq's and Qaavigarsuaq's contributions and loyalty: "Considering the rigors they endured, I don't know which is the more remarkable, that I came through the three and a half years with the same team of dogs, or with the same Eskimos. Surely, however, it is no mere sentimental gesture to point out that they had a bigger share in the outcome of the trip than I have space to show."[118]

In 1921, Rasmussen had recruited Qaavigarsuaq by taking him on a hunting excursion to test his marksmanship. After he had demonstrated his skill, Rasmussen told him that he wanted him on the expedition; his parents had already given their permission. On the expedition he was sometimes known by one of his other names, Mitiq, which proved easier for the Danish participants to pronounce.

In Copenhagen, while awaiting passage back to Greenland, Qaavigarsuaq acquired a bicycle and cut a fine figure cycling around the city. On one occasion, while at Rasmussen's home in Hundsted, he borrowed a bicycle and rode all the way to Copenhagen. He attended parties with Rasmussen, where ladies were attracted to the handsome Greenlander.

116 Makko.dk, "Hvem var Arnarulunnguaq?" English translation by Google Translate.

117 Ibid. English translation by Google Translate.

118 Rasmussen, *Across Arctic America*, ix.

Before leaving Thule, Qaavigarsuaq had fallen in love. His chosen one was Bebianne, the daughter of a West Greenlandic catechist, Enok Kristiansen, who was employed by the mission. When Rasmussen recruited Qaavigarsuaq for the expedition, the two lovers knew that they would have to endure a long separation. Bebianne picked up a small stone and gave it to the young man, saying that he should carry it with him throughout the expedition as a remembrance of their love. Qaavigarsuaq was true to his word and carried it with him everywhere. When he accompanied Rasmussen to Siberia and was detained by the Russian police, he was searched. Fearing that he would lose his stone, he hid it in his mouth. The Russian officer never found it.

It was the late summer of 1925 before Qaavigarsuaq and Arnarulunnguaq were able to return to Thule. On his arrival, Qaavigarsuaq learned that Bebianne was due to get married—to someone else—that very day. According to family lore, he ran to the church, stopped the ceremony, produced the stone from his pocket, and showed it to Bebianne. She said that he had been gone so long that she thought he had died, but her love for him remained. The wedding in progress was called off. Shortly thereafter, Qaavigarsuaq and Bebianne were married.[119]

The couple had eight children. They lived at many locations in the Thule district: Uummannaq, Qeqertarsuaq, Savissivik, Moriusaq, and Qaanaaq. Able to read and write, Qaavigarsuaq taught these skills to others. Following Rasmussen's death, he penned an article about Rasmussen and the expedition, which was translated and published in Danish. He passed away in Qaanaaq in August 1978, but was buried in Uummannaq, the place that he had loved the most.

It was autumn of 1924 when Peter Freuchen bid farewell to his four Inughuit travelling companions at Cape Seddon on the Greenland coast. Ice had prevented the *Søkongen* from landing them at their preferred destination of Cape York. A long journey north along the coast of Melville Bay was ahead of them. It was well into winter before they finally reached the homes from which they had departed almost four years earlier.

As a child, Puursimaat had been a favourite of Rasmussen, who treated him almost as a foster child. His wife, Aqattaq, was the youngest member of the expedition and the least experienced as a traveller. She had often remained behind at Blæsebælgen on Danish Island to look after the place while others travelled. On their return to Greenland, the couple had a son, Minik, born in 1925. Aqattaq was the first of the Inughuit participants to die; she succumbed to tuberculosis in Siorapaluk on August 8, 1932. Puursimaat subsequently remarried, to a woman named Naduk, who died in 1939. He lived on until 1975. Inuit in Arctic Bay, Canada, remembered him fondly

119 They were married on November 29, 1925. The story is told in Olsvig, "Hvem var de to inughuit," 136-144.

from his lengthy stay at Uluksan in 1924; a number of Inuit children were named in his honour after his death.

Arnannguaq and Aaqqiuq's daughter Navarana, born at Danish Island on August 9, 1923, was baptized when they returned to Greenland in 1925. She died in 1933. A second child, Mikissuk, was born in 1927. In 1930 Aaqqiuq, a veteran of many expeditions throughout the High Arctic prior to the Fifth Thule Expedition, joined an expedition led by German geologist Hans Krüger. The party of three—Krüger, Aaqqiuq, and a Dane, Åge Rose Bjare—departed the RCMP detachment at Bache Peninsula, Ellesmere Island, on March 19, heading westward. After two support sledges manned by Inughuit turned back in Eureka Sound, the party was never seen again. Inspector Alfred Herbert Joy, who searched in vain for any trace of them, described Aaqqiuq as "a thoroughly capable man. He is a first-class hunter, and an excellent dog driver, and a good and cheerful worker. He has done much travelling with white men, and has always given entire satisfaction."[120]

Arnannguaq never remarried. She died of influenza in 1955.

The financial compensation the Inughuit received for their participation in the expedition remains a mystery. Qaavigarsuaq complained to his biographer, Hans Larsen, that he received no payment for his years of service, but that he received two hundred Danish kroner, a paltry sum, each Christmas for the first few years after his return.

Qaavigarsuaq's daughter Regine observed: "When you think about how much the Fifth Thule Expedition has contributed to science, we find it very strange that our parents and the other Inughuit have never been visibly honored. They were awarded the silver merit medal, but we do not even have a memorial of them, and one can wonder why that is so. . . . Without Inughuit, the Fifth Thule Expedition would not have come to realization, so one can wonder where they are in our history."[121]

"His Importance Cannot Be Weighed in Words Alone"

Knud Rasmussen had launched his three-year expedition to Arctic North America with the promise of testing the theories of his early mentor, Hans Peder Steensby, on the inland North American origins of the Inuit.

Throughout the expedition, his faith in that theory remained unshaken. His first major excursion away from Danish Island was to the Inuit inland to the west of Hudson Bay, people he named collectively the "Caribou Eskimos." He wrote of what he learned there: "We had not been long among the Caribou Eskimos before

120 Alfred Herbert Joy, quoted in Barr, "Hans K. E. Krüger," 287.

121 Regine Kristiansen, quoted in Kleist, "The Expedition."

we became aware that we had before us a primitive culture that had originated in the interior. This culture was not only the most original we had hitherto met on all our travels, but—and this to us was of still greater interest—all the particulars we collected there very soon convinced us that we were on the way towards solving one of the most important of the Expedition's problems."[122]

Two years later, he travelled along the coast of the western Canadian Arctic and Alaska, where he encountered Inuit cultures quite different from those he had observed in the central and eastern Canadian Arctic. In particular, he noted that "Alaska has been the scene of much conflict, not least as a consequence of the natural conditions and the entirely new possibilities of a previously unknown form of marine hunting." His view of Steensby's theory had evolved to include not only a migration of Inuit from inland America to the coast, but then a migration west to Bering Strait, before a renewed migration from Alaska spread Inuit as far to the east as Greenland. He imagined that "crowds of primitive Eskimos" migrated to the area around Baillie Island before heading west, and that those journeys "necessitated great revolutions in their vocational technique."[123]

"We must assume," he continued, "that when they came into this land and for the first time looked out over the open sea, where not only small seals but also white whales, walruses and [bowhead] whales appeared as quarries, it would not be long before they put to sea in the kayaks which were originally built for use in fresh-water lakes." He went on to speculate on the eventual awareness of new inventions needed for the hunt—the skin boat, the throwing harpoon, the throwing board, the float to buoy up harpooned animals. "These developments," he told us, "would have proceeded through several generations."[124]

In his popular book *Across Arctic America*, published three years after the conclusion of his sled journey, he remained unshaken in his belief in Steensby's theory and summed it up succinctly:

> The conclusion was inevitable that originally all the Eskimos were land hunters, and that a portion of them later turned to hunting sea-mammals. . . . The aboriginal Eskimos developed a special culture around the big rivers and lakes of the northernmost part of Canada. From here, they moved down to the coast, either because they were driven by hostile tribes or because they had to follow the caribou in their migrations. They developed the first phases of a coastal culture at the Arctic Coast of Canada, most probably between Coronation Gulf and the Magnetic North Pole.
>
> From here they wandered over to Labrador, Baffinland, and Greenland, to the east, and westward, reached Alaska and the Bering

122 Rasmussen, "Caribou Eskimos," 6.

123 Ostermann and Holtved, "Alaskan Eskimos," 20.

124 Ibid.

Sea. Around the Bering, with its abundance of sea-mammals, they had their Golden Age, as a coastal people.

From here a new migration took place, for what reason we cannot know, but this time from the West to the East.[125]

And yet he—and Birket-Smith—were wrong.

There were many reasons to dispute the conclusions reached by Rasmussen and Birket-Smith. Birket-Smith had studied the historical record, which did not indicate that there were any Inuit living inland before the nineteenth century, and simply ignored it. Rasmussen had relied on his collection of folklore; much of it differed considerably from that of the coast-dwellers, but there were also many similarities, which he chose to attribute to modern borrowings from the coast. Both men had succumbed to the temptation to use their data to prove Steensby's theory and to ignore those aspects that didn't fit, rather than approaching the subject like an open book and letting the data shape a theory.

Ironically, it was their colleague, Therkel Mathiassen, who challenged Rasmussen's and Birket-Smith's theories on the basis of his archaeological digs. He, and others who followed him, showed that the Inuit culture had its origins in Alaska, from where it subsequently spread eastward across Canada and to Greenland. All subsequent research has borne out that conclusion. Still, Rasmussen's and Steensby's theories continued to have influence. Mathiassen himself thought that "the present Iglulik culture must be regarded as an inland culture which has acquired a marine facet," but he thought that this was not necessarily as a result of migration but might be because of "simply cultural influences."[126] In addition, he may have not wanted to unduly offend Rasmussen. Three decades later, the esteemed Danish archaeologist Jørgen Meldgaard thought he detected the "smell of forest" in his work near Iglulik; he was accompanied by the Greenlandic scholar Robert Petersen, who also wrote about the "smell of forest" in certain Greenlandic legends.[127] But today, the idea of an inland origin for Canada's Inuit has no following.

It is ironic, then, that Rasmussen's conclusions on the subject of Inuit origins, which has been described as "his most cherished research,"[128] were wrong, but that we are still enormously indebted to him and his colleagues for our knowledge of the traditional pre-Christian customs and beliefs of Inuit in Canada. In 1929, Birket-Smith published the two-part work *The Caribou Eskimos: Material and Social Life and their Cultural Position*. The following year Rasmussen published *Intellectual Culture of the Caribou Eskimos and Iglulik and Caribou Eskimo Texts*. They complemented his 1929 publication, *Intellectual Culture of the Iglulik Eskimos.* Rasmussen would also publish *The Netsilik Eskimos: Social Life and Spiritual Culture* (1931) and *Intellectual Life of the*

125 Rasmussen, *Across Arctic America*, x-xi.

126 Mathiassen, "Material Culture," 239-240.

127 Petersen, "Smell of Forest," 243.

128 Burch, "Inland Eskimos," 96.

Copper Eskimos (1932). His studies *The Mackenzie Eskimos* (1942) and *The Alaskan Eskimos* (1952) were edited and published posthumously.

Before the Fifth Thule Expedition, there was no reliable information on the beliefs and culture of the inland societies of Inuit—the people called "Caribou Eskimos." Without Birket-Smith's studies, we would know almost nothing of the material culture of these people; without Rasmussen's work we would know little of their religion, nor of the beliefs of other Inuit of the northern Hudson Bay coast, the Aivilingmiut and their sub-group the Iglulingmiut, and the Inuit farther north and west on the central Arctic coast, the Mackenzie Delta, and to a lesser extent, the north coast of Alaska. The ethnographic works of the expedition should rightly be regarded as salvage ethnography, documenting some aspects of Inuit traditional culture at the last possible moment.

Rasmussen described himself in the list of expedition personnel as a "folklorist." Yet he was much more; he had the soul of a poet and revelled in collecting the life stories and legends of the Inuit. He was at his best when recording their religious beliefs and the practices of the shamans. Well before the Fifth Thule Expedition took place, Rasmussen already had a reputation as an ethnographer, though self-taught, and a writer, and had a good many publications to his credit.

The Fifth Thule Expedition was also extremely productive in the field of archaeology. The expedition's sole trained archaeologist was Therkel Mathiassen, who was often assisted by Jacob Olsen, but Freuchen and Rasmussen himself, assisted by Arnarulunnguaq, also did archaeological digs. Mathiassen's work proved the existence of a culture first excavated at Thule on the Second Thule Expedition, a precursor to modern Inuit culture. This was a prehistoric culture that developed in Alaska and spread rapidly eastward across the top of North America, reaching Greenland by the twelfth century. Mathiassen summarized it in three words as a "pronouncedly coast culture."[129] He contributed a massive volume, *Archaeology of the Central Eskimos* (1927), to the expedition reports. It served also as his doctoral dissertation at the University of Copenhagen. This work established his reputation and laid the groundwork for future Inuit archaeology. Mathiassen also published his analysis of Rasmussen's material collections from the Northwest Passage as "Archaeological Collections from the Western Eskimos" (1930).

All the reports by Rasmussen, Birket-Smith, Mathiassen, and others were issued as volumes of the *Report of the Fifth Thule Expedition*, a series of incomparable works issued over a number of years and totalling about 5,500 pages. They comprise a virtual encyclopedia of knowledge on Inuit culture in the areas of Canada—and to a lesser extent, Alaska—touched by the expedition. Some of the legends and beliefs recorded were documented nowhere else. Scientists have long recognized their indebtedness to Rasmussen. Inuit are now coming to realize their indebtedness to him as well, for the documentation he made of their ancestors' lives and beliefs.

A well-known Canadian Inuk, Abraham Okpik, commented in his auto-

129 Mathiassen, "Archaeology," 195.

biography that he was "disappointed that most high schools . . . in Inuit country don't have copies [of the Fifth Thule Expedition reports]. Here [in Iqaluit] at the library they should have them, no matter how much they cost, because this is our culture. It is people's ancestors that they are talking about. . . . You don't see those books in the libraries at all."[130]

As a result of the work of Rasmussen and his colleagues on the Fifth Thule Expedition, the National Museum of Denmark contains the largest collection of Inuit material and intellectual culture in the world. Eleven thousand archaeological artifacts were collected, along with 3,100 ethnographical artifacts, 1,975 photographs, and more than 150 drawings by Canadian and Alaskan Inuit. Birket-Smith's and Mathiassen's notebooks are also housed there. Other Danish institutions house Rasmussen's own writings and other print and photographic material. Modern digitization technology is now making these resources available to more scholars, including Inuit scholars and those at Inuit cultural organizations.

It is natural that the scientists who had lived in such close contact with the Inuit in Hudson Bay for an extended period of time would have some concern for the future of the people. Mathiassen wrote, "What the future of the Iglulik Eskimos will be is difficult to say. Will it be possible for this little tribe, five hundred people, spread over an enormous area of land, to continue being able to hold its own in the struggle for existence, or will it, like so many other primitive peoples, be swallowed up in the fight against European civilization?"[131]

Rasmussen ventured his opinions on such a question. In Alaska he had been strongly impressed by the work of the government in establishing schools for the Inuit and bringing in American teachers—even though he developed a strong dislike for some of the missionaries and what he thought was their oppression of the free will of the people. He claimed that in Alaska, over a period of thirty-five years, "a dying, degenerate and ill-treated folk had been turned into industrious, ambitious and independent people, admirable in their zeal to live according to precepts dictated to them by their teachers." He claimed that, from the outset, the school was made the centre of community life. "The rising generation speaks English fluently," he noted, "and this possesses the first qualification for meeting the competition of the immigrating whites."[132]

Rasmussen was Denmark's hero. For two decades he had positioned himself within the small nation to have an outsized voice on Greenlandic affairs. He became, in effect, the voice of the Greenlanders.

130 Okpik, *We Call It Survival*, 205-206.

131 Mathiassen, "Material Culture," 240.

132 Ostermann and Holtved, "Alaskan Eskimos," 14.

In fact, even before the start of the Fifth Thule Expedition, he was advocating for a more open approach in Greenland. "It will not be possible to preserve the Eskimos unspoilt," he wrote in the new monthly journal *Danmarksposten* in 1920. He continued, in words that may seem brutal or unfeeling, but that he felt were only realistic:

> Their culture is of a kind that will succumb to that of the white man everywhere, and to maintain it artificially for ethical or ethnographical reasons cannot be done. . . . There is no choice. In future, the lives of all primitive people are dependent only on their possibilities for development under new conditions. The way ahead must be over the dead bodies of their own race. What is important, therefore, is to give the primitive people, in their minds and character, a death which is as merciful and gentle as possible. . . . We must take away their, to our civilization, impractical culture and try to make them resemble ourselves. We must give them the white man's aggressiveness and level-headed energy, his foresight and his audacity. Only through such a metamorphosis will they be able to pass through the door that leads to new times.[133]

A year later he said blatantly, "As far as is possible we must try to make Danes of the Greenlanders. It is no use stopping half-way."[134]

What he learned on the expedition, particularly in Alaska, only confirmed the beliefs that he had held for some time: that Greenland must gradually open up to more Danish influence, and—controversially—that Danish should be the language of instruction in the Greenlandic schools, using Danish teachers, with Kalaallisut being relegated to a subject of instruction and for use in the church. On February 12, 1925, he gave a lecture to Danish parliamentarians entitled "Alaska's Present and Greenland's Future," in which he shared some of his ideas.

The expedition brought Rasmussen worldwide recognition as an authority on the Arctic, and so it was quite natural that the Canadian government, struggling to know how to administer its own Arctic territories, sought his advice. In late April 1925 he arrived in Ottawa for a whirlwind of meetings with government officials. His host was O. S. Finnie, Director of Northern Administration in the Department of the Interior, but he also met with RCMP officials and with Rudolph M. Anderson and Diamond Jenness, both of whom had been on Stefansson's Canadian Arctic Expedition.

He proposed the banning of high-powered rifles and the establishment of reindeer herds. Female infanticide was a problem in certain areas of the Arctic, but Rasmussen felt that education would solve that problem. Health care needed to be provided through the building of small hospitals. He thought the proliferation of

133 Søby, "Political Thoughts," 8-9.

134 Ibid., 9.

fur-trade posts should be curtailed and advocated for a large area to be set aside for the exclusive use of the Inuit. The following year, an Order in Council established the Arctic Islands Preserve, encompassing the whole of the Arctic Islands and a good part of the mainland. It was to ensure Inuit an area where they could live and hunt with a minimum of disturbance. Finnie wrote to Rasmussen in 1928 to thank him for his help and advice, and commented, "As the Arctic Islands Preserve covers an area of 439,105 square miles, and as it is practically all in Eskimo territory, it will at least keep that much territory for the sole and exclusive use and benefit of the native people."[135]

In *Across Arctic America* he laid out a grim prognosis for the future of the isolated societies he had studied in the Canadian Arctic: "Before many years are past, their religion will be extinct, and the white man will have conquered all, the country and its people; their thoughts, their visions and their faith."[136] And yet he remained an optimist, believing that a gradual opening up of the Inuit homelands to development under a controlled influx of non-Inuit would portend a brighter and more affluent future.

Never one to rest on his laurels, Rasmussen had ambitious plans for the future, but, he wrote, "they can only be poor in comparison with the Fifth Thule Expedition.... My field of work has been and will continue to be north of the Arctic Circle ... for it is the Eskimos that own my heart."[137]

And so a Sixth, then a Seventh Thule Expedition ensued. On the Seventh, Rasmussen fell ill in east Greenland. He was evacuated to Denmark, where he died on December 21, 1933. He was only fifty-four.

Greenlandic writer and priest Otto Rosing said of him, "His importance for Greenland and the Greenlanders cannot be weighed in words alone."[138]

---

135 Quoted in Lloyd, "Arctic Islands Preserve," 87.

136 Rasmussen, *Across Arctic America*, 386.

137 Rasmussen, quoted in Hansen, *I Knuds Slædespor*, 177. The English translation is from Bown, *White Eskimo*, 263.

138 Rosing, "Dr. Knud Rasmussen's," 64-65. Translation by Google Translate.

MAPS

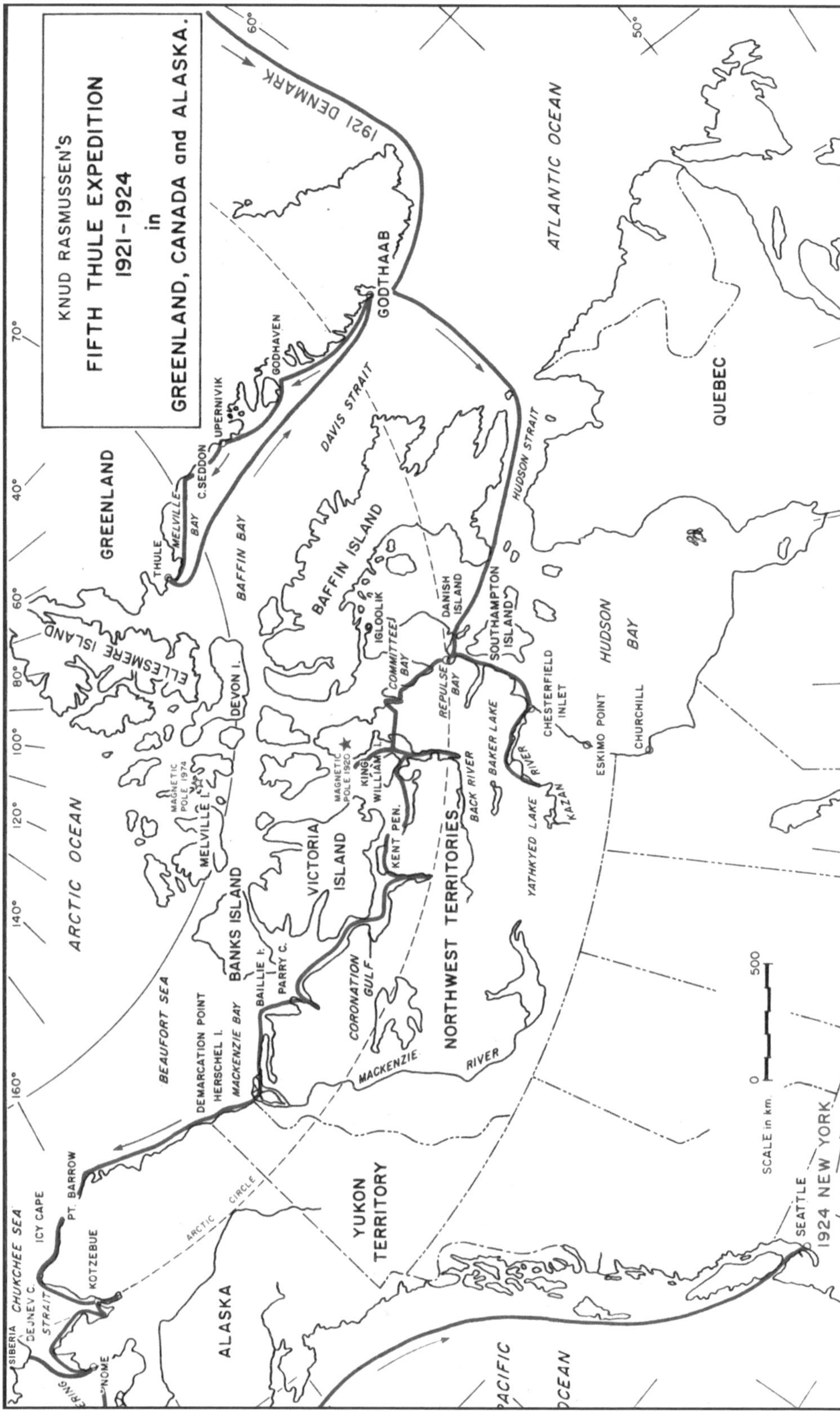

The route of Rasmussen on the expedition, 1921–24.

SOURCE: LLOYD, TREVOR. "KNUD RASMUSSEN AND THE ARCTIC ISLANDS PRESERVE." *THE MUSK-OX*, NO. 25 (1979): 88. [ROUTE ADJUSTED BY INHABIT MEDIA.]

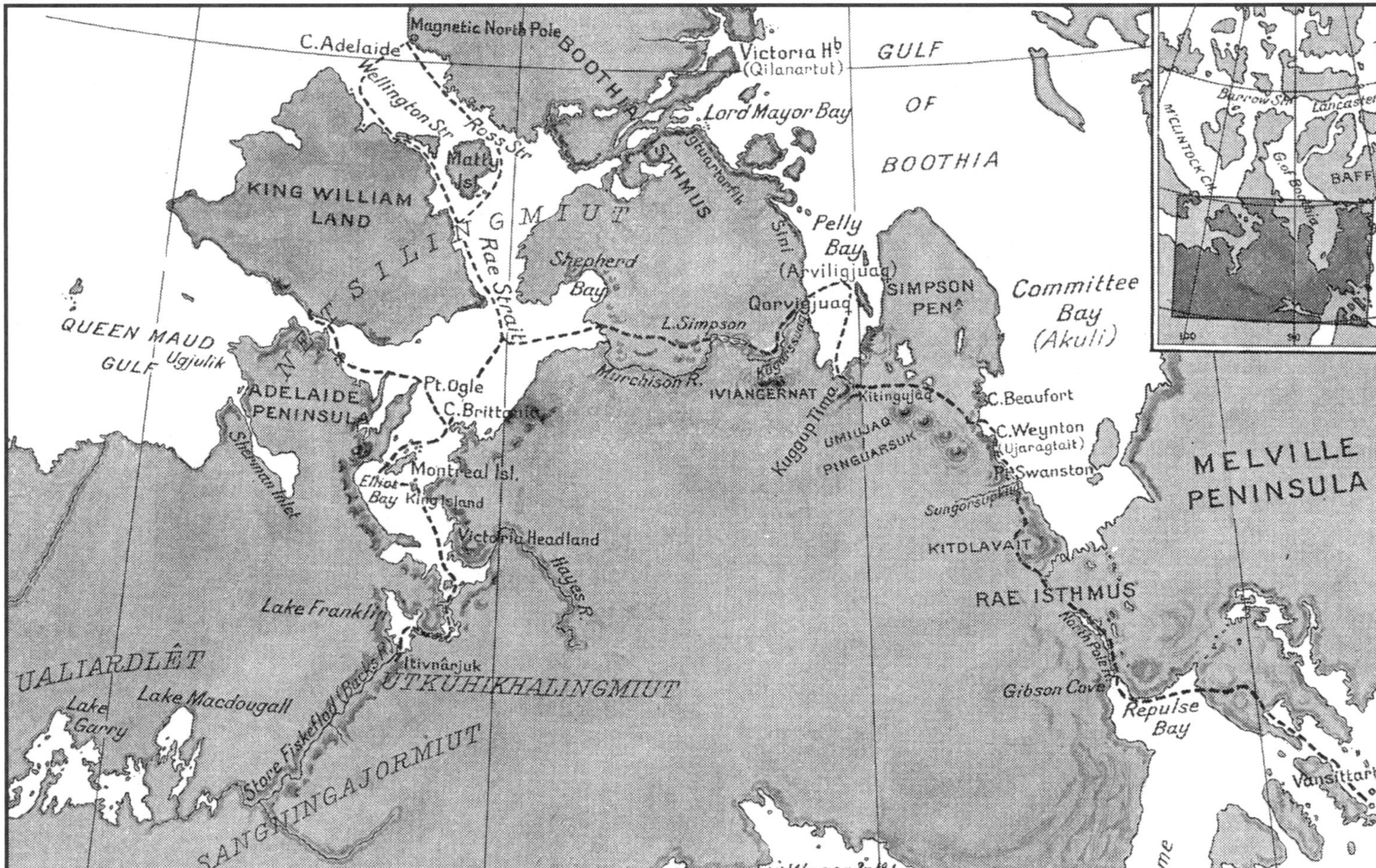

Rasmussen's route from Danish Island into and through the Nattilingmiut territory.

SOURCE: RASMUSSEN, KNUD. "THE NETSILIK ESKIMOS: SOCIAL LIFE AND SPIRITUAL CULTURE." *REPORT OF THE FIFTH THULE EXPEDITION 1921–24* XIII, NO. 1, FACING PAGE 12. COPENHAGEN: NORDISK FORLAG, 1952.

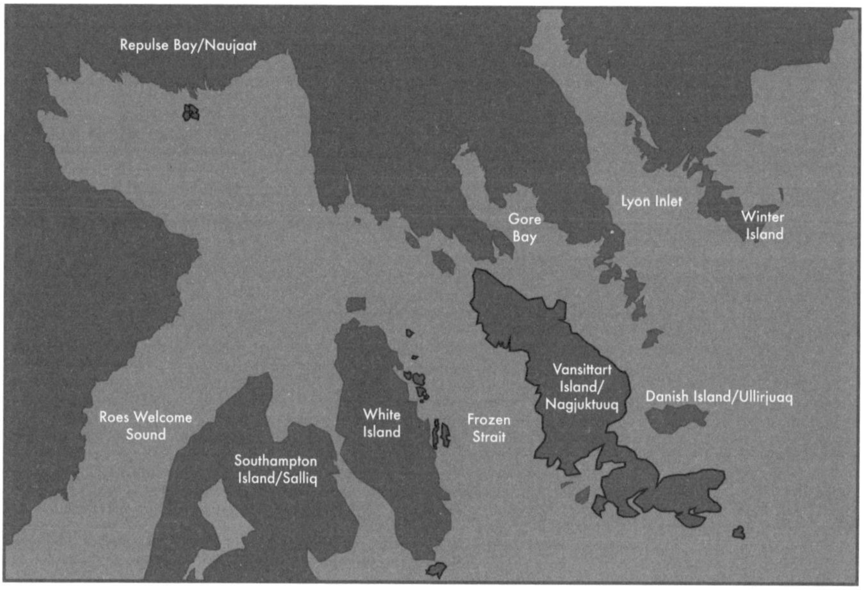

The Danish Island area.

SOURCE: ORIGINAL MAP BY INHABIT MEDIA INC.

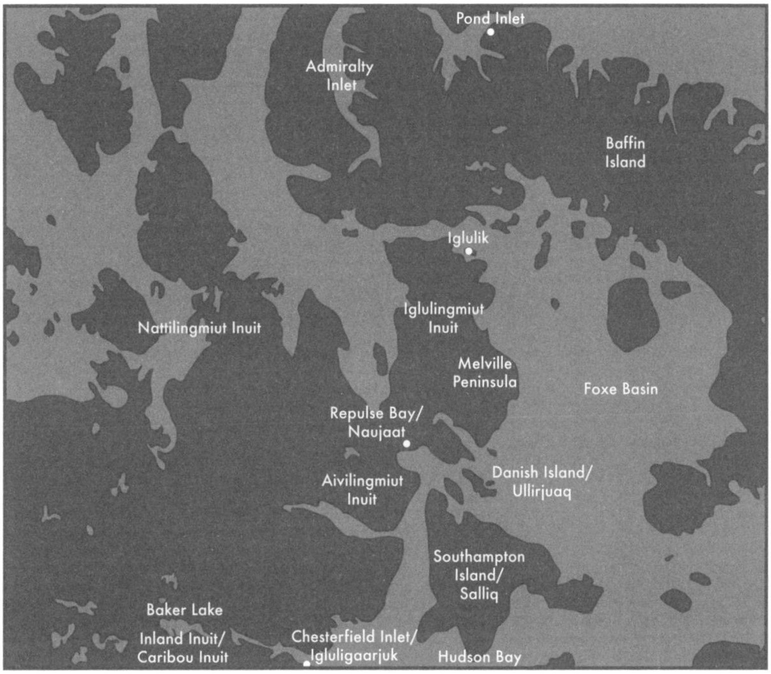

Places and cultural groups touched by the expedition in the eastern Arctic.

SOURCE: KATEUKRAINE, ID 363697151, SHUTTERSTOCK.COM.

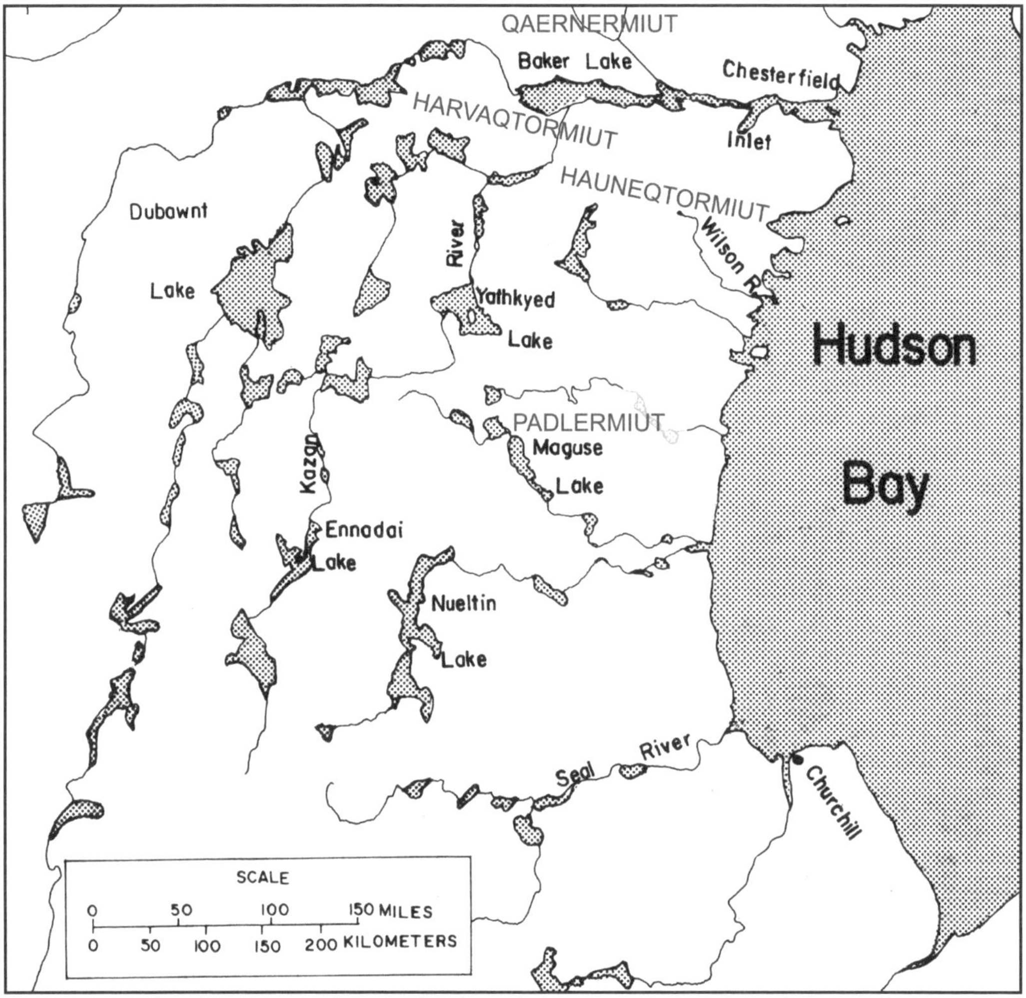

The Caribou Inuit area.

SOURCE: BURCH, ERNEST S. JR. "KNUD RASMUSSEN AND THE 'ORIGINAL' INLAND ESKIMOS OF SOUTHERN KEEWATIN." *INUIT STUDIES* 12, NO. 1-2 (1988): 83. [INUIT GROUP NAMES ADDED BY INHABIT MEDIA.]

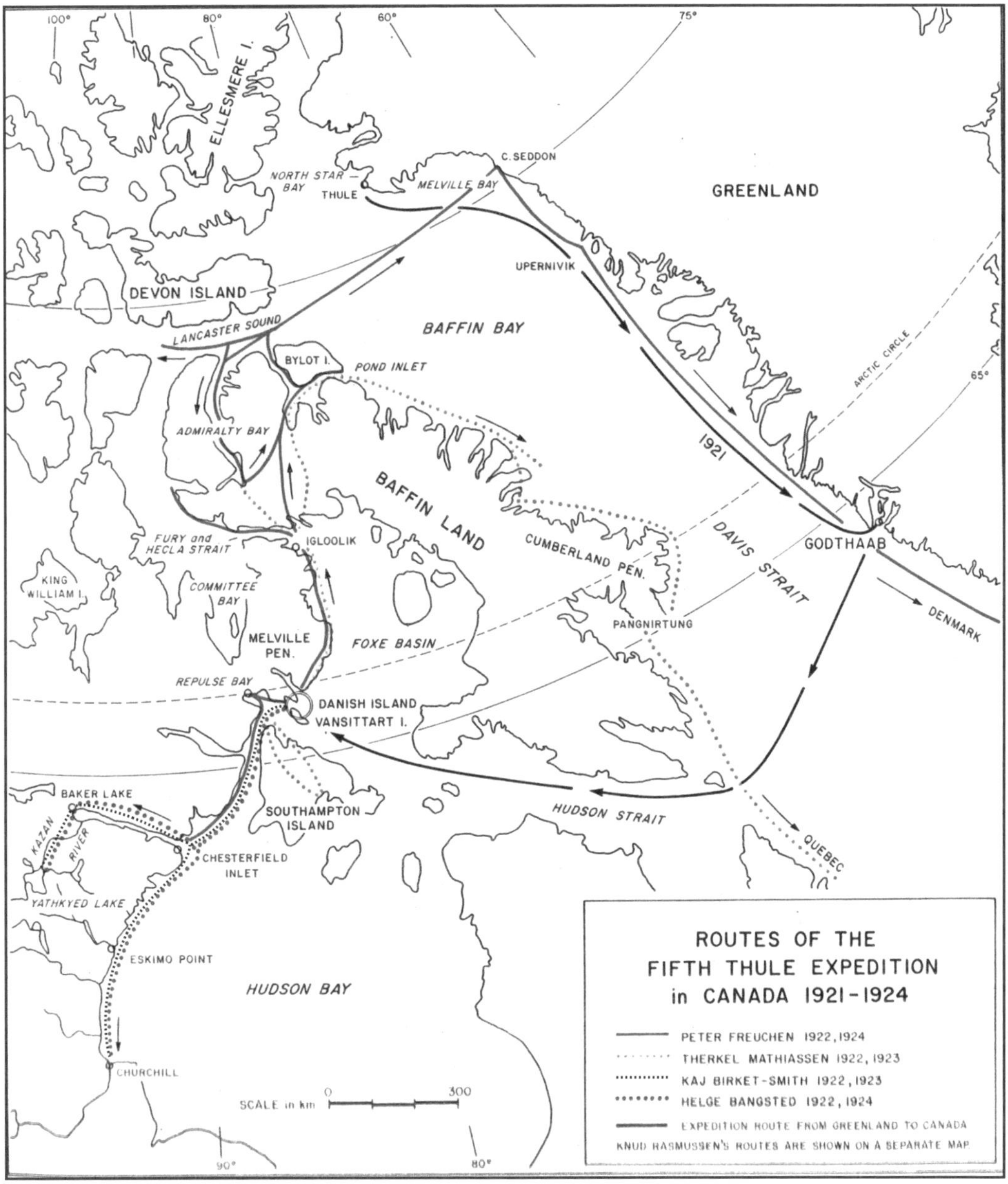

The routes of Freuchen, Mathiassen, Birket-Smith, and Bangsted.

SOURCE: LLOYD, TREVOR. "KNUD RASMUSSEN AND THE ARCTIC ISLANDS PRESERVE." *THE MUSK-OX*, NO. 25 (1979): 89. [ROUTE LINES ENHANCED BY INHABIT MEDIA.]

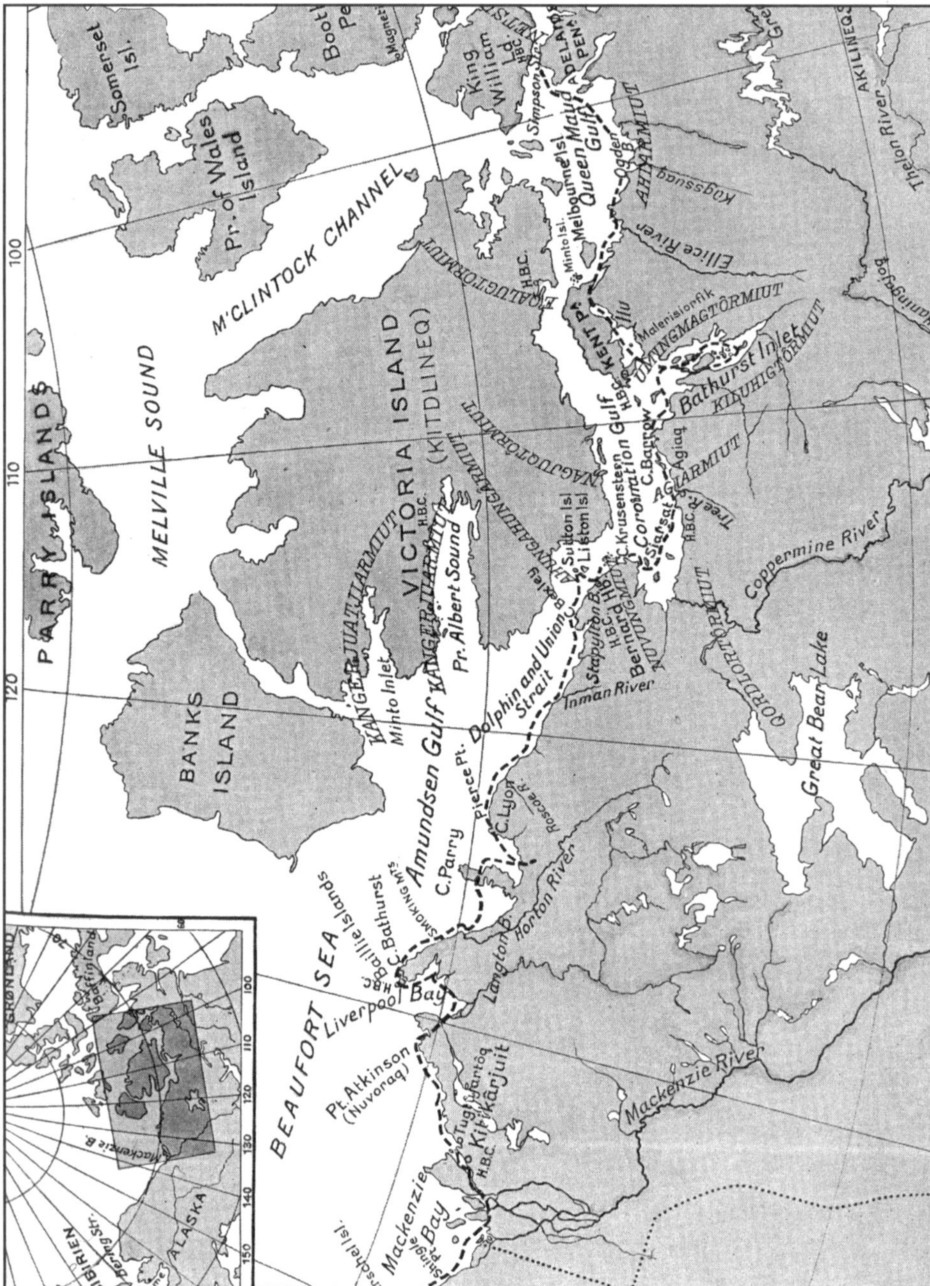

Rasmussen's route from the Nattilik area to Herschel Island.

SOURCE: RASMUSSEN, KNUD. "INTELLECTUAL CULTURE OF THE COPPER ESKIMOS." *REPORT OF THE FIFTH THULE EXPEDITION 1921–24* IX, FACING PAGE 7. COPENHAGEN: NORDISK FORLAG, 1932.

Route from Herschel Island to Nome and East Cape.

SOURCE: OSTERMANN, HOTHER, AND ERIK HOLTVED, EDS. "THE ALASKAN ESKIMOS AS DESCRIBED IN THE POSTHUMOUS NOTES OF DR. KNUD RASMUSSEN." *REPORT OF THE FIFTH THULE EXPEDITION 1921–24* X (3). 141. COPENHAGEN: NORDISK FORLAG, 1952.

PHOTOGRAPHS

Knud Rasmussen portrait.
SOURCE: PHOTOGRAPHER UNKNOWN, DANISH ARCTIC INSTITUTE. RESOURCE ID 1185.

Knud Rasmussen's birthplace in Ilulissat (then Jakobshavn), Greenland. It is now a community museum.
SOURCE: PHOTOGRAPH BY KENN HARPER.

Knud Rasmussen dressed for Arctic travel.

SOURCE: KNUD RASMUSSEN SELSKABET. PHOTOGRAPH BY LEO HANSEN.

Knud Rasmussen in a pensive mood.
SOURCE: KNUD RASMUSSEN SELSKABET.
PHOTOGRAPH BY LEO HANSEN.

Portrait of Knud Rasmussen looking to the left in profile.
SOURCE: PHOTOGRAPH BY THERKEL MATHIASSEN, DANISH ARCTIC INSTITUTE. RESOURCE ID 146016.

Hans Peder Steensby, a Danish scholar whose theories on Inuit origins influenced Rasmussen.

SOURCE: ROYAL LIBRARY, COPENHAGEN. PORTRÆT AF H. P. STEENSBY F. 1875.03.25 D. 1920.10.19 GEOGRAF. DP030720. PHOTOGRAPHER UNKNOWN.

Rasmussen with Ib Nyeboe, Chairman of the Thule Committee.

SOURCE: KNUD RASMUSSEN SELSKABET. PHOTOGRAPHER UNKNOWN.

Danish and West Greenlandic expedition personnel. Back row left to right: Kaj Birket-Smith, Therkel Mathiassen, Helge Bangsted. Front row left to right: Peder Pedersen (captain of the expedition ship), Knud Rasmussen, Peter Freuchen, Jacob Olsen. Photographed in Nuuk before the expedition left for Canada.
SOURCE: PHOTOGRAPHER UNKNOWN, DANISH ARCTIC INSTITUTE. RESOURCE ID 269069.

Peter Freuchen portrait in Greenland, 1913.
SOURCE: PHOTOGRAPH BY JOHN HØEGH, DANISH ARCTIC INSTITUTE. RESOURCE ID 120472.

Peter Freuchen standing outside Blæsebælgen on the Fifth Thule Expedition in 1922.
SOURCE: PHOTOGRAPH BY THERKEL MATHIASSEN, DANISH ARCTIC INSTITUTE. RESOURCE ID 147016.

Kaj Birket-Smith smoking his pipe.
SOURCE: PHOTOGRAPH BY THERKEL MATHIASSEN, DANISH ARCTIC INSTITUTE. RESOURCE ID 147023.

Knud Rasmussen and the ethnologist Kaj Birket-Smith.
SOURCE: PHOTOGRAPH BY THERKEL MATHIASSEN, DANISH ARCTIC INSTITUTE. RESOURCE ID 269074.

Knud Rasmussen and Helge Bangsted at work in Blæsebælgen.
SOURCE: PHOTOGRAPH BY THERKEL MATHIASSEN, DANISH ARCTIC INSTITUTE. RESOURCE ID 269073.

Therkel Mathiassen portrait, circa 1921.
SOURCE: MATHIASSEN FAMILY, VIA WIKIMEDIA COMMONS.

Jacob Olsen.

SOURCE: PHOTOGRAPHER UNKNOWN, DANISH ARCTIC INSTITUTE. RESOURCE ID 269043.

Qaavigarsuaq was a young man when Rasmussen recruited him as a key member of the expedition team.

SOURCE: PHOTOGRAPH BY THERKEL MATHIASSEN, DANISH ARCTIC INSTITUTE. RESOURCE ID 269075.

Arnarulunnguaq poses for a photograph at Danish Island.

SOURCE: PHOTOGRAPH BY THERKEL MATHIASSEN, DANISH ARCTIC INSTITUTE. RESOURCE ID 85.

Aaqqiuq and his wife Arnannguaq were Inughuit from northern Greenland who worked for the expedition.
SOURCE: PHOTOGRAPH BY THERKEL MATHIASSEN, DANISH ARCTIC INSTITUTE. RESOURCE ID 147135.

Aaqqiuq chewing skin to make it supple for a whip, in front of the expedition's library in Blæsebælgen.
SOURCE: PHOTOGRAPH BY THERKEL MATHIASSEN, DANISH ARCTIC INSTITUTE. RESOURCE ID 269078.

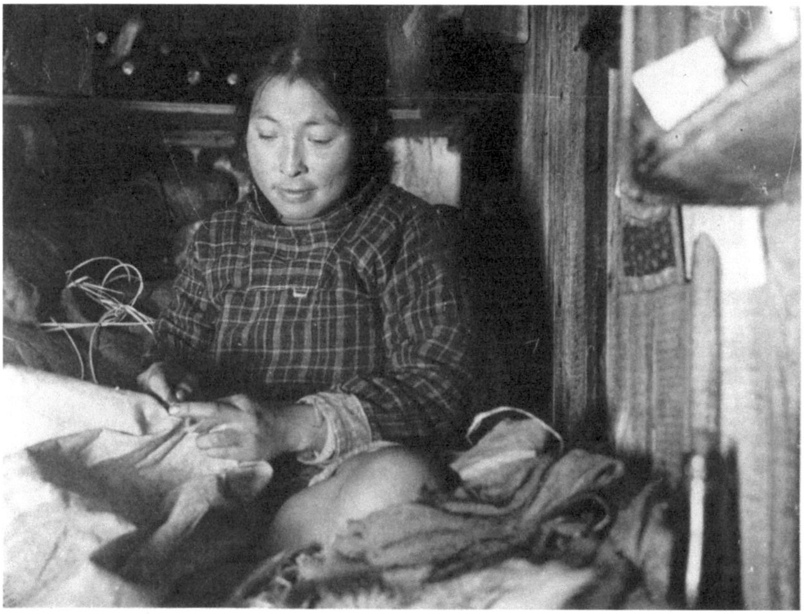

Arnannguaq sewing in the expedition headquarters of Blæaebælgen.
SOURCE: PHOTOGRAPH BY THERKEL MATHIASSEN, DANISH ARCTIC INSTITUTE. RESOURCE ID 147034.

Aqattaq, the youngest member of the expedition, was still a teenager. She was married to Puursimaat.
SOURCE: PHOTOGRAPH BY THERKEL MATHIASSEN, DANISH ARCTIC INSTITUTE. RESOURCE ID 147033.

Puursimaat and Aqattaq, a young couple from Thule in northern Greenland, worked for the expedition.
SOURCE: PHOTOGRAPH BY THERKEL MATHIASSEN, DANISH ARCTIC INSTITUTE. RESOURCE ID 147026.

Arnannguaq on the left, Arnarulunnguaq on the right. Aapaq, an Iglulingmiutaq, in the middle with an unidentified child.
SOURCE: PHOTOGRAPH BY THERKEL MATHIASSEN, DANISH ARCTIC INSTITUTE. RESOURCE ID 147048.

Aua and his wife Urulu inside their snowhouse.
SOURCE: PHOTOGRAPH BY THERKEL MATHIASSEN, DANISH ARCTIC INSTITUTE. RESOURCE ID 147071.

Knud Rasmussen, Orulu og Ava tegnet af Jens Rosing

Greenlandic artist Jens Rosing designed a postage stamp featuring Aua and Urulu in 1979 to celebrate the 100th anniversary of the birth of Knud Rasmussen. He added Rasmussen, who was not present in Mathiassen's photograph upon which the stamp is based.
SOURCE: KENN HARPER COLLECTION.

Urulu, wife of Aua.
SOURCE: KNUD RASMUSSEN. *INTELLECTUAL CULTURE OF THE IGLULIK ESKIMOS, REPORT OF THE FIFTH THULE EXPEDITION 1921-24*, VOL. VII, NO. 1. COPENHAGEN: GYLDENDALSKE BOGHANDEL, 1929, FACING PAGE 49. PHOTOGRAPHER PROBABLY THERKEL MATHIASSEN.

Aapaq, daughter of Aua and Urulu, in 1921.
SOURCE: PHOTOGRAPH BY THERKEL MATHIASSEN, DANISH ARCTIC INSTITUTE. RESOURCE ID 147043.

Ivaluarjuk, Aua's brother, was a marvellous storyteller whom Rasmussen considered the geographer of the Iglulingmiut.
SOURCE: NATIONAL MUSEUM OF DENMARK, DEPARTMENT OF ETHNOGRAPHY, NO. 1315. PHOTOGRAPHER PROBABLY THERKEL MATHIASSEN.

Tagurnaaq, whose name means "the shy one," was anything but shy. She loved to talk and told Rasmussen many stories.

SOURCE: KNUD RASMUSSEN. *INTELLECTUAL CULTURE OF THE IGLULIK ESKIMOS, REPORT OF THE FIFTH THULE EXPEDITION 1921-24*, VOL. VII, NO. 1. COPENHAGEN: GYLDENDALSKE BOGHANDEL, 1929, FACING PAGE 17. PHOTOGRAPHER PROBABLY THERKEL MATHIASSEN.

Qingailisaq, an angakkuq, photographed on November 23, 1901, wearing the coat made by his wife, Ataguarjugusiq, depicting his encounter with an ijiraq.

SOURCE: MYSTIC SEAPORT MUSEUM. PHOTOGRAPH ACCESSION NUMBER 1966.339.68. PHOTOGRAPH BY CAPTAIN GEORGE COMER.

George Cleveland, whaler turned trader, was the manager of the Hudson Bay Company's post at Repulse Bay.
SOURCE: PHOTOGRAPH BY THERKEL MATHIASSEN, DANISH ARCTIC INSTITUTE. RESOURCE ID 157661.

Hudson's Bay Company post at Repulse Bay in 1922.
SOURCE: PHOTOGRAPH BY THERKEL MATHIASSEN, DANISH ARCTIC INSTITUTE. RESOURCE ID 147058.

Drawings by Aapaq, the daughter of Aua. In the centre is a four-legged mountain spirit that she saw one night.

SOURCE: KNUD RASMUSSEN. *INTELLECTUAL CULTURE OF THE IGLULIK ESKIMOS, REPORT OF THE FIFTH THULE EXPEDITION 1921–24*, VOL. VII, NO. 1. COPENHAGEN: GYLDENDALSKE BOGHANDEL, 1929, FACING PAGE 129.

Musk-ox hunt.

A bear breaking into a tent and attacking a child.

Breathing-hole hunting. Drawn by Taparte.

Drawings by Tapaqti.

SOURCE: KNUD RASMUSSEN. *INTELLECTUAL CULTURE OF THE IGLULIK ESKIMOS, REPORT OF THE FIFTH THULE EXPEDITION 1921–24*, VOL. VII, NO. 1. COPENHAGEN: GYLDENDALSKE BOGHANDEL, 1929, FACING PAGE 225.

Hunting scenes, drawn by Ujarak.

A hunting scene drawn by Ujarak.

SOURCE: KNUD RASMUSSEN. *INTELLECTUAL CULTURE OF THE IGLULIK ESKIMOS, REPORT OF THE FIFTH THULE EXPEDITION 1921-24*, VOL. VII, NO. 1. COPENHAGEN: GYLDENDALSKE BOGHANDEL, 1929, FACING PAGE 224.

Niviatsarnaq, an Aivilingmiut woman whom the whalers nicknamed Shoofly, displays her elaborately beaded clothing.
SOURCE: A.P. LOW. *THE CRUISE OF THE NEPTUNE*. OTTAWA: GOVERNMENT PRINTING BUREAU, 1906. FACING PAGE 168. PHOTOGRAPHER UNKNOWN.

Aullanaaq, on the right, nicknamed "John L." by whalers, worked as a guide for many of the expedition members. He was the son of Niviatsarnaq.

SOURCE: NATIONAL MUSEUM OF DENMARK, ETHNOGRAPHIC DEPARTMENT, M531. PHOTOGRAPH BY PETER FREUCHEN.

Umik, the prophet from Pond Inlet who took his version of Christianity to the Iglulingmiut.

SOURCE: NATIONAL MUSEUM OF DENMARK, ETHNOGRAPHIC DEPARTMENT, NO. 826. PHOTOGRAPH BY THERKEL MATHIASSEN.

A camp of Iglulingmiut in the early 1920s. The flags over the snowhouses indicate that the inhabitants are Christian.

SOURCE: NATIONAL MUSEUM OF DENMARK, ETHNOGRAPHIC DEPARTMENT, NO. 86. PHOTOGRAPH BY THERKEL MATHIASSEN.

Father Arsène Turquetil, Roman Catholic missionary at Chesterfield Inlet.

SOURCE: *ESKIMO MAGAZINE*, DECEMBER 1955, PAGE 4. PHOTOGRAPHER UNKNOWN.

Igjugaarjuk, a powerful shaman of the inland Paallirmiut, told Rasmussen about his initiation as a shaman.

SOURCE: KNUD RASMUSSEN. *OBSERVATIONS ON THE INTELLECTUAL CULTURE OF THE CARIBOU ESKIMOS, REPORT OF THE FIFTH THULE EXPEDITION 1921-24*, VOL. VII, NO. 2. COPENHAGEN: GYLDENDALSKE BOGHANDEL, 1930, FACING PAGE 76. PHOTOGRAPHER PROBABLY KNUD RASMUSSEN.

Atqaaralaaq, one of Igjugaarjuk's two wives.
SOURCE: KNUD RASMUSSEN. *OBSERVATIONS ON THE INTELLECTUAL CULTURE OF THE CARIBOU ESKIMOS, REPORT OF THE FIFTH THULE EXPEDITION 1921-24*, VOL. VII, NO. 2. COPENHAGEN: GYLDENDALSKE BOGHANDEL, 1930, FACING PAGE 32. PHOTOGRAPHER PROBABLY KNUD RASMUSSEN.

Kaj Birket-Smith drew a sketch of Atqaaralaaq's facial tattoos, characteristic of Paallirmiut women.
SOURCE: KNUD RASMUSSEN. *OBSERVATIONS ON THE INTELLECTUAL CULTURE OF THE CARIBOU ESKIMOS, REPORT OF THE FIFTH THULE EXPEDITION 1921-24*, VOL. VII, NO. 2. COPENHAGEN: GYLDENDALSKE BOGHANDEL, 1930, FACING PAGE 80.

Kiguhiunaaq, an inland Inuk whom Rasmussen met on his travels.

SOURCE: KNUD RASMUSSEN. *OBSERVATIONS ON THE INTELLECTUAL CULTURE OF THE CARIBOU ESKIMOS, REPORT OF THE FIFTH THULE EXPEDITION 1921–24*, VOL. VII, NO. 2. COPENHAGEN: GYLDENDALSKE BOGHANDEL, 1930, FACING PAGE 70. PHOTOGRAPHER PROBABLY KNUD RASMUSSEN.

Iggiaraarjuk, a Nattilik Inuk who told Rasmussen about the last survivors of the Franklin Expedition.

SOURCE: KNUD RASMUSSEN. *THE NETSILIK ESKIMOS, REPORT OF THE FIFTH THULE EXPEDITION 1921-24*, VOL. VIII, NO. 1. COPENHAGEN: GYLDENDALSKE BOGHANDEL, 1930, FACING PAGE 85. PHOTOGRAPHER PROBABLY KNUD RASMUSSEN.

Urpingalik, the poet of the Nattilingmiut.

SOURCE: KNUD RASMUSSEN. *THE NETSILIK ESKIMOS, REPORT OF THE FIFTH THULE EXPEDITION 1921-24*, VOL. VIII, NO. 1. COPENHAGEN: GYLDENDALSKE BOGHANDEL, 1930, FACING PAGE 29. PHOTOGRAPHER PROBABLY KNUD RASMUSSEN.

Qaavigarsuaq (left) shares a chuckle with Qakuqtingniq, a leader of the Nattilingmiut.
SOURCE: KNUD RASMUSSEN. *THE NETSILIK ESKIMOS, REPORT OF THE FIFTH THULE EXPEDITION 1921-24*, VOL. VIII, NO. 1. COPENHAGEN: GYLDENDALSKE BOGHANDEL, 1930, FACING PAGE 409. PHOTOGRAPHER PROBABLY KNUD RASMUSSEN.

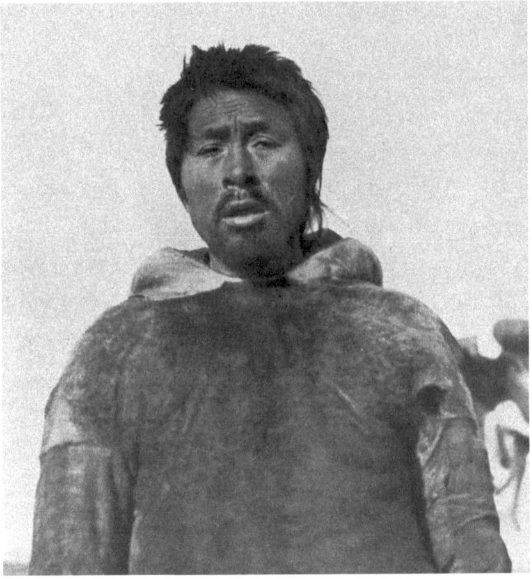

Saamik, a shaman of the Utkuhikhalingmiut, greatly esteemed by his people for his ability to kill evil spirits.
SOURCE: KNUD RASMUSSEN. *THE UTKUHIKJALINGMIUT, REPORT OF THE FIFTH THULE EXPEDITION 1921-24*, VOL. VIII, NO. 2. COPENHAGEN: GYLDENDALSKE BOGHANDEL, 1930, FACING PAGE 525. PHOTOGRAPHER PROBABLY KNUD RASMUSSEN.

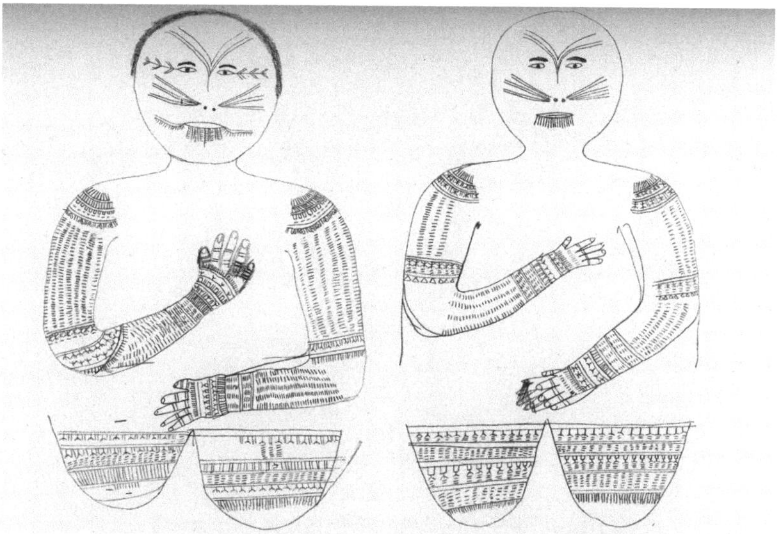

In addition to cooking and sewing, Arnarulunnguaq also assisted Rasmussen in his ethnographic work. These are drawings she made of the tattoos on the faces, arms, and thighs of two Nattilik women, Maalungiaq and Maniilaq.

SOURCE: KNUD RASMUSSEN. *THE NETSILIK ESKIMOS, REPORT OF THE FIFTH THULE EXPEDITION 1921-24*, VOL. VIII, NO. 1. COPENHAGEN: GYLDENDALSKE BOGHANDEL, 1930, FACING PAGE 312.

Hiiq, a shaman of the Umingmaktuurmiut.

SOURCE: KNUD RASMUSSEN. *INTELLECTUAL CULTURE OF THE COPPER ESKIMOS, REPORT OF THE FIFTH THULE EXPEDITION 1921-24*, VOL. IX. COPENHAGEN: GYLDENDALSKE BOGHANDEL, 1932, FACING PAGE 33. PHOTOGRAPH BY LEO HANSEN.

Hikhik was the wife of Hiiq. Rasmussen found her open-minded and helpful.
SOURCE: KNUD RASMUSSEN SELSKABET. PHOTOGRAPH BY LEO HANSEN.

Natsit, although young, had been raised by a shaman and was seen as the best storyteller among the Inuinnait.
SOURCE: KNUD RASMUSSEN. *INTELLECTUAL CULTURE OF THE COPPER ESKIMOS, REPORT OF THE FIFTH THULE EXPEDITION 1921-24*, VOL. IX. COPENHAGEN: GYLDENDALSKE BOGHANDEL, 1932, FACING PAGE 65. PHOTOGRAPH BY LEO HANSEN.

Qanijaq, with whom Rasmussen lived for a time while visiting the Umingmaktuurmiut, was wanted for murder. Rasmussen thought he was a pleasant and extremely helpful man.
SOURCE: KNUD RASMUSSEN SELSKABET.
PHOTOGRAPH BY LEO HANSEN.

Qinguruvliaq, a woman of the Inuinnait who knew all the men's songs and could help them with the words when they got stuck.
SOURCE: KNUD RASMUSSEN SELSKABET.
PHOTOGRAPH BY LEO HANSEN.

Leo Hansen joined the expedition as photographer in the central Canadian Arctic.
SOURCE: KNUD RASMUSSEN SELSKABET.
PHOTOGRAPH BY LEO HANSEN.

All four Inuit in this picture were to stand trial at Herschel Island for murder. Second from the left is Alikammiq, and third from the left is Tatamirana. They are the only Inuit ever to be hanged in Canada. Rasmussen wrote about their case.
SOURCE: KNUD RASMUSSEN. *INTELLECTUAL CULTURE OF THE COPPER ESKIMOS, REPORT OF THE FIFTH THULE EXPEDITION 1921–24*, VOL. IX. COPENHAGEN: GYLDENDALSKE BOGHANDEL, 1932, FACING PAGE 268. PHOTOGRAPHER UNKNOWN.

Herschel Island today. The buildings are maintained by Parks Canada.
SOURCE: PHOTOGRAPH BY RUSSELL POTTER.

Inuit in Point Barrow celebrate with drumming at a whale harvest festival in 1924.
SOURCE: KNUD RASMUSSEN SELSKABET. PHOTOGRAPH BY LEO HANSEN.

Dancing at the whale harvest festival in Point Barrow, spring 1924.
SOURCE: KNUD RASMUSSEN SELSKABET. PHOTOGRAPH BY LEO HANSEN.

Arnarulunnguaq, Knud Rasmussen, and Qaavigarsuaq prepare to leave Point Barrow, Alaska, in the spring of 1924.
SOURCE: SMITHSONIAN LIBRARIES AND ARCHIVES 2005-8635. PHOTOGRAPH BY LEO HANSEN.

Knud Rasmussen as a dog driver, on departure from Point Barrow.
SOURCE: KNUD RASMUSSEN SELSKABET. PHOTOGRAPH BY LEO HANSEN.

Qaavigarsuaq, Arnarulunnguaq, and Knud Rasmussen with dogs in Alaska near the end of their journey.
SOURCE: KNUD RASMUSSEN SELSKABET. PHOTOGRAPH BY LEO HANSEN.

Knud Rasmussen and Joe Bernard, owner of the vessel the *Teddy Bear*, on their voyage to Siberia.
SOURCE: PHOTOGRAPH BY LEO HANSEN, DANISH ARCTIC INSTITUTE. RESOURCE ID 131325.

Knud Rasmussen on the *Teddy Bear* en route to Siberia.
SOURCE: UAF-1993-0018-00471. JOSEPH BERNARD PAPERS. ALASKA AND POLAR REGIONS COLLECTION AND ARCHIVES, UNIVERSITY OF ALASKA FAIRBANKS. PHOTOGRAPHER PROBABLY JOSEPH BERNARD.

Knud Rasmussen and his two Inughuit companions visit Washington in 1924.
SOURCE: SMITHSONIAN LIBRARIES AND ARCHIVES 2005-8624. PHOTOGRAPH BY LEO HANSEN.

Arnarulunnguaq and Qaavigarsuaq pose in Washington with Bojesen, the secretary of the Danish legation there, in 1924.

SOURCE: PHOTOGRAPH BY LEO HANSEN, DANISH ARCTIC INSTITUTE. RESOURCE ID 122322.

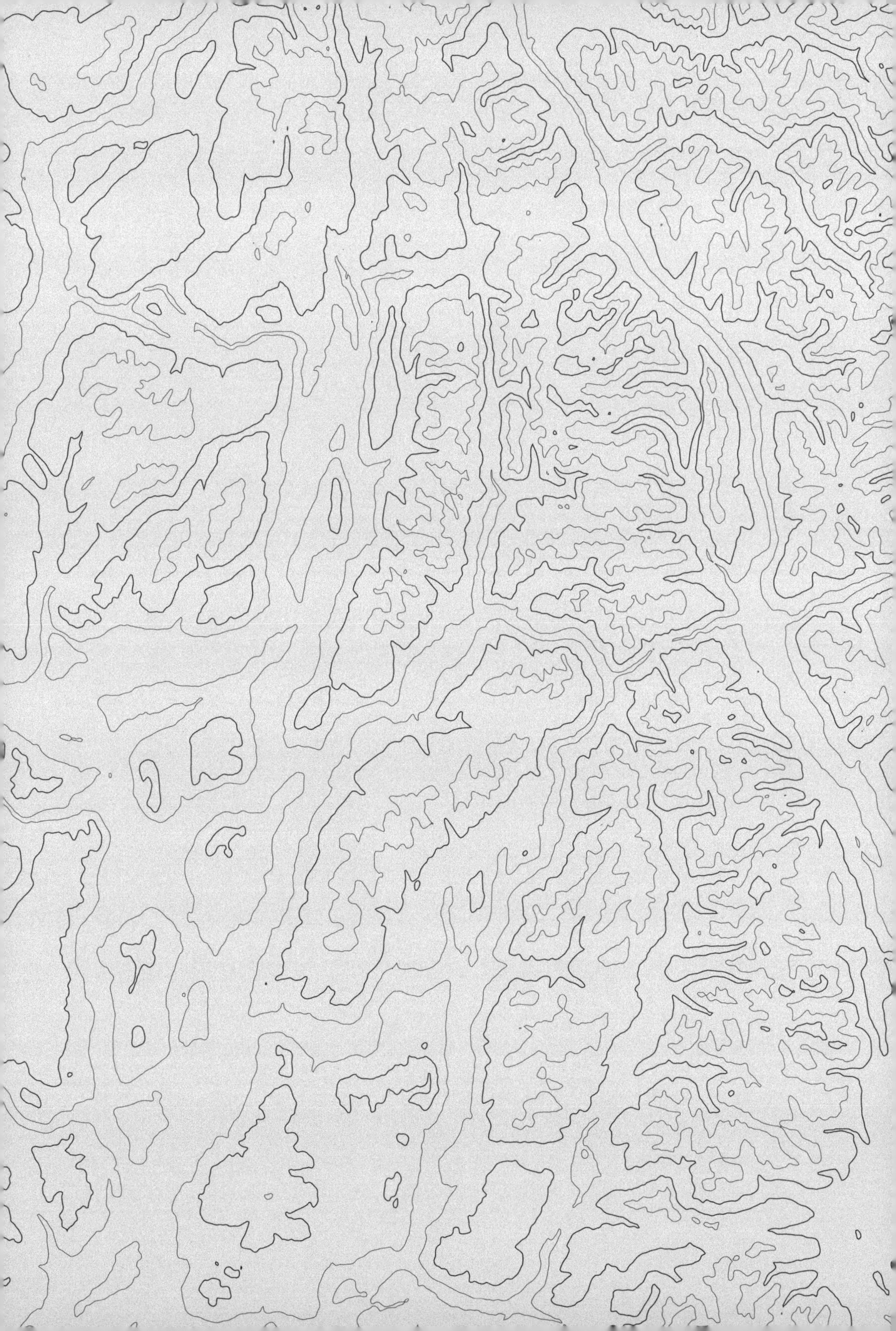

Acknowledgements

I have been interested in the Fifth Thule Expedition ever since I moved North in the 1960s, and seriously so since I became interested in Greenland in the mid-1970s. Many people have helped and encouraged me in my study of the expedition and the lives of its participants. Many of them have passed away in that half-century. Some may never have realized the inspiration they provided me. I want to specifically name those who come to mind (and apologize to those I may inadvertently have omitted).

In Greenland: Ulrik Lennert, a Greenlandic administrator in Qaanaaq when I first met him and an avid student of Arctic history, not to mention an always-gracious host; Hans Larsen, teacher and author of a Greenlandic book on the life of Qaavigarsuaq; Adam Neilsen, who taught at the Knud Rasmussen Hoyskolia in Sisimiut when I knew him; Karl Elias Olsen from the same institution; Pujo Olsen, a Greenlandic linguist and friend; Nuka Møller, linguist, scholar, and friend; Mari Kleist and Kennet Pedersen, Ilisimatusarfik/University of Greenland; Amaunnalik, an Elder in Qaanaaq who passed away many years ago—she once told me, when I was sitting reading a paper, that I sat just like Peter Freuchen, whom she had known in her childhood; Inuutersuaq, a community leader from Siorapaluk and the historian of the Inughuit; and Imiina and Qaarqutsiaq, Inughuit hunters.

In Denmark: Knud Michelsen, relative to, and biographer of, Knud Rasmussen; Navarana Freuchen, granddaughter of Peter Freuchen; Robert Petersen and his brother H. C. Petersen, both Greenlandic scholars; Regitze Margrethe Søby; Claus Oreskov of Knud Rasmussens Selskab (The Knud Rasmussen Society); Bent Nielsen and Anne-Mette Randrup-Jorgensen of the Arktisk Institut; Peter Dawes of the Geological Survey of Denmark and Greenland; and Birgitte Sonne, Institute of Greenlandic and Arctic Studies, University of Copenhagen, retired.

In North America: Igor Krupnik of the Smithsonian Institution, with whom I worked on a publication devoted to the Fifth Thule Expedition; John MacDonald, writer, thinker, and raconteur with many years' Arctic experience; Larry Audlaluk, resident of Canada's most northern community and a student of expedition history; Monty Yank for his help on some of the finer points of geography in the Repulse Bay area; Bernadette Miqqusaaq Dean, cultural activist and student of the expedition; and Brendan Griebel, Kitikmeot Heritage Society.

And as always, my wife, Kathleen Lippa, for her never-ending love, not to mention her patient tolerance of my Arctic intellectual passions.

Glossary of Inuktitut Words

Pronunciation Guide:

"a" is pronounced "ah"
"i" is pronounced "ee"
"u" is pronounced "oo"
"ai" is pronounced "eye"
"au" is pronounced "ow"
"q" is a uvular sound pronounced farther back in the throat than "k"
"r" is a uvular sound pronounced farther back in the throat than English "r"
"ll" is pronounced "bl" or "dl," depending on the dialect
Double vowels are held longer than single vowels

For more resources on how to pronounce Inuktitut words, visit inhabitmedia.com/inuitnipingit.

Word	Definition
Ahiarmiut	people from Ahiaq
ahiarmut	solitude
Aivilingmiut	people from Aivilik
Aivilingmiutut	the Inuktitut dialect spoken by the Aivilingmiut
Akilinermiulerssaarut	Report of the Canadian Inuit
Akilinirmiut	the people on the other side of the water (historic Greenlandic term for Canadian Inuit)
Akukitturmiut	people with small *akuq* (the back flap on the back of their parka); (traditional Canadian Inuit term for Greenlanders)
Akukittut	the people with short flaps on their parkas (traditional Canadian Inuit term for Greenland and for Greenlanders)
Aleut	language spoken by the Aleut people; the people of the Aleutian Islands

amaut	a woman's parka with a pouch for carrying a child
angakkuq	shaman
angakkut	shamans
aqausiq	pet name
Arviligjuarmiut	people from Arviligjuaq
aua	little helping spirit
Harvaqtuurmiut	the people of the rapids or whirlpools
Hauniqtuurmiut	the people of the place with bones
Hila	the spirit of weather (synonymous with "Sila")
iglu	snow house
Iglulingmiut	the people from Iglulik
Iglulingmiutaq	a person from Iglulik
ijiqqait	beings living in the hills; mountain spirits ; shape-shifters
ijiraq	being living in the hills; a mountain spirit ; a shape-shifter
Ilisaijikutaaq	name, meaning "the tall teacher"
Ilivilirmiut	the people from Ilivilik
inua	an object's owner or lord; the spirit of something
Inughuit	the Inuit of north-western Greenland, formerly called "Polar Eskimos"
Inuinnait	Copper Inuit
Inuktun	the Inuit dialect of the Thule district
inuktuumajuq	an eater of human kind
Inupiaq	Indigenous person of northern coastal Alaska; a dialect spoken by an Inupiaq

Ipiliqihunga	I am choking
irinaliut utiqtuq inungminut	magic words that rebound upon their master
Kalaaleq	a West Greenlander
Kalaallisut	a Greenlandic dialect of the Inuit language
Kalaallit	Greenlanders
kamiik	a pair of skin boots
Killinirmiut	a sub-group of the Copper Inuit
majuaqtuq / majurartuq	climb
majulajuit	those who want to go to heaven (also spelled *majulassunik* or *majulasut* in Greenlandic)
majulajuq	one who wants to go to heaven
Nattilingmiut	the people from Nattilik
Nattilingmiutaq	a person from Nattilik
Naujaarmiut	the people from Naujaat
Nuliajuq	spirit who governed access to the animals of the sea
Nuvungmiut	people from the point
Paallirmiut	the people from Paalliq; the people of the willow thicket
pelrartut	the white men who once visited the Nattilik country (literally translates to "those who starved")
Pinga	a spirit; the one up in the sky who was the guardian of all life, both animal and human
pittailiniq	taboos
Puatugi	Black people (literally translates to "Portuguese")
qaaqsiluni (qarrtsiluni)	one waits for something to burst

Qairnirmiut	an inland group of Inuit; the people of the flat land or bedrock
Qallunaaq	white person
Qallunaat	white people
qanukiaq	I wonder
qaumaniq	enlightenment
Qikiqtarmiut	the people from King William Island
qujannamiik	thank you
qulittaq	parka
qulliq	seal oil lamp
Sila	the spirit of weather (synonymous with "Hila")
siqqitirniq	conversion ritual
sirnaarniq	a feeling that ensures an Inuk will always side with their family
Tahiujarmiut	the people from Tahiujaq
Takannakapsaaluk	the great woman down at the bottom of the sea who rules over all the beasts of the sea
taqqutit	wick trimmers for blubber lamps
Tikirarmiut	people of the small point of land
Tikitaq	the point which rounds out like a forefinger
Tipjarsi	something along the shore that was washed up by the waves
Tununirmiut	the people of the Pond Inlet area
tuurngait	spirit helpers
tuurngaq	a spirit helper
umiaq	a skin boat
umiat	skin boats

Umingmaktuurmiut	muskox people (a sub-group of the Copper Inuit)
Utkuhikhalingmiut	people from Utkuhikhalik
Yupik	one of the Indigenous languages of Alaska; a person who speaks Yupik
Yupiit	plural of *Yupik*

References

The American Museum of Natural History. "The Eskimo Collection from Hudson Bay." *The American Museum Journal* III, no. 1 (January 1903): 6-9.

Awa, Salome. CBC Radio, *As It Happens*. November 25, 2015. https://www.cbc.ca/radio/asithappens/as-it-happens-wednesday-edition-1.3336554/nunavut-family-outraged-after-fashion-label-copies-sacred-inuit-design-1.3336560.

Bangsted, Helge. *Diary II, Fifth Thule Expedition* (diary, unpublished).

Barr, William. "The career and disappearance of Hans K. E. Krüger, Arctic geologist, 1886-1930." *Polar Record* 29, no. 171 (1993): 277-304.

Bernard, Joseph F. "In the Arctic with Knud Rasmussen." *Joseph Bernard Papers,* Archives, Elmer E. Rasmuson Library, University of Alaska Fairbanks. n.d.

Boas, Franz. "Second Report on the Eskimo of Baffin Land and Hudson Bay." *Bulletin of the American Museum of Natural History* XV, (1907): 371-570.

Bown, Stephen R. *White Eskimo: Knud Rasmussen's Fearless Journey into the Heart of the Arctic*. Madeira Park, B.C.: Douglas and McIntyre, 2015.

Burch, Ernest S., Jr. "Knud Rasmussen and the 'Original' Inland Eskimos of Southern Keewatin." *Études Inuit Studies* 12, no. 1–2 (1988): 81-100.

Carpenter, Edmund Snow. "Aivilik Relations with Neighboring Eskimos (Okomiut)." *Edmund Snow Carpenter Papers*, National Museum of Natural History, Smithsonian Institution. 1950.

Cavell, Janice, ed. *Documents on Canadian External Relations, The Arctic, 1874-1949*. Ottawa: Global Affairs Canada, 2016.

Christensen, Flemming. "Jeg er hadet af missionen og elsket af eskimoerne. Kan jeg forlange mere" [I am hated by the mission and loved by the Eskimos. What more could I ask]. *Tidsskriftet Grønland* 2-3 (1986): 63-74.

Clabaut, Armand. "Bishop Turquetil, First Bishop of the Eskimos." *Eskimo* 38 (December 1955): 3-11.

Cory, T. L. Written correspondence from T. L. Cory to O. S. Finnie. September 12, 1922. LAC, RG85, Vol. 607, File 2580.

Deputy Minister of Justice. Telegram from the Deputy Minister of Justice to Judge Dubuc. June 8, 1923. LAC, RG85, Vol. 607, File 2580.

Driscoll, Bernadette. "The Inuit Parka: A Preliminary Study." Master's Thesis in Canadian Studies, Carleton University (unpublished), 1983.

Ducharme, Lionel. "Knud Rasmussen and his visit to Chesterfield Inlet in 1922." *Eskimo*, New series 14, Fall-Winter (1977-78): 3-10.

Eber, Dorothy. *When the Whalers Were Up North: Inuit Memories from the Eastern Arctic.* Montreal: McGill-Queen's University Press, 1989.

Evaluardjuk, Deborah. "Noah Nashook." *Inuktitut* 71 (1990): 39-55.

Freuchen, Dagmar, ed. *Peter Freuchen's Adventures in the Arctic.* New York: Julian Messner, Inc., 1960.

Freuchen, Peter. *Arctic Adventure: My Life in the Frozen North.* London: William Heinemann Ltd., 1936.

—. *Vagrant Viking: My Life and Adventures.* New York: Julian Messner, Inc., 1953.

Gulløv, Hans Christian. "The Concepts of Paleo- and Neo-Eskimo Cultures: The Danish Tradition from H. P. Steensby and His Students, G. Hatt, K. Birket-Smith, and Th. Mathiassen, to Their Successors, H. Larsen and J. Meldgaard." In *Early Inuit Studies: Themes and Transitions, 1850s-1980s*, edited by Igor Krupnik, 139-164. Washington, D. C.: Smithsonian Institution, 2016.

Hansen, Leo. *I Knuds Slædesspor* [In Knud's Sled Tracks]. Copenhagen: Westermann, 1953.

Harper, Kenn. *Minik: The New York Eskimo.* Hanover, N. H.: Steerforth Press, 2017.

Hastrup, Kirsten. "Knud Rasmussen: Explorer, Ethnographer, and Narrator." In *Early Inuit Studies: Themes and Transitions, 1850s–1980s*, edited by Igor Krupnik, 111-135. Washington, D. C.: Smithsonian Institution Scholarly Press, 2016.

Isuma. "Therkel Mathiassen character outline." http://www.isuma.tv/inuit-culture-education/therkel-mathiassen-character-outline. Accessed January 2, 2022.

Jenness, Diamond. *Eskimo Administration: II.* Canada. Montreal: Arctic Institute of North America, 1964.

Jones, Renée Fossett. "The Keewatin Inuit and Interband Trade and Communications, 1717-1900." Master's Thesis, Department of History, University of Manitoba (unpublished), 1989.

Kleist, Mari. "'The Expedition would not have succeeded without them:' The crucial role of the Inuit/Inughuit participants of the Fifth Thule Expedition across Arctic North America, 1921-1924." Lecture presented at the Smithsonian Arctic Studies Center, December 15, 2021.

—. "The Fifth Thule Expedition and the Indigenous Participants who made it Possible," *Alaska Journal of Anthropology* 19, no. 1&2 (2021): 37-55.

Kristiansen, Arrutaq. "K'avigarssuak, Knud Rasmussen's rejsekammerat" [Qaavigarsuaq, Knud Rasmusen's travel companion]. *Slaedesporet* 31 (March 2012): 183-194.

Larsen, Hans. *Qaavigarsuaq: piniartorssuup Avanersuarmiup Qaavigarsuup inuunermini eqqaamasaminik unikkaavi* [Qaavigarsuaq: the life and memories of Qaavigarsuaq, the great hunter of northern Greenland]. Nuuk: Atuakkiorfik, 1999.

Laugrand, Frédéric, and Jarich Oosten. *Inuit Shamanism and Christianity: Transitions and Transformations in the Twentieth Century*. Montreal: McGill-Queen's University Press, 2010.

—. *Inuit, Oblate Missionaries, and Grey Nuns in the Keewatin (1865-1965)*. Montreal, McGill-Queen's University Press, 2019.

Lidegaard, Mads. "Arnarulunnguaq," Dansk Kvindebiografisk Leksikon. https://kvindebiografiskleksikon.lex.dk/Arnarulunnguaq. Translated by Google Translate. Accessed 2023.

Lloyd, Trevor, comp. "Station Diary, Danish Island," in *Trevor Lloyd Papers*. Trent University Archives, file 87-014-6-15. n.d.

—. "Knud Rasmussen and the Arctic Islands Preserve." *Musk-Ox* 25 (1979): 85-90.

Makko.dk (Blog om Grønland). "Hvem var Arnarulunnguaq?" [Who was Arnarulunnguaq?] In http://makko.dk/greenland/hvem-var-arnarulunnguaq/. February 17, 2019. Accessed December 3, 2021.

Malaurie, Jean. *The Last Kings of Thule*. New York: E. P. Dutton, 1982.

Mary-Rousselière, Guy. "Monica Ataguvtaluk, Queen of Iglulik." *Eskimo* 16 (March 1950): 11-14.

—. "Father Gasté Meets the Inland Eskimos." *Eskimo* 57 (December 1960): 3-15.

—. "History of a Case of Cannibalism in Baffin Island." *Eskimo* 81 (1969): 6-23.

—. "The Fifth Thule Expedition as Seen by the Eskimos." *Eskimo*, New series 11, Spring-Summer (1976): 19-25.

Mathiassen, Therkel. "Foreløbig Beretning om Femte Thule-Ekspedition fra Grønland til Stillehavet: Arkaeologi" [Preliminary Report on the Fifth Thule Expedition from Greenland to the Pacific Ocean: Archaeology]. *Geografisk Tidsskrift*, 27 (1924): 201-208.

—. *Med Knud Rasmussen Blandt Amerikas Eskimoer* [With Knud Rasmussen Among America's Eskimos]. Copenhagen: Gyldendalske Boghandel, 1926.

—. "Archaeology of the Central Eskimos." *Report of the Fifth Thule Expedition 1921–24* IV (1-2). Copenhagen: Nordisk Forlag, 1927.

—. "Material Culture of the Iglulik Eskimos." *Report of the Fifth Thule Expedition 1921–24* VI (1). Copenhagen: Nordisk Forlag, 1928.

—. "Archaeological Collections from the Western Eskimos." *Report of the Fifth Thule Expedition 1921–24* X (1). Copenhagen: Nordisk Forlag, 1930.

—. "Report on the Expedition." *Report of the Fifth Thule Expedition 1921–24* I (1). Copenhagen, Nordisk Forlag, 1945.

Michelsen, Knud. *Knud Rasmussen: Ambassador on Dog Sled.* Ottawa: Federation of Danish Associations in Canada, 2021.

—. "Plans for the Fifth Thule Expedition and the Great Sled Journey Across Canada and Alaska." *Alaska Journal of Anthropology* 19, 1-2 (2021): 24-36.

Nielsen, Bent. "… for mig en Oplevelse, jeg næsten ikke tør tro paa" [… for me an experience I hardly even dare to believe]. *Tidsskriftet Grønland* 5-6. (2007): 233-249.

Niviatiaq, Suzanne. "Ananaga Inungmik Nirilaursimanivina" [About When My Mother Ate a Human Being]. *Inummarit*, 1973.

Okpik, Abrahan. *We Call It Survival*, ed. Louis McComber. Iqaluit: Nunavut Arctic College, 2005.

Olsen, J. P. Jacob. *Akilinermiulerssârut* [Report on the Canadian Inuit]. Nuuk, Det grønlandske Litteraturselskab, 1927.

Olsvig, Ivalo Katrine Birthe Foget. "Hvem var de to inughuit Arnarulunnguaq of Qâvigarssuaq Miteq?" [Who were the two Inughuit, Arnarulunnguaq and Qaavigarsuaq Miteq?] *Tidsskriftet Grønland* 67, 3 (September 2019): 136-144.

Ostermann, Hother, ed. "Alaskan Eskimo Words." *Report of the Fifth Thule Expedition 1921–24* III (4). Copenhagen: Nordisk Forlag, 1941.

—. "The Mackenzie Eskimos. After Knud Rasmussen's posthumous notes." *Report of the Fifth Thule Expedition 1921–24* X (2). Copenhagen: Nordisk Forlag, 1942.

Ostermann, Hother, and Erik Holtved, eds. "The Alaskan Eskimos as Described in the Posthumous Notes of Dr. Knud Rasmussen." *Report of the Fifth Thule Expedition 1921–24* X (3). Copenhagen: Nordisk Forlag, 1952.

Petersen, Robert. "J. P. Jacob Olsen, en Grønlænder i Arktisk Canada" [J. P. Jacob Olsen, a Greenlander in Arctic Canada]. *Tidsskriftet Grønland* 8 (1958): 295-302.

—. "On 'Smell of Forest' in the Greenlandic Myths and Legends." In *Fifty Years of Arctic Research*, 234-248. Copenhagen: Department of Ethnography, The National Museum of Denmark, 1997.

Pratt, Kenneth L. "Tracking Najagnir: A Shaman's Encounters with Murder, Western Law, the Lomen Brothers Company, and Knud Rasmussen." *Alaska Journal of Anthropology* 19, 1-2 (2021): 141-159.

Rasmussen, Knud Johan Victor. "Dagboger fra Den Litterære Grønlandsekspedition" [Diaries from the Literary Expedition to Greenland]. No. 8 (September 1904). Knud Rasmussens Arkiv (Knud Rasmussen Archive), Det Kongelige Bibliotek (The Royal Library), Copenhagen.

—. "Efterladte papirer, Dagbøger fra den 5. Thuleekspedition 1921-24, Dagbog 8, Diverse optegnelser fra East Cape" [Papers left behind: Diaries from the Fifth Thule Expedition 1921-24, Diary 8, Various records from East Cape]. Royal Library of Denmark, Manuscript Collection.

—. "Forslag til en dansk etnografisk Ekspedition til Central-eskimoerne" [Proposal for a Danish Ethnographical Expedition to the Central Eskimos]. *Geografisk Tidsskrift* 20 (1909): 92-94.

—. *Fra Grønland til Stillehavet, Rejser og Mennesker fra 5 Thule-Ekspedition 1921–24* [From Greenland to the Pacific Ocean. Travels and People from the Fifth Thule Expedition, 1921-1924]. 2 vols. Copenhagen: Gyldendal, 1925-1926.

—. *Across Arctic America: Narrative of the Fifth Thule Expedition*. New York: G. P. Putnam's Sons, 1927. (References are to the 1989 reprint by Greenwood Press.)

—. *Inuit Nunáinik K'aujatdlainialungneĸ* [An Attempt to Reach all Inuit Lands]. Copenhagen: Bianco Lunos Bogtrykkeri, 1928.

—. "Intellectual Culture of the Iglulik Eskimos." *Report of the Fifth Thule Expedition 1921–24* VII (1). Copenhagen: Nordisk Forlag, 1929.

—. "Iglulik and Caribou Eskimo Texts." *Report of the Fifth Thule Expedition 1921–24* VII (3). Copenhagen: Nordisk Forlag, 1930.

—. "Observations on the Intellectual Culture of the Caribou Eskimos." *Report of the Fifth Thule Expedition 1921–24* VII (2). Copenhagen: Nordisk Forlag, 1930.

—. "The Netsilik Eskimos: Social Life and Spiritual Culture." *Report of the Fifth Thule Expedition 1921–24* VIII (1-2). Copenhagen: Nordisk Forlag, 1931.

—. "Intellectual Culture of the Copper Eskimos." *Report of the Fifth Thule Expedition 1921–24* IX. Copenhagen: Nordisk Forlag, 1932.

Rosing, Otto. "Dr. Knud Rasmussens Betydning for Grønland og Grønlænderne" [Dr. Knud Rasmussen's Significance for Greenland and the Greenlanders]. *Geografisk Tidsskrift* 37 (1934): 64-65.

Schwalbe, Daria Morgounova et al. "The Fifth Thule Expedition's Siberian Legacy." *Alaska Journal of Anthropology* 19, 1-2 (2021): 175-193.

Shokarev, Sergei Y. "Dezhnevo (Kengisqun): The Westernmost Point of the Fifth Thule Expedition." *Alaska Journal of Anthropology* 19, 1-2 (2021): 194-210.

Søby, Regitze Margrethe. "Knud Rasmussen's Political Thoughts on a Greenlandic Greenland in Cooperation with Denmark." Unpublished, circa 1990.

Steensby, Hans Peder. "An Anthropogeographical Study of the Origin of Eskimo Culture." *Meddelelser om Grønland* 53 (1916/1917): 39-228.

Stefansson, Vilhjalmur. *My Life with the Eskimo*. New York: Macmillan, 1913.

Tapatai, Louis. "Akulak, the Shaman." *Inuttituut* (Winter 1972): 7-12.

Trébaol, Father Jean Marie. "Genealogical compilation from the Liber Animorum of St. Etienne Mission of Igloolik." Unpublished, 1957-1958. Translated from French in 1983, translator unknown.

Tremblay, Alfred. *Cruise of the Minnie Maud: Arctic Seas and Hudson Bay, 1910-11 and 1912-13.* Quebec City: Arctic Exchange and Publishing Ltd., 1921.

Treude, Erhard. "The work of Knud Rasmussen in the Canadian Arctic as described by RCMP Inspector Stuart Wood." *Études Inuit Studies* 28, 2 (2004): 185-201.

Tungilik, Victor, and Rachel Uyarasuk. *The Transition to Christianity*. Edited by Jarich Oosten and Frederic Laugrand. Iqaluit: Nunavut Arctic College, 1999.

INHABIT MEDIA
IQALUIT • TORONTO